Mountain Upside Down

by

John Toren

John Toren

NODIN PRESS

ISBN-0931714-99-0

Nodin Press is a division of Micawber's, Inc.
530 N. Third Street, Suite 120
Minneapolis, MN 55401

for Hilary,
whose enthusiasm,
support, and participation
make it all worthwhile.

Acknowledgements

I have digested, pondered, and recast countless friendly and challenging conversations in the course of fashioning these essays, and it seems to me, in fact, that writing is nothing other than a more formal and exacting, if less convivial, form of talking. The central role played by my wife Hilary in the development of these pieces should be obvious to anyone who opens the book. I would also like to single out in particular Tim Wahl, John Steininger, and Gene Sylvestre, as spirits whose continuing insight, commentary, and criticism have been priceless. Many of the values I've attempted to conjure are exemplified by the beloved Curlew Club, whose members include Carol Wahl, Keith Kroschel, and Gayle Anderson, and our long-standing Christmas Club, in which Rocky and Greg Daigle, Becca and David Menken, Shiela Wolk, and Jim and Debbie Ingebretsen figure prominently. I ought to mention distant friends Dave Jensen, Rollo Hebert, and Joe and Debby Blackshear, and others near at hand, including Don and Sherry Ladig and Dana and Mary McDill, as well as the giddy and hilarious Formerly Bookmen group that includes Mary Beth and Glenn Freeman, Maria Bianchi, Rick Johnston, Richard Stegall, Annie Klessig, Lisa Legge, Guy Neske, and Carol Jackson. The Water Garden Group of Michel Ravaz, Renie O'Dougherty, Jeff and Fran Mittelmark, Marnie Larkin, and Brian Iwamoto deserves a special note, and among other friends too numerous to name I'd like to single out John Kudrle, Bill Roth, Bill Mockler, Joyce Skokut, and Ann Penaz. It's been a great pleasure to work with my old friend Norton Stillman in putting this book together, and it would be impossible to overstate the unending interest and support of both the Toren and the Sylvestre clans.

Table of Contents

THE UNFORTUNATE MACARONI.

Pub accor to Act. Feb V 6 1772 by Marty Strand

Introduction: Cultural Requirements

O ne morning not long ago I received a plain white pamphlet in the mail, no more than a few pages long, with the title *Cultural Requirements* printed on the cover. "A great subject, a great format! This is a work I should have written," I muttered to myself, cursing my indolence, as I popped the staple off. "For isn't this the thing we all *need* to know? How to live? How to participate fully in the life of our culture?"

Opening the pamphlet, I was relieved to find that it had been sent to me by a local nursery in the hope that a plant I'd purchased there recently wouldn't be returned dead, accompanied by a refund request. The title of this little work gnawed at me, however, like an elusive Zen koan, and, after a good deal of serious inattention, I began to discern where the rub lay. The horticulturalist uses the phrase "cultural requirements" to describe what type of culture a plant requires; that is to say, what conditions are most likely to further its health and development. When that same phrase, "cultural requirements" is applied to the human realm, a degree of ambiguity immediately presents itself. Human culture, unlike plant culture, is something we not only draw sustenance from, but also contribute to. We nurture culture both within ourselves and in our interactions with others; we become "cultured" in a way that a mugo pine, for example, does not, and on occasion we also find ourselves defending culture against the ever-present threat of its decline, decay, or inertia. As often as not, when we speak of our cultural requirements, we're referring, not to what we need *from* our culture, but to what we have been called upon to do on *behalf* of our culture, so that it may thrive. The orientation has been reversed.

Whether we're drawing from it or contributing to it, we no sooner raise the issue of cultural requirements than we find ourselves facing the question, "Which culture?" Since the rise of the counter-cultures of the sixties, young men and women have taken pleasure in identifying themselves with fragments of culture that differ at least slightly from the norm. Some of these sub-cultures have been self-consciously aesthetic in orientation—the Beats, the Hippies, the Punks—while others

4

have appeared naturally with the growing self-awareness and pride of ethnic groups. Journalists enjoy exposing the bourgeois conventionality that underlies many of these ostensibly radical deviations from the norm, yet clearly a more diverse array of lifestyles is *visible* nowadays than at any time in the past, and this makes it difficult to generalize about anything "cultural."

We have long since reached the point, in fact, where diversity itself is taken as a mark of cultural distinction; whether such diversity is a good thing or a bad thing remains a matter of dispute. In a recent study with the evocative title *Bowling Alone*, Robert D. Putnam analyzes what he sees to be a serious decline in community participation among Americans. Fewer individuals volunteer to work for political campaigns, join the PTA or the Elks Club, or bowl in leagues, than they did fifty years ago. (How come is it, then, that I still have such a hard time getting a lane on Wednesday night?) The book is filled almost to excess with graphs. There is even one that charts the correlation between watching television and gesturing obscenely at other drivers on the freeway! Evidently the more TV you watch, the more you curse.

The result of Putnam's many surveys and analyses, simply put, is that among each of twelve activities considered to be "community-building," from attending public meetings to going to church to reading the newspaper, the younger the age-group, the less the degree and avidity of participation. This may be a serious problem. On the other hand, (and this does not appear to be one of Putnam's categories,) it may be that people simply have more durable friendships than they used to, and therefore feel less need for joining associations. Or they may be forming organizations the existence and nature of which sociologists remain unaware. Then again, people may simply be too busy nowadays driving their children to hockey practice to participate in community life as fully as they would like in other ways.

On a different level of analysis, the historian Jacques Barzun, in *From Dawn to Decadence*, decries the tendency of we "modern" folk to take a relatively narrow range of experience as our own "personal" culture, and in so doing, lose sight of the broader spectrum of shared cultural artifacts and institutions which make up the social fabric.

> *Culture—what a word! Up to a few years ago it meant two or three related things easy to grasp and keep apart. Now it is a piece of all-purpose jargon that covers a hodgepodge of overlapping things. People speak and write about the culture of almost any segment of society: the counter-culture, to begin with, and the many sub-cultures: ethnic cultures, corporate cultures, teenage culture, and popular culture.*

Clearly Barzun intends, in his weighty and often entertaining book, to locate and corral the underlying values which, though they once girded our culture, have long since wandered up the back-canyons of the increasingly sparse and desert-like cultural landscape.

It might be suggested, on the contrary, that the history of modern times in the West has been marked less by cultural consensus than by heated conflict *between* distinct religious, political, and ethnic interests. The single most valuable result of this conflict, for all the violence and ugliness involved, has been an increasing commitment not only to tolerate, but actually to sustain a wide spectrum of values and ideals under the rubric of liberal individualism. Although some will continue to contest this cultural drift, it seems to me that the proliferation of provincial, ethnic, and "counter-" cultures marks the enduring success, rather than the incipient demise, of a broader liberal *ethos*.

This point was admirably expressed in one of the classic works of the sixties, Harvey Cox's *The Secular City* (1965). Cox argues that secularization, urbanization, and social atomization are good things, in so far as they allow us greater freedom to cultivate and enrich those relations and interests that genuinely appeal to us. Impersonality and disengagement may characterize our brief interactions with business associates, grocery cashiers, and other urban functionaries, few of which we'll ever get to know well; but we are subsequently able to devote our free hours to a wide array of social activities, making friends here and there with others with whom we share perhaps esoteric interests and enthusiasms which only large population centers can sustain. Although Cox's concern is rooted in theological as well as merely social issues, in the "fate of man" as well as merely the condition of culture, the upshot of his analysis is that "personal culture," far from being a contradiction in terms, constitutes a kind of fulfillment of the project initiated by the Western liberal tradition. Our relationships become deeper and more humane in the modern urban environment, as peculiarities and excellences of personal character are given greater opportunities to develop through expanded social interaction and greater access to the *stuff* of culture: information, education, art.

Cox's image of the secular city, peopled with individuals striving to come to a fuller knowledge of themselves and their place in the universe, with perhaps only a dim recognition of what the enterprise entails, is one that I find attractive, because it grants to even the most shallow, mindless, and self-centered activities the dignity of having a role to play in a very grand project. I take comfort in this thought, because, although I like to think that I take the issue of personal culture, (which to my mind is the same thing as cosmic orientation,) seriously, I have no way of knowing whether my own efforts to develop culturally have been successful. In any case, though I may be accused of political apathy, self-indulgence, elitism, or abject social irresponsibility, I feel no shame in admitting that I am simply not *worried* about culture.

What worries me is that in the end, culture, in its kaleidoscopic wonder and brilliance, will somehow evade my grasp.

A few years ago, in an effort to chronicle my own progress toward a fuller understanding of the *stuff* of culture, I undertook to write and print a seasonal pamphlet devoted to an array of subjects germane to this issue–history, cooking, metaphysics, film, nature, literature. Computer technology made this a relatively easy thing to do, but my inspiration came from the eighteenth century, when pamphleteers churned out ragged essays combining observations of daily life and cracker-barrel philosophy in a way that we've rarely seen since. It seemed to me that somewhere between Diderot's *Advice on an Old Dressing Gown* and Hume's *Essay on Human Understanding* lay a field of inquiry that was simultaneously personal and analytic, readable yet at least occasionally overarching and "deep." I had no illusions as to the marketability of my own little feuilleton; it was simply great fun to write and produce, and it also allowed me to get a few things off my mind.

I chose the title *Macaroni* for the publication, and this too has a connection with the eighteenth century. In the days of Johnson and Boswell the noodle we call macaroni was largely unknown in England. Wealthy travelers returning from the Continent took pleasure in eating the exotic dish they'd met up with in Italy, just as we eat sushi today. There was an aristocratic club in London called The Macaroni Club, in fact, and the word was soon being used to describe anyone who was foppish, affected, or painfully refined.

Today all of this must seem a little ridiculous. Macaroni has long since become a plebian dish, often poured from a little blue box along with powdered cheese in a foil envelope. And yet, although its social *cachet* has plummeted, macaroni remains exactly what it was in the eighteenth century: an inexpensive, easily stored, starchy foodstuff suitable to be mixed with a myriad of simple or exotic sauces.

Were the fops of the eighteenth century wrong to elevate the lowly noodle to the level of an elitist social symbol on the basis of its Mediterranean exoticism? I don't know. In any case, macaroni has long since returned to vogue in diverse forms under the name of pasta, and even the lowly macaroni-and-cheese now appears as a kind of comfort food on the menus of retro-restaurants, in the company of meatloaf and chicken pot pie. In its simplicity, durability, elegance, adaptability, and even grandeur, it both encompasses and transcends the highs and lows that have been inflicted on it in the course of its history. Its refinement, rusticity, and enduring adaptability speak directly to the heart of human experience—and if you think I'm waxing poetical here, let me remind you that a style of writing driven by exaggeration and giddy ornamentation is sometimes referred to as "macaronic."

The essays in *Mountain Upside Down* (which also has to do with highs and lows, now that I think of it,) originally appeared in *Macaroni*. They've only been simplified, shortened, and re-arranged.

It may strike you that the cultural *stuff* that attracts my attention is more often rarefied than common or popular–more often "high" than "low." There's a reason for this. It is of the essence of culture, I think, in its nutritive capacity, to be exemplary rather than typical or symptomatic. Those who argue differently face a Catch-22, the illogicality of which has not in any way diminished its popularity as a journalistic hook. It goes like this:

A) Culture is in decline. Look at TV, look at films, etc.

B) But no, look at this fine book, or this jazz performance.

A) Yes, but the things you've just mentioned aren't truly repre*sentative*. The masses know nothing about them. They're the tastes of an elite. Therefore, culture is in decline.

The flaw in this line of analysis stems from a stubborn determination to equate mass culture, which is only occasionally significant, and exemplary culture, which may well be unpopular or obscure in its day, although it increases in significance with the passage of time. Anyone who expects popular culture to rise to the level of that body of resilient works of art and thought, few in number in any given era, which, having retained their vigor through time, supply us with a vision of the past, is bound to be disappointed. No one in our day is likely to be as cryptically profound as Heraclitus, as proper as Confucius, as compassionate as Christ, as noble as El Cid, as observant as Jan van Eck, as cosmic as Giordano Bruno, as feverishly romantic as Cervantes, as clever as Shakespeare, as sublime as Mozart, as charismatic as Napoleon, as melancholy as Leopardi, as guileless as Therese of Liseaux, as intellectually perverse as Wittgenstein, or as humane as Jean Renoir. When we examine the climate of our own times the commonplace habits and artifacts we meet up with daily or read about in the papers, and not the isolated ideas and images that posterity will remember us for, tend to dominate our field of view. Therefore, it would appear that our culture is "in decline." It's a simple matter of perspective.

On the other hand, it needs to be acknowledged, I think, that if popular culture is almost invariably mediocre, because "mediocre" means average and what's popular is average, it also tends to be vital, because it trades in basic human emotions, giving less thought to historical precedents or refinements of style than to the question of whether a thing will sell. The relatively unreflective orientation of this broad stratum of culture—its concern for immediacy of effect—often results in artifacts whose shallowness and predictability are evident to us even at the moment we're enjoying them. Yet it occasionally produces exemplary ideas or images as well, which may, with the passage of time, become the enduring artifacts of a bygone Golden Age. The tragedies of Sophocles and Euripides, the poems of the Carmina Burana, Verdi's operas, Charlie Chaplin's films were all very popular in their day, although they shared that popularity with countless now-forgotten works. We continue to enjoy and study them today, not because they were once popular, but because they still move us.

In short, enduring cultural forms arise both from the midst of popular culture, and also from individuals working in isolation, gearing their expressions to the sensibilities of an elite, or perhaps attending to an utterly private and personal muse. In the end neither popularity nor obscurity has much of a bearing on the value of anything.

Who is to say, then, what has value and what doesn't? In a society like ours, anyone can, and almost everyone does. Opinions are everywhere. If we find one slant uncomprehending or offensive, there's nothing to stop us from turning elsewhere. Our tastes are never so firmly grounded as we like to believe in any case. The ceiling of the Sistene Chapel and the child's drawing on the refrigerator door are not equally well done, but they challenge us with equal force to see and feel honestly, and they both make manifest an impulse, and a universe, that's larger and grander than either of them. At times we prefer one, at times another. The large and the small, the dramatically expressive and the instinctively humane, the historically prominent and the quietly domestic—it's all part and parcel of that cultural fabric which nourishes us, and which it is our cultural requirement, in turn, to support and extend.

Nicolas of Cusa, writing at the end of the fifteenth century, argued that the infinitely large and the infinitely small amount to the same thing, which is God. It's a thought worth pondering; yet I must say that in the end the idea of "infinity" in either form, being mathematical and abstract, leads us away from the truth. Whatever else he, or she, (or they?) may be, God is not an abstraction. Nothing real is abstract.

I'm more inclined to endorse the remark of Thomas Aquinas that "we know God implicitly in everything we know." But this slant presents us with problems as well. Perhaps we ought to dispense with the theological nostrums altogether, (though they're always there, in the logical substratum of our personal attempts to show or to explain the way we feel about things) and merely echo the sentiment of a talented and now slightly obscure French novelist (Henry de Montherlant) who once wrote—

> Life is a wonderful thing. When you turn it over and examine it thoroughly, when you see that which is, you feel like getting down on your knees. That which is—three remarkable syllables!

Far be it from me to suggest that life is a paradise, a pastoral arcadia or a new Cythera where intellectual stimulation, physical pleasure, material prosperity, and social harmony flow like wine from an enchanted fountain. Yet it seems to me we're moving in that direction. All the evidence supports my position. I'm referring not only to the evidence of history, (dark as it may sometimes be) but also to the natural observed tendency of the human heart to orient itself favorably toward "the Good."

The Mail Run

I drive up the hill through banks of fog. The sun is just now rising above the trees on the far side of Zenith Avenue. White fog on either side of the road, then, and amber fog ahead; the air is cool, it's no wonder I'm giddy and amazed. The ash trees in the park, once pathetic seedlings standing in awkward isolation from one another, like hesitant children on the first day of school, have become tall and well rounded and collegial. Cars approaching down the boulevard make no sound in the thick air, though the window is open, and suddenly armies of geese loom on the far side of the intersection, long black necks arching beautifully in the mist like a scene from a Wagner opera. Summer is activity, fall is poetry. (Winter is inescapable, no need to put a name to it, or to give it a thought.)

I seldom stop at the top of the hill. A glance to the left as I reach the crest, and then a swooping right turn and down along the parkway into the city. A left on Plymouth Avenue, and I'm headed into the sun again down semi-deserted streets, past apartments, binderies, low concrete structures where they manufacture nameless things, and then another right turn onto Second Street North. Magic city, aging brick warehouses, empty weed-covered fields with long-abandoned railroad tracks embedded in them. Some of the fields have been converted into parking lots. Some of the warehouses are now apartments and condos. Yes, people work and even live down here. I pass the Star Tribune warehouse, Open U, and the Guthrie Experimental Stage. The Mississippi is flowing quietly (and massively) only a block away. The Lindsay Brothers Building, and then Creamettes, where macaroni for the millions, made of wholesome North Dakota durum wheat, is being boxed and shipped, day and night.

But the people I see on their way to work as I move through the silent streets that parallel the abandoned tracks don't work at Creamettes. They work downtown or in the studio businesses (designers, architects, photographers, media specialists) that have moved into the warehouses abandoned by the jobbers of agricultural implements who've long since gone out of business, or left the city for modern one-floor suburban buildings. It's a neighborhood of age and intellect and neglect, but all I think about as I drive east down First Street is the sky to the east, the light and the freshness of the morning, the crudescence of the aging brick, and the beauty of the women and men in stiff or slightly elegant clothing on their way to work downtown.

I envy these people, albeit only very slightly. I envy them because they're doing important things, you can tell that by the way they dress. Then again, I suppose anyone whose life we don't know well tends to appear statuesque and "together." We retain this feeling from the Greeks, perhaps, who felt that any passing stranger just *might* be a God. No doubt the people I see on the street look beautiful largely because they've just a few minutes earlier made themselves presentable, and I, who know nothing about them, see only the unfathomable opacity of their mask, their strangeness, amid the utilitarian buildings, the New Age coffeehouses, the clumps of yellow gumweed, and the orange plastic cones demarking the construction zones where more new condos are about to go up.

No one would guess just to look at me, as I motor east down First Street with plaintive French songs (Poulenc: perfect for the fog) playing on the tape player, that I, too, am doing something important. I'm going to get the mail.

Yet it isn't so hard, after all, getting the mail. You park in the ramp at the large Ziggurat-like facility, (there was once talk of moving the post office out into the suburbs, too) you climb the steps and enter the building, walk down the hall, turn left at the door, then through the big swinging doors: the mail will be sitting on the floor beside the Blumberg mail in a dirty gray sack. A short skinny guy with a waxy yellow flat-top, an earring, and a two-day stubble will be sitting on a stool reading the paper. "Have a good 'un," he'll remark absent-mindedly without looking up as you grab your bag and heave it to your shoulder, trying to get a firm grip on the small metal clasp that keeps the bag closed as you depart. But the bag may not be there, especially if you're early, as I often am. In that case the man will descend from his stool and shout "Jack, Bookmen's here," and then he'll say to you, "It'll be just a minute." Jack, a gray-haired, tired looking man with old-fashioned silver glasses, will gather the ropes up and bring the bag over, dropping it at your feet with a non-committal, if not distinctly hostile, "There you go," and return to his station.

I don't know what's wrong with Jack. Too many years of long nights at the post office? Not getting to drive to work in the morning fog, sun in the face, geese on the boulevard, beautiful buildings and people everywhere?

On my way back down First Street I pass Origami, (good sushi) the former Allied Van Lines Building (new home for the Theatre de la Jeune Lune), The Prairie Star Coffeehouse, then the handsome multistory labyrinth of the International Design Center. (Give me oak, ash, maple, birch, cherry, butternut–anything but teak!)

Turning south on Third Avenue I approach Moose & Sadie's Coffeehouse, where two or three people sit at small black tables on the pavement high above the street, reading the paper or looking out past the parking meters toward the eastern horizon. That's where I'd like to be sitting, although the bloom of the morning is so fleeting that perhaps it's better to be moving purposefully through it with a sack of mail on the seat beside you than to watch it disappear from the neighborhood bit by bit. I occasionally park and climb the concrete ramp that leads up to the sidewalk and the door to the cafe, to pick up a currant scone and an iced cappuccino or a double shot of mocha. The people there don't know me, I'm not a *regular*. I smile, they smile, we're trying. Then they turn and go about their work, hardly alert enough at times to get the job done as they lurch down into the refrigerator for the milk or slam the instrument that holds the wet grounds violently against the side of a metal sink. I wait patiently; I look at the chalkboard menu, the clock. Tee-shirts with the black and white Moose & Sadie's logo hang from a pole above the cash register. Bags of coffee beans for sale on the sill.

I used to half-expect someone to burst into the dark confines of the narrow wood-floored room from the street and greet a friend:

A: Hey! Look at this. I ran across a volume of Carlo Betocchi's poems last night at B & H.

B: Hey, great find! How do they sound?

A: I don't know. They have a Leopardi lean, maybe, less modern than Montale. Spare and melancholy. Here, I'll read you one. (And he begins in a slow, sure, and slightly comical voice:)

> I asked you what those flowers were,
> whose rare indigo faded
> on the yellow underbrush
> between the limed high walls
> behind the house, close to the rusted chicken-wire
> of the small garden of a few cabbages,
> their leaves gnawed by the hail.
> You answered:"They are wild chicory—
> so I called them as a little girl!"
> In the dry hot air they quivered
> on the stems in meager clusters—
> far from the heaven, whose language
> they stammered in bewilderment
> on earth and in the soul.

B: Hey,that's not bad. Almost like Machado in his Soria days.

A: (shaking his head doubtfully) I don't see the resemblance.

B: The key phrase, I think, is—

A: I know what you're going to say: rusted chicken wire.

B: No, it's—

"Here's your coffee. A currant scone?" And I turn to pay my bill.

17

When I pick up the thread of the conversation again it's:

B: Did you see the Chang/Agassi match?

A: I've got to tell you, I miss the Europeans. Think of Edberg, Lendl, Forget, Becker. These guys had *stature*–

B: Guy Forget had stature?

A: Call it a nervous stature–

B: What about Muster then? There you have stature… of a sort.

A: All I'm saying is that the Americans seem better or more interesting when they're struggling to…

This coffeehouse conversation never takes place, however.

When you get the mail in to work, then you sort it. Orders in one pile, everything else in the other. The orders you bring in to Jeanine, who's eager to begin entering and processing, and is very glad to see you so early. The rest of the mail–the checks, the bills, the advertisements, the catalogues, the magazines, the private documents from the accounting firm–go back into the canvas bag, to be deposited on Arlene's desk. When she sees the size of the bag Arlene will grimace and say "Oh brother, I'm going home," but she sorts and distributes just as well as the last receptionist, probably better.

At the coffee machine I run into my old friend John. He's excited about a new recording of Anne-Sophie Mutter singing Swedish art songs that he received the night before from his record club. "Oh, I was going to ask you," he says, "My son Brian is doing a report on mythology. I thought it would be interesting for him to do something about Dionysus, or Pan down in the swamp gathering reeds for his pipes; the contrast with Apollo, you know. But where is it in Nietzsche that he talks about all that?"

"The Birth of Tragedy," I take a wild guess. "But don't forget, John, Apollo was the god of music. And during the winter months Dionysus took over control of the temple at Delphi. The symbiosis between the two was very close. Calasso says... " And so the work day begins.

Only one thing bothers me about getting the mail. Nothing ever comes for me. A postcard once a year from my friend Steve in New York, telling me which matches he saw at the U.S. Open. More frequently a customer service questionnaire from Browning and Ferris Waste Disposal Systems: "Is the garbage man courteous and helpful?" "Do your dumpsters have any rough or dangerous edges?" Nevertheless I relish the morning drive, the ritualistic transfer of sacred bundles, the fog, the pink clouds, the jangling and poetic music on the car stereo, and then the friendly circuit through the warehouse where I work, and where I know all the people, and they still look beautiful.

Gila Panic

Pan has always struck me as a scruffy, second-rate god, as indeed he may well have been, but in his guise as the god of the sudden, groundless fear that grips travelers in remote and desolate places—the god of *panic*, in short—he's come upon me many times. Hilary and I are in the habit, when we travel in the Southwest, of pulling off on seldom traveled forest and desert roads to camp, miles from the nearest dwelling, telephone, or streetlight. It's legal, it's free, and the settings are frequently beautiful and sometimes majestic. Yet our enjoyment of such *ad hoc* campsites is invariably undermined by the irrational thought that we're about to be murdered. It's the rule, rather than the exception, that no sooner have we set up our little blue tent than some stranger will wander dangerously close, and on those occasions when one doesn't actually appear, the likelihood that he will makes for a fitful and uneasy sleep.

Not long ago we set up camp at just such a site a few miles south of the Gila Cliff-dwellings in southwest New Mexico. We'd taken the road to the ancient site from Silver City, forty-four miles north through ponderosa forests with the landscape becoming more open and beautiful as the elevation rose. The cliff dwellings themselves are set in a canyon rising from an expanse of meadow. The hike up the canyon was shady, with wildflowers and birds at every turn. Cutting back across the open, sun-exposed face of the rock we reached the caves.

I've seen so many of these cliff-villages over the years that all I could think of was "Looks like Tonto National Monument, but no jojoba bushes." Not that I wasn't moved and intrigued by the two large openings in the rock, the exaggerated overhangs, and the crumbling stone walls. One T-shaped window opening suggested the influence of the Chaco culture to the north. The volunteer ranger from Vermont, who was having trouble locating Ben & Jerry's Ice Cream at the supermarkets nearby, lectured us briefly before setting us loose to stumble, climb, and poke our way like children through the plazas, rooms, and courtyards of a two-family village inhabited seven-hundred years ago by people who knew neither how to read nor write, though they undoubtedly knew how to hunt, and to pray.

"What do you think these people thought about all the time?" an elderly woman with wild white hair and sturdy canvas pants said in a loud voice further amplified by the smoke-blackened walls of the overhanging cliff. I was the only person standing nearby. Startled, I was uncertain whether she expected me to respond. "The same things we think about," she continued after a pause, looking out from the shadows toward the glaring sun and the stunted trees on the opposite face of the canyon. "Getting a good girl to marry your son, finding a good boy for your daughter."

Well that's an interesting perspective, I said to myself. I was going to ask, "But what about the ones who didn't have children?" but she had climbed up a ladder and down into a grain storage chamber out of sight, and I let the issue drop.

Having driven so far up into the mountains we decided to hike up a creek to a natural hot springs in the woods above the visitor's center, following a trail cursorily described on a mimeographed sheet with the title "Short Hikes in the Gila Wilderness." The woman in the gift shop warned us that to reach the springs you have to cross the river twice, but neither the woman nor the trail guide saw fit to mention that there is more than one trail leading up into the woods from the trailhead. When we'd reached the spot designated on the map we found paths leading off in several directions, and all of them seemed to be making for the creek. We followed the most conspicuous one through the tangled creek-bottom underbrush until we reached the river itself, which had overflowed its banks and was coursing vigorously through the bushes along the shore.

How deep was the river? The water was thick and brown, we couldn't tell. Up to the knees? Certainly. Up to the waist? Very likely. Would we make it across unharmed? No doubt. Would camera and binoculars make it across undamaged? Perhaps not. Would the hot springs be hot when we got there, with all that rainwater running over and past it? Who could say?

We returned to the car, foregoing our dream of a good hot soak in the shadows of the pines, and began our return trip out of the valley and then down through the mountains, on the lookout for likely side-roads with secluded camping spots.

The road we finally hit upon followed a creek, and it was so bad that I pulled our rented car off into the grass at the first rocky plunge into the creek-bed. (Rule number one: Always pull your car off the road, however remote it may seem. Someone will soon be coming by.) We carried our gear around the next turn, where the land rises and another stream joins the first at the face of a handsome sandstone cliff. There we found a flat, grassy meadow surrounded by birch and pine between the two streams. It was a beautiful site. Others had camped here. The two streams made a pleasant gurgling sound. Sunlight beamed on the flank of the cliff. Hummingbirds were feeding in the shadows on the far bank.

The tent was up, I was on the verge of scrounging for wood to build a fire, when I heard the low drone of an engine. Airplane? No, a green jeep was coming very slowly down the narrow rutted two-track road from the shadows of the pine forest above us. As it came around the final corner into view I scrutinized the people inside. An Indian family, probably Zuni, all of them small-boned, lean, and alert. What had they been doing up on that mountain road? Nut-gathering? Poaching? Hunting down livestock for an employer? They didn't look like they were returning from a picnic. Two young boys were bouncing excitedly in the back seat, but their father looked stolidly straight ahead as he passed us moving at a crawl, as if the nuances of the heavily rutted road were too treacherous to be neglected for even a moment. With his thin face, shaved head, big ears, shiny olive-colored skin, and bulging eyes, he reminded me of no one so much as a latter-day Niccolo Machiavelli. Not a happy association. His wife glanced at us and smiled as they passed—I had waved briefly at the passing vehicle—but that change in expression, although it rose from a natural and spontaneous social impulse, was brief and hesitant.

Once we'd eaten a cold dinner of sausage and bread on the river bank, washed down with a cup of lukewarm bourbon and water, we walked up the road through the shadows of the woods to see what might be up there. The road got narrower and the woods thickened. Someone had built a fine split-rail corral a few turns upstream.

"It's reassuring to see something so well-made and sensible and humane out here in the middle of nowhere," Hilary said, and I had to agree. Nature is beautiful and mysterious, but it's also a little creepy, especially at night.

I got up before dawn. The dew was heavy, I could see my breath as I crawled out of the tent. The stream was still gurgling away. I felt stupidly happy to be standing in the darkness beside that little stream with another day of adventure ahead. Walking down the road to the smaller stream, I could see that our car was still parked where I'd left it, a distant patch of white amid the trees in the pre-dawn light. Later, higher up on the ridge, we watched the sun rise and spread itself across a blanket of blue cotton fog that had engulfed the valley.

Back in Silver City, we had breakfast at the Corner Cafe. The coffee was hot and good.

My aunt used to teach school in Silver City. I was tempted to ask one of the waitresses if she'd known her.

Return to Zuni

New Mexico Highway 53 runs right through the center of dusty Zuni Pueblo. The road is lined with gas stations, jewelry shops, and craft supply stories. Zuni is the largest of the pueblos in the Southwest and the tribe is widely considered to produce the finest craft work.

It would be easy to visit the craft-shops at Zuni and think you've seen the pueblo. Ramshackle adobe dwellings spread haphazardly back from the highway in both directions, many of the streets are nothing more than spaces between buildings, and the buildings often sit at odd angles to one another, which makes it difficult to tell whether you're entering the village or just driving up into someone's front yard. On our first visit to Zuni we had nosed our way through the village without coming upon either the plaza or the old church. We were determined this time to see them both.

The plaza in Zuni is where the famous Kachina dances are held every year. Photos from the Curtis era show it to be a multi-leveled courtyard on the architectural order of Taos pueblo, but when we finally located it, having asked several teenagers returning home from school where it was, it turned out to be nothing more than a space between two buildings, open to the east, with several narrow alleys running into it from other directions. From one side of this earthen courtyard you can look down into the weed-filled confines of the graveyard that extends out from the old mission church. By virtue of the same propinquity, the roof of the church would be a very good place from which to watch the seasonal dances that lie at the heart of the Zuni faith.

We entered the unlocked church expecting little and were surprised to see, high overhead on either side of the nave, a series of stunning murals depicting Kachinas engaged in dances, processions, and offerings. The figures are life-sized, vividly rendered, and proportionally exact. The costumes are wild and colorful and the masks are bizarre, although the murals are obviously sober and serious in intent. The background paintings of the surrounding countryside are also very well done. Considered as a group, they made the Roman Catholic "stations of the cross" paintings that were hanging in thin wooden frames on the walls beneath them look tepid, anthropocentric, and slightly pathetic in comparison. Well, the passion of Christ is a pathetic thing, by definition: The two words—passion and pathetic—have the same root. If the Zuni figures look childishly vigorous and flamboyant, with their grotesque masks, dramatically striped clothes, feathered headdresses, staffs, and leggings, all the same they appear to be doing something important and sacred. The figures in the stations of the cross, on the other hand, seem to be doing something stupid and wrong, while Christ himself merely suffers it all with an agonized but obviously superior "they know not what they do" expression on his face.

Far be it from me to suggest that a religion based on supplicating nature is better than one based on the moral anguish of humanity's imperfect yet spiritually active and striving nature. But judging from the evidence of the old mission church at Zuni, it makes a better mural.

I might as well add here that in so far as I understand it, the Zuni religion isn't based on supplicating nature. It's rather that in Zuni life clans, individuals, and superhuman entities exist in a web of inter-related forces and obligations that needs to be ritualistically maintained to insure that things continue to prosper. Of course it may be argued that Christianity rests on a similar foundation: if everyone behaved with perfect charity toward everyone else the Kingdom would be upon us. The Zunis believe harmony can and perhaps will be maintained, however, while Christians are committed to the belief that due to our fallen nature, we're constitutionally incapable, as individuals or as a group, of maintaining it.

A man was sitting with his back to the altar near the front of the nave, reading a newspaper. As we approached him he looked up and Hilary made a remark about the beauty of the murals. "I painted them," he informed us matter-of-factly. "I've been working on them for twenty-seven years." We asked him if he'd tell us who the figures were, and what they signified. In the end we chatted for an hour, and he told us a good deal not only about the murals, but also about himself (orphaned at five, dishonorably discharged from the Korean war, drinking, confusion, re-evaluation, listening to the elders). He told us about the clans, the societies, and the tribal initiations. (The green altar on the upper left section is an exact reproduction of the altar in his medicine lodge.) We left the church feeling that we'd made some sort of genuine contact, however superficial, with the ongoing life of the village.

Nevertheless we could not resist a final visit to one of the craft shops out on the highway before heading north to Gallup. I'd long been mildly interested in picking up a Zuni fetish; they're sold at every craft and art store in the

Southwest. There are so many available, however, and they come in so many shapes, colors, and sizes, that choosing one over another had long since come to seem like an arbitrary matter to me. Meanwhile, the notion that any one of these thousands of animal images could possess even an iota of sacred power was growing ever more doubtful. I was determined that if and when I purchased a fetish, it would be of the old, rough-hewn style, and not the new, more elaborate and intricate, but patently touristic and artificial one. I was also committed to buying it in Zuni. My fanciful hope was that some event would take place by which the

fetish would *chose me*, and this, in fact, is what happened.

The fetishes at the Turquoise Trader are stored in long low-sided wooden boxes behind the glass doors

of a display case. All the bears are in the first box, all the turtles in the next, etc. I opened the case and began poking around desultorily among the little stone creatures, most of which are less than two inches long. I pulled one out to take a better look. It was in the old style, with an offering of turquoise and pipestone pebbles strapped to its back. (You make an offering to the image, and it rewards you with its power.) "What is that, a badger? I've never even seen a badger," I mumbled to no one in particular.

"That's not a badger; that's a wolf," said the saleswoman who had come up behind me.

"Well, I have seen a wolf," I said.

Oberg Mountain Road. 8:00 A.M. January 1, 1996.
Fresh snow in the pines. I was just getting out of the car when
I saw two gray dogs, one smaller and blacker than the other,

climbing up the embankment from the woods onto the unplowed road fifty yards ahead of me. But where was their master? Where was the dog-sled? It took me only a split-second to realize that these creatures weren't dogs, but wolves. I was standing beside the car with the door open, I couldn't believe my eyes, yet at the same time I was taking in every detail—the dark, solemn look, the hanging head and tail, the large size, the frosty fur. They looked at me for a few seconds, and then they slowly and deliberately turned and began to walk up the unplowed road. I howled as convincingly as I could. They both turned their heads, and then continued their retreat with only an occasional backward glance. Majestic, unperturbed, or merely sleepy? I don't know. But as I watched them I felt that subtle frisson that comes with the recognition that you're in the presence of something rare and sacred, and that the moment at hand is unlikely ever to be repeated. They're still there, you can see them growing smaller as they pad silently toward the bend in the road, the ridge. These are wolves.

Just then two young backpackers muscled their way past me toward the display case and I was left holding an unrecognizable wolf fetish with a very long nose and a short thick tail. I liked it. I bought it. Wolf may or may not be my power symbol, but I'm taking it as such until something better comes along. And the fact that the animal in question has actually shown himself to me helps me to overcome a natural reluctance to *play* at other people's religion.

In the pamphlet that came with the stone carving I read that Wolf represents swiftness, or the East. (Early riser, morning light.) Also, hunting. (Nietzsche's Big Hunt!) Further on I read:

> *The Zunis consider those things that are least understood and*
> *most mysterious as the most sacred and powerful. Because*
> *animal ways can never be truly understood by humans, animals*
> *represent unknown powers to the Zunis. As man tries to grasp*
> *forces which are beyond his immediate control, he looks to*
> *animal spirits as a bridge to the distant, greater powers.*

There is wisdom in this remark. We don't understand nature, and we never will. This is made very plain by the dismal plaques to be found on every nature trail you come upon in the West. These plaques will tell you about the cross-bedding in the limestone, or the role of fires in the forest succession, or the importance of preserving the cryptobiotic mass on the desert floor. Many of them carry a latent or explicit message—Watch out, Leave things alone, Everything works fine when you're not here! But I have never read a sign that explained to me where the feeling of awe, mystery, and beauty comes from that envelopes both the landscape and myself time and again in the mountains and deserts, along the rivers, under the bluffs.

Someday I'll be walking along a mountain trail through the woods and I'll see a sign:

Every emotion is a presence— Alain.

Coming out onto a luscious meadow there will be a second:

And what, then, is emotion? "Briefly, it is a preparation of the human
body, an incipient way of acting which, in anticipation of its object, is
on the point of doing what it would do if the object were there."

But what of that emotion which is the response to an object? "My heart leapt to my throat when I caught sight of..." and so on. Can emotion be the anticipation, and also the recognition of the "presence" itself? Well, why not? Mystery, panic, exhilaration—something *elicits* these emotions. Something there or something not there.

Finally coming out to the edge of the cliff, from which the entire spread of the canyon can be seen, there will be a third sign, which says, simply:

LOOK.

Picnic Fare,

or,

a Recipe for Friendship

I suspect that for as long as human beings have pondered the cosmos, time itself has occupied a central place in those speculations. Paintings in caves, rocks aligned to mark the seasons, the burial of the dead: What is at issue here, other than memory, durability, change, and the passage of time? It may be intriguing to consider, in fact, whether self-awareness and an awareness that *time is passing*, are one and the same thing.

To notice and mark the passage of time is one thing, however; to capture or even to describe that passage is something else again. The analytic investigation of this common and elusive entity, time, has, from Zeno's day to our own, produced a variety of intriguing paradoxes and evident contradictions. It's become popular in recent times to refer to the "space-time continuum," as if, by using this phrase, we'd finally put some polish on the issue, and yet the idea that space and time are inextricably intertwined and "moving" together along a seamless track is just as strange as any other. Space doesn't really *move*, after all, and neither does time. Things move through space, and this takes time. The simplicity of this observation borders on the moronic, I realize, but there isn't much more we can say.

As a further twist to the curious situation we find ourselves in, it's often been noted that things can easily be moved back and forth through space, while time always moves in the same direction. If I rearrange the furniture in the living room and find the result unsatisfactory, it doesn't require a great deal of effort to restore the room to its original configuration. Recapturing the time I've lost during all the re-arranging is simply not possible.

Yet it strikes me that even this distinction is more apparent than real. When we move furniture, the couch may collapse, and in all likelihood there'll be a gouge in the hardwood floor before we're through with all the re-arranging. And if we do decide to move things back the way they were, the fact that we've tried, and failed, to introduce a new arrangement to the room will give the original setting an entirely different feel. Oh my God! We're stuck with this?

On the other hand, time can, I believe, occasionally be "recaptured." This happens when we get together with old friends, for example. The setting (the space) may be incongruous—an airport lobby, an unfamiliar bar—but the effect is one of reviving time by reconnecting with those who've shared important experiences with us. The years simply fall away. This is not really a "going back," however, but a catching up. We move ahead in time, ineluctably, and I guess it's just as well that we do, because the best things in life, of which friendship is certainly one, are rooted in ongoing activity. When we get together with our friends, often men and women we've known for years, there's no need to explain or conceal much of anything. In one another's presence we unlock a zone of shared time within which interactions take place with absolute security and freedom. Our past returns to life, while the future loses its harsh and fearful contours. Everything dissolves in a lovely and gratifying "now" that seems limitless in extent.

Strictly speaking it's not merely time, however, but common experience, that friends share with one another. The specific content may be nothing more significant than an appreciation of textiles, Wagnerian opera, or golf. In approaching this shared matter friends invariably exhibit a contrast in temperaments and perspectives, sometimes subtle, sometimes dramatic, and this is what leavens the relationship.

Plato raises the question in one of his dialogs whether, in friendship, like attracts like or unlike. He rejects both possibilities in the end, without, however, arriving at the sensible conclusion that friendship is a potent and ongoing dialectical interchange of like with unlike which requires both intimacy and distance to sustain itself. The intimacy, the contact, generates the shared "stuff" of the relationship. The distance, the space, allows us to evaluate and integrate that experience, rather than merely being swept up by it and later deposited in a heap.

Space and time, unlike and like, a coming together and a moving apart: I guess life is like a giant accordion learning how to play itself. And never the same tune twice!

It's a very hot day; there's an oppressive, quivering, heaviness to the air. Throughout the city air-conditioners are roaring. I'm enjoying my own little oasis of cool, I'm listening to some innocuous Italian lute music and thinking about space, time, and picnics. Not about *having* a picnic, but simply about the picnic itself as a social (and metaphysical) activity. There are few activities more conducive to the growth and sustenance of friendship, I think; few that allow us so effortlessly to slip the bonds of space and time. Any extended food-event with friends is likely to incorporate reminiscences, small-talk about films, how the kids are doing, or the events of the day, and that good-natured gustatory sharing that has given us the word *companion*: "he (or she) with whom we share bread." What makes the picnic unusually powerful and appealing, I think, is that it removes the burden of last-minute preparation from the event while adding an element of atavistic nature-play that may actually constitute a brief but genuine "going-back-in-time." There are no hosts and no guests. A picnic is a blissful interlude, in short, for the creation of which only three things are required, and everyone knows what they are: a bucolic setting, a mess of food, and friends.

THE SETTING

It shouldn't be difficult finding a place to settle down for an outdoor meal. Whatever feels right is right. Yet it seems to me that the finest picnic spots almost invariably have greenery, a degree of privacy, and a view. The greenery allows us to imagine that we've escaped the pressures of modern life and returned to the pastoral ease of Theocritus and Virgil, of Giorgione and Monet. In imagining this, we succeed in doing it, and the companionship of our friends, who are bent on the same retreat, makes the transformation all that much more convincing. Utter wilderness will not do, however. It's hard to get to, dangerous to be in, and these facts make the repast itself more of a practical necessity than an aesthetic lark. The thought that sooner or latter we've got to "get back" clouds the event as well.

On the other hand, those picnics that take place on picnic tables amid noisy throngs of strangers at the beach or in a city park, usually in the hot sun, with charcoal fumes, lime-colored Frisbees, barking dogs, and blaring radios tuned to all the wrong stations–those picnics seldom attain the degree of privacy and repose that allow us to feel that we have actually "gotten away." They can be fun, especially if we and our chosen *famiglia* can generate sufficient racket to sustain the hegemony of our own sector of the social space, but it's a giddy, hectic kind of fun in which the restorative murmurs of friendship's supple flow are all but drowned in the crashing surf of an appealing, but broader and far less personal humanity.

Greenery, then, in the midst of civilization, but at the same time slightly removed from it. And there must be a vista.

If I insist on this point, it's because it seems to me that unlike a sit-down dinner, where the focus is on food and conversation directed back and forth between friends across a table, often with some degree of heat, a picnic is, or ought to be, more poetical, expansive, and diffuse. We flop on the ground, crossing our legs, or sprawl awkwardly with one stiff arm holding our torso more or less upright. We point this way and that, one minute facing toward one another, while the next we're looking off across the lake or down into the valley we've perched ourselves above. The ambiance of a picnic is enhanced, I think, by the interludes when we fall silent, wrapped in our private thoughts, dreaming dreams of beauty and indolence and mutual affection as the wine flows and exotic morsels of food disappear into our mouths one after another. Life should be like this all the time.

A bluff on the east bank of the Seine a few miles south of Rouen. Hilary and I picked up our rental car in the city, and almost immediately stopped at a grocery store to purchase wine, cheese, and rabbit paté. We snake our way onto a back road above the river, where French workman are realizing their dreams of a second home by means of concrete blocks, PVC pipes, and plaster, and hike down through tall grasses to the edge of the bluff. The blue sky, the gentle curve of the river flowing down from distant Paris, the classical red-brick chateau peeping out through the trees on the plain just below us, the sweep of the landscape, the exquisite quality of the inexpensive foods we've just spread out on the ground, make us feel that we've stumbled into a Shangra-La of European civility. Which in fact we have.

But you don't need to travel halfway around the world to find a proper setting for a picnic. One of the finest here in Minneapolis is on the west bank of the Mississippi just upstream from the Plymouth Avenue Bridge. The old Grain Belt brewery rises to the north across the river. Forklifts scurry back and forth in the lumberyard directly across the way. A barge may pass, huge and primitive and slow, or maybe two barges piggy-backed in front of an antique tugboat. To the south the buildings of downtown Minneapolis glisten in the evening sun. The green lights on the suspension bridge spanning the river have come on, seagulls pass, and a killdeer is peeping shrilly on a narrow strip of beach somewhere nearby. The bank, though steep, is grassy, and the ash trees planted along the boulevard will be a forest someday.

Another fine spot is on the hill north of the Lake Harriet Rose Gardens. Park in the lot by the rock garden, then walk around the lake. It will take you forty-five minutes, it will build your appetite, and you'll feel the full force of colorful urban activity that you'll only catch glimpses of from where you're going to sit. From the gradual rise of the hill you can see the perennial gardens spreading out beyond the classic fountain with its statues imported second-hand from New York City. The lake shimmers through the trees, couples wander here and there amid the garden beds, pausing to observe a chrysanthemum or a peony. Children run and shriek.

Or take a canoe and put in on the west side of Cedar Lake. Cross the lake and enter the dark weedy channel that connects it with Lake of the Isles. Once you've emerged from the channel into sunlight again, you'll pass under a Beaux-Arts bridge into the larger lake, along the banks of which people are jogging, fishing, and feeding geese. Now head for the bridge you see in the distance to the right of the wooded island. A hundred feet to the right of the bridge you'll see a grassy patch hidden from the paths above by a row of honeysuckle hedges. Beach the canoe and get out. Unfold your blanket and open the basket: you're there.

WHAT'S IN THE BASKET?

A successful picnic meal can consist of nothing more than a stack of ham sandwiches slathered with mustard and chopped onions, a bag of potato chips, and a six-pack of beer. But the exotic atmosphere that's sometimes lacking in a familiar local setting can be evoked by easy-to-prepare European foods. A slice of pâté, a wedge of Brie, a container of sliced apples and a baguette will do the trick with minimal effort. On the other hand, a classic picnic spread might well include several of the following Mediterranean delicacies.

tzatziki

A depressingly weak version of this tasty white sauce is available in tiny paper cups to be drizzled on gyros sandwiches in Greek restaurants and fast-food concessions everywhere. The real thing is very easy to make, however, and it tastes much better. You simply take a quart of whole-milk yogurt and drain it for a few hours through a strainer lined with a dishtowel, putting a bowl under the strainer to catch the juice. The longer you wait, the thicker the yogurt becomes, although two hours should be sufficient for the task. Next, put the yogurt in a bowl and add two cucumbers that you've peeled, grated, and perhaps even drained to remove the excess water. Mince four or five cloves of garlic and add them to the white paste along with enough dill to have an effect. Add two tablespoons of olive oil and chill.

To serve tzatziki you can either spread it with a knife onto French bread or set the bowl out onto the picnic blanket to dip wedges of pita into. Either way, you'll probably end up dreaming of the dull clank of distant cowbells on windswept Greek islands at sunset, or better yet, of the Aristotelian scheme of elements. The coarse bread is EARTH, the aromatic dill is AIR, the virulent garlic is FIRE, and the cool cucumber, of course, is WATER.

What, then, might the yogurt itself be? In the system of the ancient Greeks the yogurt, which is mysteriously generated from goat's milk and invisible floating yeasts, embodies the flowing, chaotic energies of the cosmos from the midst of which life in its varied and miraculous forms emerges.

I read that in a book somewhere.

gazpatcho

They call it a liquid salad. They being the Spanish, who combine fresh tomatoes, green peppers, cucumbers, garlic, and onions—all diced until they're pulp—with tomato sauce, wine vinegar, salt, cayenne pepper, sugar, olive oil, and a mess of herbs including masses of fresh parsley and just the right amount of that dangerous leaf, tarragon. Gazpatcho has zing. You can serve it in bowls or in paper cups along with chunks of buttered bread or homemade croutons. Stale bread is often added right into the soup. In fact, although we think of gazpatcho as a kind of tomato soup, bread and vinegar have traditionally been considered the two essential ingredients.

It's even been suggested that the vinegar-soaked bread offered to Christ on the cross was an early form of gazpatcho!

Here are the approximate proportions:

2 lb. fresh or canned ripe tomatoes
1 green pepper, cut into bits
1 large onion, similarly chopped
2 cucumbers, peeled and diced
4 tablespoons red wine vinegar
1/4 teaspoon tarragon
1/4 teaspoon sugar
2 or more cloves garlic, chopped
1 cup tomato juice or ice water (to thin)

Add a handful of chopped parsley and whir these ingredients in a food processor, a little at a time if necessary, until they form a smooth paste. Add salt and olive oil to taste. Toy with the vinegar and tarragon until you've got them just right. Add crushed ice to cool the mixture in a hurry, or to keep it cold on your way to the picnic site.

garbanzo salad

The city of Florence is often referred to as the cradle of the Renaissance, and with good reason. Dante, Michelangelo, Giotto, Machiavelli, Botticelli, Guicciardini, Cavalcanti, Alberti, Donatello: Florentines one and all, or Tuscans at any rate. The Sienese are also Tuscans, of course, although the art of their city long remained rooted in the Gothic world. Whatever tone they adopt, Tuscans are well-known not only for artistic brilliance, but also for their love of beans—so much so, in fact, that other Italians refer to them as *fagioli*, which is to say "bean-eaters."

I've often wondered, twisting the opener around yet another can of garbanzo beans, as the sky grows pink in the west and my rubbery legs, wearied from a long hard day on the loading dock, cry out for the relief of a tiny glass of cheap Chianti, might there be a connection? Brilliance and beans?

In any case the canned bean, and in particular the canned garbanzo bean, has much to offer. Somehow, all the processing and canning heat leave the garbanzo unfazed, like a Florentine architect in the face of a tempting but awkward civic commission. You open the can, you drain and rinse the beans, you put them in a large bowl, and you're on your way to a simple yet substantial dish.

Once the beans are in the bowl, chop the onions, red, white or yellow, and mix them in. Chop and add some parsley, and douse the whole with olive oil, balsamic vinegar, pepper, and salt. As a final touch press a clove or two of garlic and a bit of sage, either powdered or crumbled, into the mix. Bits of sweet red pepper, fresh or canned, would also be nice. Pour yourself another glass of that cheap Chianti, put "Ecco la Primavera" on the stereo (but of course, you've been listening to it the whole time, I should have known!) and open your volume of Cavalcanti's sonnets at random:

> Flowers and green are such a part of you,
> with every lovely thing that shines on earth,
> your presence makes the sun less bright and true,
> and he who does not see you has no worth.

This simple salad makes a wonderful picnic dish. As an alternative, you might consider putting the beans into a food processor and mashing them into a paste; add salt, 1/2 cup of olive oil and three cloves of chopped garlic, and serve with wedges of pita bread.

It may strike you that the recipes I'm offering here are a little vague or slapdash. Yet I have it on the highest authority that this is also how they do things in Tuscany. In his colorful book *A Tuscan in the Kitchen* Pino Luongo describes a simple salad almost identical to mine, using phrases like "…if you don't like onions leave them out" and "Add the vinegar splash by splash, drop by drop… You splash, you mix, you taste. When it's right for you, stop." Surprisingly, Luongo says nothing about sage. Well, I can't do anything about that.

I'm preparing a treatise, drawing on the work of Francesco de Sanctis, Etienne Gilson, and other distinguished scholars, in which I suggest that the Beatrice who so inspired Dante in his *La Vita Nuova*, and who guided him in the final segment of his immortal *Comedia*, was not, in fact, a woman he saw in the street in Florence and doted on for the rest of his life, as the libidinous have argued. Nor, as religious scholars have consistently maintained, was she the concept of spiritual beatification itself. I believe, and am well prepared to demonstrate, that Dante's Beatrice was in fact nothing other than a symbolic, hermetic, name for that humble, and yet altogether lovely and satisfying bean, the garbanzo.

peperoni alla Siciliana

The aroma produced by a red bell pepper grilled over the burner of a gas range on the end of a fork, or charred in the broiler on a piece of tin foil, is strange and evocative— something on the order of burning sweetgrass. The poet Gerard Nerval would not, perhaps, have taken drugs or wandered all the way to Turkey in search of exotic experience had he been in the habit of grilling red peppers on the charcoal brazier in his lonely garret in Paris:

> *Respect an active spirit in the beast:*
> *each flower is a soul open to Nature;*
> *in metal dwells a mystery of love;*
> *"All things are sentient!"And mold your being.*

Red peppers don't need to be peeled to be enjoyed, however. To make a satisfying picnic topping, grill or broil four of them until they're black and soft. Then cut them into thin strips, either peeled or unpeeled. Next, slice and sauté a large onion in some olive oil, along with three cloves of chopped garlic. Cover the mess and cook it gently, adding a bit of water if it gets dry, until the onions are very limp. Then put in the pepper strips and 2 tablespoons of balsamic vinegar, and cook some more. Finally, put in a tablespoon of dry oregano, a handful of pitted and chopped Kalamata olives, one can of drained, chopped anchovy fillets, and 2 tablespoons of rinsed, chopped capers. Continue cooking over low heat for twenty minutes. Then cool. Adjust the oregano, salt, and oil to suit your taste.

Spread this colorful stringy vegetable paste over thick slices of French bread. A melange of flavors will linger in the mouth and throat. Fruit and flesh and oil and spice, charcoal and sweetgrass. It's a simple thing to make, yet eating it is like eating poetry itself.

eggplant caponata

The dishes I've been describing attack the sour, salty, garlicky regions of the palate. The following dish, which is also from Sicily, is no less sharp, but it has a pronounced element of sweetness as well. It's almost a chutney, and it would go nicely with a store-bought meal of paté, Brie, bread, and grapes or sliced apples. It takes time to make, however. I recommend you do what the Sicilians do: they make large batches of caponata when the eggplants are ripe, and they store it in earthenware jars. (Or try the refrigerator.)

To make caponata you must first prepare a charcoal fire and then grill three pounds of sliced, oiled eggplants along with two pounds of similarly prepared onions until they're cooked through to the point of being largely black. The carboniferous matter adds significantly to the flavor of the dish. (You can also do this in the broiler, but the result will be less flavorful.) When they've cooled, coarsely chop the slices and set them aside.

Next, combine the following ingredients in a mixing bowl:

    1 tablespoon cocoa
    1 15 oz. can chopped whole tomatoes in heavy puree
    1/3 cup dried currants
    1/2 cup olive oil
    1 tablespoon rinsed capers
    15 pitted and sliced green olives
    15 pitted and chopped Kalamata olives
    1/2 cup balsamic vinegar

Add the chopped eggplant and onions to the mixture, toss to combine, and check to see if the balance of flavors is sound. If necessary, add more vinegar, a splash at a time.

Caponata tastes better after it's been sitting on the kitchen counter for a while. Make it in the morning while listening to Darius Milhaud's *Le Bouef sur la Toit*, and serve it with crackers or bread on a hill overlooking the river in the evening, before you regale your friends with that long anticipated recitation, from memory, of the tenth of Horace's first collection of Epistles:

> *Fuscus, you love to live in the city: I DON'T.*
> *But good afternoon, anyway. I hope you are well.*
> *It's the only difference between us, this city vs. country—*
> *For in all else we're practically twins or brothers-in-mind...*
> *But while you keep to the nest, I praise the brooks*
> *Flowing through the sweet countryside, its*
> *stones overgrown*
> *With moss, its delightful groves. Need I say more?*
> *I begin to live, I reign, as soon as I've left*

The very same things you people praise to the skies—

And so on. But perhaps your friends have grown tired of these performances, and have chosen instead someone else's recitation, albeit with the aid of a printed text (well, the poem is much longer!) of Ronsard's "The Salad":

Wash your hands, get them good and clean,
Hurry and find a basket, friend, Jamyn;
Let us gather a salad, and so unite
To our passing lives this season's fruit.
With a straying foot, a roving eye,
Here, there, in a hundred out-of-the-way
Places, at the top of a bank, across a narrow
Ditch, or in a field left fallow
That of itself, never disturbed
By the plow, bears every kind of herb—
I'll go this inviting way alone.
And you, Jamyn, take that direction...

(Here Ronsard inserts a lengthy description of various French herbs.)

Then, reading the ingenious Ovid,
The splendid verses where he is Love's guide,
Step by step, still rambling, let us go
Back home. Rolling our sleeves to the elbow,
We'll wash our greens handful by handful
In the sacred waters of my beautiful
Fountain, blanch them in salt water, stir
And sprinkle them with red wine vinegar,
Richen them with the good oil of Provence.
Oil that comes from the olive trees of France
Ruins the stomach, it is so inferior...

It may seem odd to you that I'm interjecting bits of obscure poetry into a fairly straightforward rundown of familiar and easy picnic recipes. But the verses I've singled out have been written in distant times and places to celebrate the very things we're celebrating—food, friendship, beauty, nature, indolence. Art halts Time, or at the very least, it allows us to become comfortable in that mysterious and ineluctable stream. Horace, Cavalcanti, Ronsard, Nerval: They felt what we feel. Lines like *Let us gather a salad, and so unite / To our passing lives this season's fruit...* reinforce our own sense of the significance of being together in the midst of nature's recurring cycles.

It's true, we could just as well be discussing episodes of "Seinfeld" or "NYPD Blue." But these realms of allusion don't carry quite the same resonance, I'm afraid, nor do they bring us into contact with the pastoral dimension I'm attempting to evoke. There are no pastoral sit-coms, at least not since "Northern Exposure" went off the air. And, when all is said and done, the reason we know who Horace, Ronsard, and Nerval are, hundreds or even thousands of years after the fact, is that they expressed themselves with a classical perfection that we largely lack. They rode Time's arrow, they positioned themselves at Archimedes' point. They lifted the earth, not with an imaginary lever, but with a string of imaginatively chosen words.

bruschetta with summer tomatoes

There was a time when pesto ruled the Western world. Maybe it still does. But at the risk of betraying the very spirit of the age, let me suggest an alternative use for that fresh basil you picked up at the farmers' market the other day for fifty cents a bag.

I would like to believe that the word *bruschetta* is related to the English word *brusque*. The English word, though of uncertain origin, appears to be derived from the Italian word *brusco*, which means variously "tart, unripe, rude, peevish, ill-tempered, roughly hasty." What the modern Italian word bruschetta actually means I have no idea, but I do know what it is: a piece of toasted bread into which raw garlic has been rubbed. It's a crude, hasty, morsel of food that serves marvelously as a means of transport for the dishes I've just been describing, and no topping fits it better, I think, than a mix of coarsely chopped tomatoes, raw garlic, fresh basil, olive oil, and salt, in the following proportions:

> 2 lb. tomatoes, chopped
> 30 fresh basil leaves, chopped
> 5 cloves finely chopped garlic
> 1/2 cup olive oil

Mix these ingredients together, pile the red-green pulp onto the toasted slices of bread that have been rubbed brusquely with raw garlic, and shovel them one after the other into your mouth. As the mass of tomatoes diminishes, begin dipping the bread into the bowl, where the garlic, oil, herbs, and vegetable juices have accumulated.

If summer has an essence, then perhaps it's to be found at the bottom of that bowl.

But what, exactly, is an essence? I can well imagine this question arising at the end of a summer picnic, when the nighthawks have begun to swoop and cry and the wine is dwindling in the glass. The *essential* differs from both the accidental and the incidental, being fully adequate to embody or at the very least evoke the thing itself, while remaining purer, deeper, and simpler. The theatrical director who sets his production of *Hamlet* in China is suggesting that the particulars of time, place, and custom are not "of the essence" of the drama. The art instructor who advises her students to do a series of drawings with a rude stick (as one of mine once did) is suggesting that fancy tools have less to do with the essence of artistic expression than do vision and execution. A picnic without food, on the other hand? A poker game without chips? Such things are inconceivable. The food, the chips are essential to the matter at hand.

Philosophers have frequently challenged the concept of essence, however, suggesting that everything is unique, and in any case we never know what a thing is until we see what it does. Yet while it may be true that we never know a thing's essence fully, we do see what things do, time and again, and we can form an idea of what they're like with some degree of accuracy as a result. As we ponder a thing's essence, we're seeking to grasp not its general nature, but its inner core and most ample expression, as if to impress upon ourselves its enduring reality, stripped of both speciously abstract and tiresomely incidental effluvia.

Surprising as it may seem, essences are invariably a matter of detail. The poet in her garret summons images to evoke, by means of disparate particulars, the essence of a feeling, a relationship, or an event, not quite knowing what she's after. The historian seeks to convey, by means of a few well-chosen incidents, the atmosphere of a remote *milieu*. The middle-aged couple takes their children to the ballpark, attempting to add to the storehouse of family memories while feeding their own nostalgia as well.

On the other hand, it often happens that a day goes by filled with irritating interruptions, confused initiatives, and mindless obligations, or with accidents pure and simple— things that were *not supposed to happen*. We crave the essential, and we recognize it when it appears because it swings us easily into a more harmonious and invigorating position with respect to our surroundings, our companions, and ourselves. The vast and varied particulars of our lives appear to have come together, for once, in a single image, event, situation, or exchange.

The word "essence" also refers to a smell, of course. Drive into the parking lot of any perfume factory in Grasse, with the Mediterranean sparkling in the distance, and you'll see the copper stills that were once used to reduce the lavender, jasmine, rose petals, or lilacs into concentrated essences. These scents have the power to send us into realms of beauty and longing that are both heavenly and inexplicable. Are flowers really that important to anyone? If so, then perhaps it's because the various phases of our own precious past may be evoked by evanescent natural scents. The essence of childhood is grandma's soap, the essence of adolescence is cut grass on the baseball field, the essence of college is cheap incense, the essence of early parenthood is baby powder and poop, the essence of European travel is diesel exhaust and espresso.

Essences are both definite and elusive, in other words, which is why we love them. They subvert the analytic intelligence, and bring us face to face with the sweet nothingness of the past in its most vague and concentrated form. They touch us in the deepest place.

The essence of summer in the bottom of a bowl of sopping garlicky tomatoes? Well, why not?

picnic wines

The classic picnic wine, although almost no one serves it, is a rosé made from the grenache grape. Once we've admired the rosy color, however, and reassured one another that, yes, there are dry, well-made, rosés on the market, we're likely to admit that either a hearty red or a fresh, well-balanced white would be a better choice for the occasion.

It seems to me that any of the several cheap white wines from central Italy—Frascati, Orvieto, Vernaccia de San Gimignano—compliment the sharp, bold, herby dishes we've been describing nicely. Their neutral, and in some cases even slightly sour taste makes many cheap California whites seem confused and presumptuous in comparison. In fact, they can often relay an austere medicinal shiver that effectively cuts and compliments the garlicky, tomato tastes and prepares the palate for another bite. Drinking Frascati, we think of Rome; Orvieto, and we think of that city's delightfully painted cathedral facade; a sip of Vernaccia de San Gimignano, and the medieval towers that loom above that politically insignificant town superimpose themselves on the skyscrapers we see in the distance across the lake.

A well-chilled bottle of Côte de Ventoux, on the other hand, from the Luberon region of Provence, will have us spouting Petrarch. Petrarch was the first man to climb Mont Ventoux, in 1327. In so doing, he became the first man in modern times to actually climb a mountain just for fun. When he reached the top he reached for the pocket edition of St. Augustine's *Confessions* that he carried everywhere (so we're told) and, opening it at random, he read:

> *Men go far to observe the summits of mountains, the waters of the sea, the beginnings and the courses of the rivers, the immensity of the ocean, but they neglect themselves.*

Petrarch was not the first man to climb Mont Ventoux, however. On the way up he met a shepherd who had already been to the top, many years earlier, and had, so he said, got nothing out of it except torn clothes and a firm resolution never to go there again. (Maybe the shepherd had brought along the wrong book!)

Any affordable white wine with the word "Mâcon" on it, designating it as a Chardonnay from that village in the lower reaches of Burgundy, would make a fine choice, as would any wine from a reputable Burgundian shipper—Verget, Louis Latour, Joseph Drouhin—with the aword "Chardonnay" or "Bourgogne" on the label.

Among hearty picnic reds don't overlook two offerings from Greece, the Naoussa and the Paros. There are plenty of Chiantis on the market, all of which may be worth trying at least once, although I would recommend the chunky wines from the heal of Italy's boot as well, the Rosso del Salento and the widely available Salice Salentino.

A Rhone red would be a good choice for a summer picnic. Be on the lookout for a wine from one of the villages north of Chateauneuf du Pape—Gigondas, Rasteau, Vaqueyras, or Seguret. California also produces plenty of robust reds and Rhone-style blends.

A RECIPE FOR FRIENDSHIP

The food has been prepared, the wine selected. You've chosen a site; yes, but where is everybody? Where are all your friends?

There is no recipe for friendship. None that I know of, at any rate. Friendship is both voluntary and exclusive, and every friendship is unique. Some are complex and silky, others are simple and harsh. For this reason, you don't actually "win" friends, nor do you "make" friends, the way a woodworker makes a birdhouse, first selecting the pattern, then purchasing the materials, etc. You find yourself becoming friends with someone in the context of vague, unnamable spirits, and the freedom and complexity of the process is the source of both its enormous potential for emotional satisfaction and its no less pronounced volatility. Building a birdhouse is one thing, after all; getting a bird to nest in it is something else again. The difficulties multiply when we pause to consider that we're not only the builder of birdhouses, but we're also the birds. From civility to courtesy to cordiality we hop our way along one another's oddly-crafted perches, tentatively exploring, until at last, if all goes well, we exchange visits, or better yet, take flight together, climbing and swooping and chattering like swallows.

Among seasoned friends all of this has long since become second nature, but it may be worth noting that at every stage in its development friendship requires not only an exploratory openness, but also a degree of self-consciously maintained respect and distance. Enthusiasm, like depression, is contagious, but it can also be an obnoxious quality, and few things in personal life are so problematic as the reckless self-expression we inflict on those we truly love and trust.

On the other hand, friendship does and must bring us out of ourselves into a shared and at least slightly celebratory atmosphere that's always implicitly spiritual. The goddess of the hearth isn't dead, nor the god of springs, of spices, of wine, of mountaintops. The muses attend us when we sit on the grass in front of the bandstand passing dishes and plates of food while the sun sets and the music drifts out across the lake. Romance, conversation, art, athletic competition, we've forgotten the names but the spirits that animate these things are the ones that make us want to live. The great picnics bring these elements together and elevate them to the level of poetry. The setting, the food, the conversation—might I here add a final element to the mix? I'm referring to poetry itself. Bring the right book—Petrarch brought Augustine, Ronsard brought Ovid—and you can nudge your gathering beyond chow and gossip to a more distinctive and memorable level, and it doesn't really matter if anyone's listening. Poetry opens us to a land of images above sense, where everything is fraught with a meaning that eludes us, though it clearly includes us, and the meaning is always the same: beauty and strangeness are very closely allied; time is something...but it isn't everything. Have another pickle. Take another look around.

MINOAN LINES

Not long ago Hilary and I spent a few weeks exploring the islands and villages of Greece. Yet reading books about Greece doesn't remind me of being there at all. On the other hand, when I open a book of poems by the French surrealist poet Jules Supervielle, I'm thrown back immediately into the world of elemental feeling that the Greek environment evokes:

> Love flashes across the
> falling saline masses
>
> and joy is evasive as melancholy.
> One enters as if entering
>
> a church under cascades of shadows
> noiseless and foamless.

> *A liner in its fiery berth*
> *Burns away the chains of earth.*
>
> *The anchor's hoisted, on each arm*
> *A mermaid wriggles with alarm,*
>
> *Jumps back into the ocean, so astounded,*
> *She's not aware of being wounded...*
>
> *The high seas come on board, disguised*
> *As blind men with briny eyes.*
>
> *And in the gulf of space, at last*
> *They slowly climb the mizzenmast.*

In short, Greece is a dream.

It would be a mistake to imagine, however, that there is anything disjointed or bewildering about the experience of traveling in Greece, or that the dream in which the Greek countryside envelops the traveler is one of mindless escape from the pressures of urban life. It's only that being in Greece gives one—it gave me, at any rate—a feeling of vivid and elemental contentedness that I have not experienced to the same degree in any other place. Past and future dissolve. The next meal, the next hike, the next ruin? They're all simply variations on the single meal/hike/ruin that is Greece, into which one drifts willingly and of which one never tires.

Whether the Greece I'm about to describe resembles the Greece familiar to current-day residents of Athens, Thessaloniki, or Rhodes, I have no idea, but I can state with some degree of confidence that 'my' Greece is not a merely touristic one. My interest in the country was kindled at an early age, watching "Epic Theater" productions of *Hercules Unchained* and *Jason and the Argonauts* on TV or at Saturday matinees. The green Aegean water of *Jason*, that Ray Harryhausen classic, made a deeper impression on me, I think, than did the famous sword-fighting skeletons.

At the age of twelve I gave a book report on an abridged version of *The Odyssey of Homer*, which didn't go well. I'd stopped reading the book halfway through, irritated that the character named in the title–Homer–hadn't appeared yet, and was put into an awkward situation when my English teacher asked me to relate the tale of Penelope and her weaving (which comes at the end of the book) to the class.

Another element was added to my picture of Greece by way of a rugged two-volume edition of Plato's dialogues that stood on the shelf at home, water-stained halfway up the spine by the rainwater that periodically swept down the driveway and into the basement of our house. Not that I learned anything specific about the True, the Good, or the Beautiful by examining these works. But I was impressed by the way Plato raised and sometimes resolved challenging issues of meaning and value in an atmosphere of gentlemanly seriousness and ease making use of everyday speech and drawing examples from the world of horsemanship and potting.

Our senior class put on a production of Sophocles' *Antigone*; I was assigned to make the plaster statues that stood on the pedestals on either side of Creon's throne room. But the breakthrough came during my freshman year in college. I had intended to study mathematics, but early on in my freshman year I registered for a class in Greek history for which the instructor demanded that we not only read Herodotus's *History* cover to cover, but also supply detailed notes demonstrating that we'd actually read it. How could any form of mathematics compare in interest with the richness, drama, and detail of that first historian and anthropologist of the West? Although I soon transferred my abiding interest from the ancient world to the richer and more complex world of Modern Europe, my choice of language was

Classical Greek. I found the script mysterious and fascinating, and because I was shy (and therefore reluctant to speak up in class) the fact that no one knows how ancient Greek was actually pronounced appealed to me. But more important than anything, I think, was the fact that while my friends were still learning how to say "The bakery is closed on Sunday, but my aunt lives right down the street," in German or Serbo-Croatian or French, I was already reading the lyric fragments of Sappho and Archilochos, and examining, with Plato, the question of whether like prefers like or unlike.

All that was a long time ago. But these things stay with you. In our travels Hilary and I have focused our attention on the centers of the modern world—Paris, Rome, London, Madrid—scurrying out for greater or less periods of time to Normandy, Provence, Burgundy, Andalusia, or Wales. Greece was simply too far away, too expensive to get to, and too set off from Europe to be a viable destination. There was also a lingering apprehension that too much time and history stood between the Greece of the temples and the poetry, and the Greece we'd be likely to meet up with on the streets of Sparta or Nafpaktos. Was Greece too hot? Too dirty? Too touristy? If so, then why did everyone who went there, from whatever walk of life, seem to love being there so much? The question became one, not of "if," but of "when." One must go to Greece.

II. A Cicerone

In 1993 a book-length meditation on Greek mythology by the Italian publisher and bibliophile Roberto Calasso, *The Marriage of Cadmus and Harmony*, was translated into English. An early review in *The New Republic* enticed me; a lengthy profile of the author in *The New Yorker* stunned me. Calasso's grandfather had been a friend of the greatest mind of the early twentieth century, Benedetto Croce. Calasso himself had absorbed Proust in the French by age thirteen. On the other hand, one of his great joys (or so the article reported) was writing blurbs for the books his firm publishes. "The game is this: to write something that actually has substance but write it in a way that will make a casual reader curious and will also inspire a bookstore owner in the smallest provincial town in Italy to order the book."

I bought Calasso's book on Greek mythology, and I found it to be unlike anything on the subject I'd ever read, except perhaps Ovid's *Metamorphoses*. It was a retelling, but also a rethinking and a reliving of the polytheistic life experience. Saturated with obscure illusions and arcane meta-psychological asides, it carries the reader nevertheless, by virtue of sheer brio, to a state where the academic question of "what the Greeks once thought" gives way to the more personal and mysterious issue of how we ourselves are tied to the cosmos, to the animal kingdom, to the cycles of growth and decay that give our lives structure and meaning. At lighter moments Calasso dilates provocatively on the interminable tussles between narcissism and self-knowledge, heroism and hubris, jealous territoriality and erotic expanse that the Greeks themselves explored with striking imaginative force.

The Marriage of Cadmus and Harmony isn't a travel book, however. It has neither geographical references, nor chapter-headings, nor an index. Yet it was the single work we turned to again and again on our trip in our efforts to make contact with the lore that would give a specific locality atmosphere and meaning.

These investigations took time, needless to say. We sat for hours under a cypress tree above the temple of Apollo at Delphi absorbing the curious history of turtles and snakes, mountain nymphs and raving sibyls, which underlies that most sacred site in Greece. We spent an entire afternoon on the steps of the Temple to Zeus in the Arcadian groves of Olympia, reciting to one another the history of the Olympic games, and the more remote and interesting events that make up the story of Pelops, Hippodamia, her incestuous father Oenomaus, and the double-crossed charioteer from whose dying curse the whole gruesome story of the House of Atreus devolves. Well, for many years Calasso and his wife spent the entire month of August in Olympia—it's the least we could do in return.

The final event, trivial in itself, which helped turn our attention in a serious way toward Greece once and for all, was this: Until a few weeks before we purchased our tickets we'd been planning to go, not to Greece, but to northern Spain, to walk the pilgrim trail to Compostela, under the inspiration of a copy of James Bentley's *The Way of Saint James*. There happens to be a picture of a frosty, wet, slate-gray church on the dust jacket of this book with an expanse of snow-covered mountains in the background. One Sunday morning in January, while we were shaping fantasies of exotic places into concrete plans of action against the harsh realities of the Minnesota winter, I happened to glance at that picture, and turning to Hilary I said, "Do we really want to go to the mountains of northern Spain at the end of March?"

III. Hospitality & Light

Two things that all the guidebooks to Greece discuss, but few succeed in conveying the character of, are the hospitality and the light. In *The Greek Islands* Lawrence Durrell touches upon the latter quality when he writes:

> *The light! One hears the word everywhere "To Phos" and can recognize its pedigree—among other derivatives is our English word "phosphorescent," which summons up at once the dancing magnesium-flare quality of the sunlight blazing on a white wall; in the depths of the light there is blackness, but it*

is a blackness which throbs with violet—a magnetic,
unwearying ultra-violet throb. This confers a sort of brilliant
skin of white light on material objects, linking near and far,
and bathing simple objects in a sort of celestial glow-worm
hue. It is the naked eyeball of God, so to speak, and it blinds
one.

It's possible that the subtle effects of the Greek light worked
their magic on us unawares, yet it seems to me that in early
April the Greek air is full of the smoke of burning olive grove
and vineyard prunings, as well as humidity coming in off the
sea, where the winter rains have not yet subsided. Then
again, it may be that having spent a good deal of time in the
crystal light of the Colorado plateau of northern New Mexico,
which is not only clear and dry but also seven-thousand feet
above sea level, the light of Greece seemed nice to us...but not
that nice.

This is not merely a question of aesthetics. It's integral to the
Greek experience. Calasso writes at one point in *The Marriage
of Cadmus and Harmony:*

> *By the time of the tragedians, 'dios' has come to mean*
> *nothing more than "divine," in so far as it is "a property of*
> *Zeus." But in the Homeric age 'dios' means first and foremost*
> *"clear," "brilliant," "glorious." To appear in Zeus is to glow*
> *in light against the background of the sky. Light on light.*
> *When Homer gives the epithet 'dios' to his characters, the word*
> *does not refer first of all to what they may have of "divine,"*
> *but to the clarity, the splendor that is always with them and*
> *against which they stand out.*

It may be that the Greek light charmed us in spite of
ourselves, for the landscape, the countryside, did possess an
inexplicably heroic, elemental, and brilliant caste. On the
other hand, the Greeks we chatted with in Athens and

elsewhere were deeply apologetic about the haze, the clammy mist, and the cool air—"It's usually sunny and hot at this time of year. We're very sorry, you should come back again in June," as if they were personally responsible, as individuals, for making sure that we, their visitors and guests, were enjoying our stay.

Which brings us to the subject of Greek hospitality. The travel guides uniformly describe a degree of friendliness toward foreigners among the Greeks that has no parallel in other European countries. "The Greek reputation for hospitality is not a myth. Greece is probably the only country in Europe where you may be invited into a stranger's home for coffee, a meal or even to spend the night." Well, Hilary and I have been invited into the homes of strangers in both England and France. But the tone of relations between visitors and natives in Greece is definitely distinctive. A superficial run-down of the differences the traveler is likely to encounter might run as follows: The English are tickled that we Americans, their country cousins, can be so guileless, brash, and interesting. The French treat you with either chilly formality or bemused respect and interest, but in either case you sense it's nothing personal. In Germany people try hard to please, but in a slightly sly and obsequious way that conveys the message, "Yes, we can and will be nice to you, because we're good Europeans; but in point of fact we're better than you, it's you who should be being nice to us." In Italy spontaneous niceness and enthusiasm is widespread, because individualistic Italians have no doubt that if you get to know them you'll be charmed by them, but the general run of interactions is on a level of absent-minded *sprezzatura*. Foreigners may come and go but the Italians are really only interested in one another.

In Greece things are a little different. There one feels an instinctive need on the part of shopkeepers and waiters and taxi-drivers and passers-by to be judged hospitable, warm, loving even, because this is what life demands of all of us. It's as if the German's desire to please were stripped of its underlying insecurity and combined with the Italian's irrepressible self-confidence, from which the narcissistic element had miraculously been removed. One senses swimming in the depths of a Greek's dark eyes, layer upon layer of hurt, anger, abnegation, and adjustment. From the domain of inarticulate wisdom they've fashioned for themselves in response to both their tragic history and their uniquely fierce temperament, they welcome you heartily.

In his book *Hellas* Nicholas Gage reports that to be the guest of a Greek is easy, to be the friend of a Greek is very hard. I seem to have been constructed the other way around. I am not warm or hospitable by nature, I'm cautious about getting to know people, I value formality highly, presuming it isn't unctuous or stiff. On the other hand, I like to think that once I've become friends with someone the friendship will endure, and I have almost enough friends of ten and twenty and even thirty years to prove it. (One can never have too many friends.) In all of this I resemble the French, I guess, who refer to one another by their last names for years on end, more than I do the Greeks. Effusions of hospitality embarrass me a little. Stolid Nordic that I am, I know I'll never be able to return such displays with sufficient warmth and energy to be convincing, although in my heart of hearts the love I feel may be deep and pure.

In the restaurants and hotels of Greece this did not present a problem, by in large. You come, you eat, you sleep, and then you pay, in an atmosphere of genuine but not demanding congeniality. What worried me (albeit only slightly) was a stop we were planning to make at the Hotel Pan in Delphi. A friend had recommended that we stay there: her great-aunt owned the place. Would the family roll out the red carpet for us, once they knew that a relative had recommended them to us? And if they did, what would the experience entail? Would we be worthy of it, or would we shame ourselves egregiously? As it turned out, that single stop set the seal on our entire visit, giving us the sense that the little niceties we experienced in Greece on a daily basis were but morsels of a greater abundance of good feeling just waiting to be tapped.

The Hotel Pan sits on the downhill side of the main street of Delphi amid a long row of similar hotels, tavernas, and tourist boutiques. The gently curving street is mildly attractive. A good deal of construction was in progress when we arrived, in preparation for the tourist season, although there were few tourists around at the time. Restaurants stood empty.

We parked directly in front of the door to the hotel, checked in, and were given what may well have been the best room in the place—it was the only one that had an unobstructed panoramic view of the valley. After a trip to a nearby grocery store we settled in for the night, eating dinner on the small balcony of our room while we looked out across the descending landscape to the distant town of Itea and the blue curl of the Gulf of Corinth twenty miles away. We could hear the sounds of children playing in the distance. An elderly couple worked unhurriedly in their tiny yard thirty feet below us, clearing dead vines and debris from the surface of a stone wall, while another couple, unseen in the depths of an apartment across the street, was engaged in a lively dispute that grew more heated as the evening progressed. Goat bells echoed faintly from the depths of the long valley, their haunting tintinnabulations seemed to be coming from everywhere at once. Smoke curled up from the shadows of red-tiled roofs to meet the last rays of the declining sun, which, as it slipped from view, brought the graceful interplay of the hills to the west into increasingly dramatic relief. Blue to purple to black, the land tightened itself up while the distant waters of the gulf grew brighter and more silvery as if in reply. The lights of Itea began to twinkle, the stars came out, the ouzo in the bottle made its way into our glasses, we discussed our lives and our families and ourselves and our disappointments and our aspirations under the auspices of a Twilight God which was among the most powerful and enchanting we'd ever met up with. "Why can't everyone be this happy?" we asked ourselves, "Why can't everyone we love be here with us tonight?"

The following morning we ate breakfast in a long cozy pine-paneled room with traditional fabrics hanging on the walls. When we'd finished eating I said to the man serving us (who'd checked us in the previous afternoon) "Excuse me. We know one of your relatives. Dimitria, Susie's daughter." His already cheerful face brightened and he said, "I'm Yanni. I'm Susie's cousin." He shook hands with both of us and went back into the kitchen, where we could hear him exclaiming to someone in Greek exactly who had come to stay with them. A few minutes later a short elderly woman with a shock of thick black hair and large fluid eyes came up to our table and, standing between our chairs, she smiled and laid a hand firmly on each of our shoulders. She told us her name. We smiled and told her who we were, entering by fits and starts into the sort of halting conversation you have with someone with whom you share no vocabulary whatsoever. Lots of smiles and nods, lots of warmth passing back and forth, but absolutely no comprehension on either side except that basic and invaluable recognition of mutual liking. After a while she left the room and returned with a second pot of coffee. Nothing could have pleased us more. Refills in Greece are unheard of.

As we were leaving the hotel a few minutes later Yanni stopped us in the lobby to ask if we were going to visit the sacred ruins. We told him we were, and he ran hurriedly to the adjoining shop to ferret out an English language guide to the sprawling site. When we told him we were planning to visit the little port town of Galaxidi as well later in the day his eyes lit up. "A good choice," he said, "It's a gem."

The ruins of Delphi may well be the most historically significant, beautiful, and moving in Greece. It was here that Western poetry was invented; here that rulers and commoners alike came to consult the sibyl, who delivered her prophetic pronouncements while seated on the lid of a cooking pot; here that the famous rock stood which was inscribed with the quintessential Greek maxims "Know thyself," and "Nothing too much." Today the ruins are an impressive shambles, the surrounding countryside green, unspoiled, and dramatic. There is something about the slope of the hills, the height of the cliffs, the tilt of the canyon cleft with respect to the sun, and the spread of the plain to the west, that instills a kind of awesome peace in the visitor.

We spent the morning exploring the ruins. In the afternoon we drove down to the coast, ate lunch in the shaded arbor of a restaurant in Galaxidi, and then continued a few miles further west along the coast road, with the massive snow-capped peaks of Mount Panahaikos looming up from the far shores of the glittering turquoise gulf.

Our second evening on the terrace rivaled the first, although our interest in ouzo had diminished considerably. The following morning during breakfast Yanni brought us a little plate of cookies, compliments of his mother. As he was leaving I turned in my chair and said, "I know you're busy tending to breakfast and checking out your guests, but is it possible you'd have a moment to chat with us?" He dashed back across the room, seated himself on the single unoccupied chair at our small round table, cracked an enormous smile and said, "There's always time for friends."

In the hour that followed we discussed family history, the beleaguered Greek economy, the olive harvest, and the four pasty-faced people seated at the table next to us. "They're Russians," Yanni said under his breath. "We've seen a lot of rich Russians coming through in the last few years." Hilary complimented him on his English, and asked him how he'd learned to speak so well. "In the hotel business, you meet people from all over. A young man, he wants to talk with the young women, you know. English, it isn't so difficult. "

Yanni has never been to the United States, however. He took his family to Paris for their last vacation. "With Paris and Rome and Barcelona a few hours away," I remarked, "Why fly all the way across the Atlantic? There isn't really much there."

"Well, it's a young country," he countered graciously.

In the end Yanni married a Greek girl from Thessaloniki. "Some of the men here, they married Americans," he told us, "But it's hard for the women, especially in the winter. We're a very closed society. The women stay home a lot, many of them live with their husband's mothers. There are only three American women in Delphi. They have no one to talk to." He looked down at the tablecloth, and I wondered if he was thinking the same thing I was thinking: Why can't the

American women talk to the Greek women? The moment passed, he shook his thin longish locks back from his face as if to divorce himself from the more extreme forms of traditional Greek culture, and said "I could never live with my mother." Then he smiled again and shuddered good-naturedly.

At that moment Yanni's mother appeared, gliding up to our table with tiny steps, and put her hands on our shoulders once again like a bishop. "She looks sweet," Yanni said, looking up at her across the table, "but she's a hard taskmaster, believe me." We laughed, and Hilary said, "Tell her what you just told us," and so he repeated the remark in Greek. For an instant we could see fierceness and a hint of challenge come into her eyes as she looked into the eyes of her balding fifty-year-old son, but the sweetness never left them.

We asked Yanni if the oracle which had meant so much to the ancient world still carried spiritual significance with the residents of Delphi. "Oh, certainly," he replied rising up in his chair, a little shocked that anyone would think to doubt it. I was hoping to learn more about the modern workings of that three-thousand year old institution, but just then someone called from the kitchen, Yanni looked at his watch and leapt to his feet.

"My children go to school in Amfissa, " he said. "A group of French students are visiting, they're scheduled to tour the ruins at nine, and I'm giving the tour." He held out his watch for us to see; it was well past the hour. "Are you going to be here for a while longer? I'll be back in no time," and he rushed out of the room.

But we had spent two days in the tiny village of Delphi already, and we were determined to go. While we were packing our bags, however, Yanni's mother rapped on the door of our room and then pushed it open. Standing in the doorway she bent her small stout frame at the waist like a mechanical clock-tower figure, and waiving her arms in circles in front of her she excitedly shouted a Greek phrase we didn't recognize (What Greek phrase did we recognize?) although we were sure it meant "Come!" When we arrived in the lobby with our bags an instant later she handed us a long tube wrapped in bright blue paper dotted with stylized Byzantine ships. "It's just a couple of water jugs," Yanni's brother Andreas (who was now tending the front desk) said dismissively, but his mother was excited, and so, to be honest, were we. "Should we open it?" Hilary said. "It's for you. Just take it." Andreas replied. And so we paid our bill, hugged the proprietress of the Hotel Pan for the last time, and left.

We didn't open that package until we were well on into the trip, preferring to carry it exposed in the straps of a cloth suitcase. If it were pottery, we reasoned, it would be best to keep it in its packaging. But more importantly, this bright blue package had been given to us by Greeks. To our eyes it said, "Yes, we're tourists, but we have been welcomed and entertained and showered with gifts by Greeks. Can't you see the package?" Of course, any tourist who had bought a statue or vase in the shop next door to the Hotel Pan might be carrying a package identical to ours. That thought never occurred to us. We loved the package itself, as we loved the people who had given it to us.

IV. Driving in Greece

To judge from our limited experience, rental cars aren't auctioned off in Greece after they've been used for a season or two. They don't have that pleasant smell of newness that the cars you get in Las Vegas or Denver do. Our Geo Metro was noticeably worn. But considering the reputation Greek drivers have, it made perfect sense to us that we'd be given a nicked up white tin can with 50,000 kilometers on the odometer, tired seat cushions and five manual speeds all of which seemed pretty much alike. Who could say if we'd ever make it back to Athens?

Greece has the worst accident fatality rate in Europe. The travel guides are equivocal at best about the advisability of driving. Comments in *The American Express Guide* may be taken as typical:

> *Driving in the two main towns demands iron nerves... The speed limit is 30 mph and because of the density of the traffic it is almost impossible to exceed it... (In the countryside) resign yourself to finding the slowest truck ambling along the fastest lane; this is readily accepted by the driver's compatriots who overtake him on both sides...At intersections size often comes before right of way and the smaller vehicle gets the worst of a collision.*

These sentiments are echoed by the author of the somewhat more adventurous *Lonely Planet Guide to Greece*:

> *The terrible driving evident in Athens is mirrored throughout the country—statistics show Greece has the highest accident fatality rate in Europe. Seven people are killed every day, and on weekends the number rises to 30. The greatest cause of accidents is speeding in the wrong lane...*

But my favorite description of driving in Greece is a master-piece of eloquent understatement from the *Independent Traveller: Mainland Greece*:

> *On any road, even a motorway, you should be prepared from one moment to the next for the sudden emergence of a heavy truck or farm vehicle. Remember that not even motorways have a central retaining wall and do not assume that no one would be so foolish as to overtake on the brow of a hill. In the summer, when it rains so rarely, a light shower can turn a*

road surface instantly into a skating rink. And do not imagine
that a tree will be lopped as punishment just because it has
grown tall or bushy enough to conceal a traffic light or a road
sign....As for the national temperament, the Greeks with
some justice pride themselves on the speed of their reactions.
Behind the wheel, this leads them to last-minute decisions,
compulsive weaving in and out of traffic lanes, and a
preference for sudden breaking rather than gradual
deceleration.

But perhaps the single most telling remark we encountered concerning the local hazards of driving was delivered to us by a young Swiss couple we met on one of the islands long after our rental car had been returned to the Avis garage. In the course of conversation it came out that they'd spent a year traveling through Siberia, Japan, China, Southeast Asia, and Australia, having all sorts of wild adventures along the way. Yet when we began to relate the particulars of our recent tour of the Peloponnese Peninsula they blurted out in disbelief: "You mean to say, you drove in Greece!?"

With regard to the statistics themselves I was not concerned. Greece is the poorest country in Europe. Therefore, it has the worst roads and the oldest cars. It is one of the most mountainous and the most agricultural countries in Europe. Ought we to be surprised, then, if a disproportionate number of Greeks die behind the wheel of a car? But let it be supposed that Greeks are maniacs behind the wheel. The question remains to be asked and answered, whether any self-respecting traveler, male or female, can conscionably spend the winter months absorbed in tales of the daring exploits of Heracles, Ajax, Theseus, and the rest; and then, with the arrival of spring, opt to putter across the countryside where these events took place safely ensconced behind the tinted glass of a comfortable tour bus?

In the end, it seemed to us that, dangerous or not, without a car we'd simply be unable to get to the places we wanted to get to. We were confident that as long as we could escape Athens itself in one piece we'd be fine, so we arranged to pick up our car on a Sunday morning. So far, so good. What none of the travel guides had prepared us for is how beautiful and varied the countryside actually is, or how much sheer fun driving in Greece would turn out to be.

In Greece, no one stops at stop signs. Then again, there aren't many stop signs in Greece to stop at, and they're all in English. You slow down, you look around, you continue on your way. Being a past master of the rolling stop, I found myself quite at home in this regard. Of far greater interest and importance is the fact that for a Greek driver the lines that divide the lanes serve merely as suggestions. Knowing full well that a painted line will never stop a car, the Greek driver relies upon his or her independent judgment as to which part of the road to travel on. The standard position on two-lane blacktop roads is several feet over on the shoulder, which has conveniently been made entirely level with the driving lane itself. If a car approaching from the opposite direction pulls out to pass, it will be easier to avoid colliding with it from that position; similarly, a car approaching from the rear will be able to slip by with the absolute minimum of adverse exposure to the oncoming stream of vehicles. This system of creative lane-sharing puts the entire surface of the road into effective use, but it requires that an individual operating an automobile remain alert at all times. No elbow-out-the-window, one-handed driving in Greece, at least not on the main roads. In place of such expansive and potentially mind-numbing American-style touring the Greek driver becomes caught up in an electric web of interactive forces and currents, pushing forward, hanging back, shifting nimbly from side to side in response to the changing speeds and movements of his or her fellow-motorists, not all of whom are even visible, for who can say what may be coming around the next bend? Driving in Greece is unquestionably fraught with tension, but it also brings new and delightful shades of meaning to the word *propinquity*.

What one sees out the window of a car, motoring desultorily through Laconia or the Argolis or Arcadia or  Crete, are lemon groves, snow-capped mountains, men and women riding donkeys side-saddle, herd upon herd of goats crossing the road, the pale forms of distant islands across expanses of green sea, men sitting in outdoor cafes in small groups idly fiddling with their worry-beads. You pass ter-raced vineyards, minuscule whitewashed family chapels with domed roofs, olive groves, nondescript white buildings clustered at narrow places in the road, cypress trees curling up toward the hazy blue sky, roadside shrines beyond number commemorating traffic fatalities (each with its unique collection of bottles, photographs, and curios inside); fields of yellow and white and purple wildflowers, supermarkets, gas stations, schools, wine co-operatives, dusty soccer-fields, crude rock walls, picturesque harbors cluttered with pleasure boats and fishing boats, men and women wandering up and down the roadsides in the evening twilight stuffing spring herbs into cheap white plastic bags. This is Greece. It's just like the pictures in the books, except it's going on all around

you for hundreds of miles in every direction, you can see it
and smell it and hear it and feel it, like a universe of bees
buzzing, and it's beautiful beyond belief.

V. Ships

The port city of Piraeus serves as the connecting link
between the sprawling low-rise metropolis of Athens,
where 40% of all Greeks live, and the islands that many
tourists consider the "real" Greece. (Nor is it only tourists
who hold to this view, by the way. The woman who ran our
hotel in Athens remarked to us as we were checking out,
"April is nice, but you should really come back in June.
Greece is the sea. If you can't enjoy the sea, then you haven't
really experienced Greece.")

Although they're commonly referred to as ferries, the
ships that line the harbor in Piraeus are immense. They tower
above the concrete pier, dwarfing the semi-trailers and auto-
mobiles jockeying to come on board, not to mention the
tourists rigged with colorful and expensive backpacks and the
flamboyant barefooted gypsies in their dilapidated pick-up
trucks. The mouths of these ships hang open, their interiors
are dark and cavernous. Their glistening white prows carry
names like "Candia," "Sappho," "Poseidon Express," or
"Express Santorini," while across their sheer broad sides one of
two phrases is likely to appear in large Aegean-blue letters:
Arkadian Lines or Minoan Lines. A clock on the stern hanging
just below the level of the deck tells when each ship is
scheduled to depart.

The sight of these colossal vessels, twelve or fifteen
scattered at different places along three sides of the port,
brought out a depth of infantile wonder that surprised me. This
was, I think, in part because the ships were so beautiful and
clean that for all their immensity they looked like toy ships. It
seemed impossible to imagine that things so large could

actually propel themselves in a stately way through the water. I was repeatedly surprised–they stood so tall–that when they pulled away from the dock they didn't simply flip over in the  water and disappear. What impressed me more than anything else, however, was the fact that these ships were there for the purpose of transporting, not coal or grain or container-goods, but people. Ferries for Crete, Ferries for the Saronic Gulf, Ferries for the Eastern Cyclades, Ferries for the Dodecanese. There are no signs at the port directing you to the proper point of embarkation–you have to ask around along the pier–but these are the places the ships are going to. They're dream destinations. The men and women leaning over the railings high above you–native and tourist alike–are on their way out into the sea from the foam of which our civilization, and our psyches, developed.

Once the ship passes out beyond the mouth of the harbor and begins its journey down the coast it no longer seems so immense. Dusk descends, the twinkling white suburbs of Athens spread out across the lower slopes of the purple hills, giving way in time to shadows and darkness. You explore the cafeteria, the lounges, the rear deck with its unfilled swimming pool, the upper decks with their numerous doors each one bearing a sign CREW ONLY. Black shearwaters swoop and spin just above the waves, flashing their white bellies, a large fish jumps, another leaps gracefully high into the air right behind it. Dolphins! They frolic off into the evening across the copper waves, and you can't help

thinking of the frescoes in the 3,500 year-old palace of King
Minos at Knossos that you're on your way to visit. The night
air is cold, the lounges are filled with teenagers on holiday
sipping drinks and smoking cigarettes while the television
blares the European basketball finals or a rerun of "Cheers."
Outside, you sit in plastic chairs at the very end of the upper
deck, you can see the captain on the bridge (he's watching T.V.
too) through half-shut curtains. The land, quite distant now,
slips by at an even rate, treeless and desolate. It's too hazy to
see even a single star.

I love the phrase "Minoan Lines." It's the name of the
company that owns the ship we're traveling on. Shipping is
a practical enterprise, of course, and Greece's largest
industry, after tourism, but the presence of the word
"Minoan" lends an air of archaic enchantment to it as well.
We know relatively little about what Minoan civilization was
like. It's generally considered to have been the first truly
Western civilization; so old, in fact, that even to the Greeks
of Plato's time it was shrouded in mystery and conjecture. But
from Classical times to ours Minoan civilization has always
conveyed elements of idyllic peace and prosperity, underlain
with a somewhat irrational and bizarre involvement with
bulls, labyrinths, double axes, and of course the Minotaur
himself, half-man, half-bull. These associations may carry an
intimation that what's too good is inseparable from what's
very bad. Nevertheless the archeological discoveries of the last
twenty years at Acrotiri and other sites in the Aegean have
done little to dispell the popular notion of Minoan civilization
as the historical reality upon which the myth of Atlantis was
based.

The unique blend of the practical and the dreamlike, the
ancient and the modern, the idyllic and the slightly insane,
that the phrase "Minoan Lines" evokes may explain why I was
so adamant about getting a T-shirt with that expression

printed on it, preferably in blue letters. I asked the woman at the desk at the ticket agency in Naxos town, on the island of Naxos, and she told me you could get them on the ship. I asked the purser on the ship, but he said they were not for sale: only employees of the Line were authorized to wear them. For the duration of our trip I kept a keen eye out for a cabin boy of my height and build wearing a clean new shirt but I never saw one. I inquired at several shirt-shops in the Plaka in Athens, and was told, "You'll have a hard time getting hold of that."

I'd commission a silk-screen shop to make me a set if I could find eleven friends to go in on it with me. In fact, it seems to me we ought to redesign life along Minoan lines. Don't ask me precisely what that means and you'll get your shirt.

VI. Greek Salad

The two items of Greek cooking best known on this side of the Atlantic are the Gyros sandwich and the Greek Salad. The Gyros sandwich tastes in Greece about the way it tastes in New York City or the Mall of America—hot, aromatic, spicy, covered with raw onions and dripping with runny tzatsiki. (Tzatsiki, that delectable paste made of thick yogurt, garlic, and fresh dill, deserves an essay in itself.) On the other hand, I've never had a Greek salad here at home that can compare with the ones they serve in Greece. Unlike American Greek salads, which are invariably sour, the village salads of Greece are never sour. In fact the balance of flavors in a genuine Greek salad is so subtle and complete that the first bite may seem to be lacking in something. The oregano doesn't proclaim its exotic harshness, the vinegar doesn't attack the nose and throat aggressively. (In Greece lemon juice is the more common acidulater in any case, I'm sure.) The oil is light, the olives are relatively few in number. By the second or third judiciously assembled bite, however, the onions, cucumbers, and tomato slices have come into their own, to say nothing of the feta cheese.

The second obvious difference between authentic and ersatz Greek salads concerns the cheese. Here at home the feta is invariably crumbled into the salad, in Greece it appears in a single thick slab on top of both the vegetables and the dressing. As a result it keeps its rich chunky texture. You break it off piece by piece with your fork as you eat.

The blend of flavors in a genuine Greek salad—and the ones served to us were almost uniformly superb—is as subtle and as indescribable as that of a perfectly concocted Béarnaise sauce. One can only marvel at the consistency with which, in Greece, this evidently simple dish is endowed with transcendental import. Simplicity, freshness, balance, taste. The cookbooks I've examined are of little help in uncovering the secret. I suppose the rule may be somewhat as follows: If you can't see a lemon tree, and also an olive tree, out your kitchen window, you'll never succeed in making a proper Greek salad.

This thought came to me on the sunlit terrace of the Paradise Garden Taverna, which is located in the tiny village of Apo Potemia, in the heart of the verdant Cycladic island of Naxos. We'd been told about the place by a friendly German couple sitting beside us on the rear seat of the bus from Apollonia to Chora the previous afternoon. We'd been out hiking in the hills; so had they. We asked them where they'd gone and they described an attractive route, giving special emphasis to the taverna where they'd had their lunch. The following morning we took a taxi up to the village of Melanes and retraced their steps.

I ought to mention at this point that although Naxos is the lushest of the Cyclades, by any conventional standard it would still be considered rather barren. It produces the finest potatoes in Europe, oranges and olives and lemons and grains are grown throughout the central valley, and the eastern slopes of the island are as carefully terraced as anything you're likely to see in Japan. (Odd as it may seem, Naxian potatoes are exported to Japan.) That much having been granted, the fact remains that vast stretches of the island are rocky, stark, and good for nothing but goats, or for hiking across, with the sea breeze from Egypt blowing into your face.

Our hike took us from a northern flank of the island, which has been described as "lunar," over several hills and down into the valley of the Potemias, a series of three shady villages with a stream running between them; then up and around a steep eminence called Profitis Ilias, which has a ruined castle at the top (built in 1262 by Venetian adventurers who had taken the island by storm, if you must know.) Rounding this conical hill—we never made it to the top, fatigued as we were by the salad and the bread and the tzatsiki and the retsina we'd enjoyed at the taverna a half-hour earlier—we caught sight of the beautiful highland valley called the Tragaea, where we'd planned to catch the bus back down into town. Every part of the journey was memorable, from the fifteen-foot marble statue we came upon lying half-finished in a farmer's field near Melanes, abandoned there in 575 B.C. after one of the legs broke off, to the wait for the bus in the sunny square at Filoti at the end of the day, during which we observed the bustle of the village and chatted with hikers from France and Wales about the routes they'd taken that day. But our lunch at the Paradise Garden in Apo Potamia was something else again.

As we came into Apo Potamia from the fields we saw a man below us who looked half-crazed tending a bonfire in the yard behind the church dedicated to the Panayia Zoodochus Pighi, Our Lady of the Life-Giving Spring. When he saw us approaching he made a sign with extended fingers of a man drinking, laughed knowingly and then pointed to a flight of stone steps that led down from the main road into the trees.

Following this path we came to an arched stone doorway, through which we passed into the courtyard of the taverna. To the left stood a barn-like white dining hall, obviously built to serve the needs of the entire valley, if not the entire island; to the right, in the shadows of the doorway arch, clear spring water gurgled from a pipe into a large square flat-bottomed marble pool–the life-giving spring, no doubt. Directly in front of us a pebbled terrace spread itself in all directions, with white metal tables and bright plastic chairs scattered here and there amid the orange trees.

We chose a semi-shaded table–there was no one in the place–and sat for a good long while feeling the dappled sun on our faces, listening to the buzzing bees, and taking in the sweet scent of the orange blossoms directly above our heads. Three young boys were kicking a soccer ball against a rock wall in the parking lot above the terrace. A truck pulled into the lot briefly, blaring what we took to be political slogans through a powerful loudspeaker, and then moved on. At last a woman in a gray sweater appeared from the shadows of the dining hall and approached our table.

"I don't suppose you'd be serving meals at this time of the day," I asked politely, not being entirely sure the place was even open. The woman winced, pursed her lips, and shook her head doubtfully, clearly startled by the sudden appearance of what was, I realized only in retrospect, a fairly complex English sentence. But we established lines of communication straightaway, and were soon presented with a tray loaded with tzatsiki, two salads, a basket of crusty bread, and a carafe of golden retsina.

What can I tell you at this point about the food? Or about anything? We had passed the slumbering marble giant, crossed the windswept fields, encountered the crazy fire-tender, descended the steps and touched the waters of the life-giving spring; we sat in the dappled sun of the fragrant orange blossom garden, attended by the woman of ultimate decorum. The vegetables were fresh, the dressing was subtle, the tzatsiki was thick and potent, the bread was coarse and tasty, the retsina seemed to have been drawn from a barrel held in reserve which carried the secret resins of a thousand years of wine making.

This is what we'd come for, this is the dream we'd been dreaming all our lives.

PLAYING CARDS

A playing card is a beautiful thing. Cards are also powerful within their domain, although the power varies with the number on the card. A hand of cards is like an army, then, it has weaknesses and strengths; but it would be wrong to suggest that a hand of cards symbolizes an army, any more than an individual queen or deuce symbolizes a queen or a deuce. With cards, the symbol is the reality, which is as much as to say, there is no symbol. Lovely instruments of play, ornate and inscrutable, our cards are our agents. We send them into the fray and they never betray us, never desert, never fail to exert themselves to the fullest extent of their power.

There are *other* cards, of course, working on behalf of other agents no less devotedly than are the ones we've deployed. This is what makes it a game.

Over the years anyone might be expected to accumulate a few decks of playing cards—bridge decks, poker decks, tourist decks, designer decks—but I was surprised to discover, when I rounded mine up the other day, that I've amassed twenty-two of them. To a collector of playing cards this would be a trifling number, no doubt, but it surprised me a little. Here in the pile I see journeyman decks from "Streamline" and "Bee" purchased at gas stations in Tuba City, Dubois, or Grand Marais; well-worn double decks made by Hoyle with Dutch windmills, golden retrievers, or scenes from the Grand Canyon on the back. Then there are the fancy decks made by Piatnik of Vienna. One has slightly ridiculous petty nobles on the face cards, with rosy cheeks and insipid smiles. A second set is Jugendstil Art Nouveau in design— beautiful to look at, but difficult to read or to play with.

A Piatnik deck named "Florentine" is among my favorites: although the court cards are nothing special, the backs carry exquisite floral textile patterns, brown and gold, while the faces have unusually large numbers, for those of us whose vision is not quite what it once was. Yet even this Florentine set is Anglo-American in character. King, Queen, Jack. This is the court most of us are familiar with.

In the French deck, King, Dame, and Viscount, (K, D and V) rule. In all essential respects the suits and values of the two are the same. I have three touristic French decks made of cardboard; two of them are facsimiles of decks dating from the seventeenth century, with Bayard, Blanche of Castile, Crillon, and Marguerite de Valois identified by name among the royal entourage. The third (and the most comfortable to play with) is a modern deck that says "Coins Arrondis Dorés" on the side of the box. I'm told this means "gold-edged," and the cards are indeed gilt-edged and very supple, without seeming in the least bit plastic.

With Italian cards the situation is different.

The least interesting of my four Italian decks says "Genovesi Scozia" on the box, though what makes a playing card Genoese-Scotch remains a mystery to me. Made by the Modiano company in Trieste, its design is distinguished only by the fact that there are no numbers on the faces of the cards. I would not recommend playing bridge with such a deck.

My other Italian decks lack the 8, 9, and 10. They also differ from the cards to which we're accustomed with regard to the suits. In place of hearts, clubs, diamonds, and spades, they have cups, coins, batons, and swords. Instead of king, queen, and jack they have king, knight, and knave. "Ah ha, the minor arcana of the Tarot deck," you say, and it's true. But we must remind ourselves here that the word Tarot merely refers to a deck which has been enhanced with the major arcana—the hanged man, the empress, the lovers, the chariot, etc. etc. These were the original "trumps." It is not well known, I think, that the deck with these unique trump cards (Taroccho in Italian, and before that trionfi) was used for gaming long before it was used for telling fortunes. Tarot cards first appear in the historical record in 1447. The first mention of their widespread use for divination is 345 years later, in 1781. When we say "Ah ha, the Tarot deck," therefore, all we're really saying is that this deck is of the design used during the very earliest days of European card-playing, the days of Dufay, Villon and Botticelli.

My decks of Italian cards differ from one another in design, no doubt because they're from different regions. One is Neapolitan, one Catalonian, and one Castilian. In the Catalonian deck the swords are sickles, the batons have become clubs studded with diamonds, the cups are now glass beakers half-full of wine, and the knaves have become peasant girls. In the Castilian deck the knaves are back, but the batons have become red and green bell peppers. Or maybe they're just red and green clubs. In any case, the face cards of this particular suit (peppers or clubs) are Moors.

None of these things affect the way you use the cards, but they carry a certain ancillary interest, both cultural and aesthetic.

The only game I play regularly with my Italian cards is Briscola. This is the game they play in the charming British film *Queen of Hearts*, which is well worth seeing. "Lead with the Coins, beware the King of Swords!" You can play it with a regular deck if you remove the 8s, 9s, and 10s.

In Briscola the order of the cards, from highest to lowest, is as follows:

A, 3, King, Knight, Knave, 7, 6, 5, 4, 2.

You'll note that the 3 stands just below the Ace in rank. These two—the 3 and the Ace—are also the most valuable cards to win in a trick. Each player begins with three cards (two, three, or four can play). You play a card, then you draw one from the deck. The highest card wins the trick. Whoever takes a trick leads the next one. Points are awarded at the end of the game for the counters gathered in the course of taking tricks. The value of the counters is as follows: A = 11 ; 3 = 10; K = 4; Q = 3; J = 2.

The play of Briscola is complicated slightly by the fact that, after dealing out the first three cards to each player, you flip the top card off the pack to designate trump. Even the lowest card in that suit is higher than the highest card in any other suit. You can lead trump at any time, and you can *play* trump at any time as well, until the last three tricks of the game, when you can trump only if you're out of the suit that has been lead.

The challenge of Briscola lies in "bringing home" your Aces and 3s while also trumping as many of your opponent's high-counting cards as you can. The beauty of the game lies in the fact that because you never have more than three cards in your hand at a time, the opportunities for planning ahead or strategizing are meager. You play a card, you draw a card, drifting in the quiet current of minor triumphs and set-backs. Many valuable cards fall in the last three tricks: you won't know until after the hand is finished whether or not Fate has been kind to you.

An aura of mystery, romance, and the occult surrounds the fanciful images of playing cards. This aura can be felt in a fortune-teller's tent, no doubt, but it's even stronger, I think, at an ordinary card table, where Fate, in the form of the deal, presents us with a challenge that we ourselves must seize and make the most of. The affection I feel for the women and men that sit across from me in no way undermines my desire to score, to undercut, to win; but winning is less important, in the end, than entering fully into the  ambiance of the night, the game, the fateful moment of decision, the glory and the anguish of a trick or a game won or lost. At the card table very few things matter, and many of these are beyond our immediate control. To play a game of cards (not chess, not go) is to humble yourself, therefore. Yet it seems to me that card players sing, whistle, and hum to themselves more than any other group of people. Why? Because the hand we hold, which is known only to ourselves, gives us an agenda, a route, an avenue of adventure and risk that may lead, in the end, to apotheosis, if not tonight, then some other night.

This act of "entering into" a game, of submitting to the fate of the deal, of accepting rules that limit our options while at the same time clarifying what deed or result will constitute success, seems to me to be an act of almost overwhelming import. In life this opportunity seldom presents itself quite so unequivocally. On the contrary, we often feeling we're muddling through a series of tasks the significance of which is doubtful at best. At the card table, on the other hand, though the issue at hand is unquestionably arbitrary and insignificant, it may occur to us that we're participating in an activity which, in its mystery and color, its good-natured social ambiance, its heightened emotional tenor and its unpredictable ebb and flow, is close to the heart of spirituality, of music, of that "real" life which, in taking up the game, we've deliberately withdrawn from.

This is a fact worth pondering.

How, then, do games "stand" with respect to life? In the first place, I ought to underscore the obvious point that life isn't a game. In life the options are many, the rules obscure or non-existent, the results equivocal at best. If things haven't gone your way at a round of cribbage or poker you can rise from the table with the dismissive "It's only a game," and return to a larger domain, but life isn't something you step away from with a shrug and move on to something richer and deeper. Not as far as we know. Life is inescapable. Gaming is a matter of choice.

Games, then, are a part of life that draws us into a narrower and clearer, if less significant, world within it. Yet the separation between the two is not absolute. Life intrudes in games in many ways. Consider, for example, the case of a cabal of players who gang up on a single opponent on the basis of impulses rooted less in rational considerations of a game's likely outcome than in a long unspoken history of family animosities. Here life is felt as an intrusion that unfairly tips the playing field. Similarly, natural sympathies may drive us to soften the blow of defeat on an opponent by easing up in the final stretch of a game that's already clearly won. Some Parcheesi players have great difficulty sending *anyone* back home, although this common act not only undercuts the progress of an adversary but also results in valuable extra moves for themselves. There are occasions when considerations of this kind are not only fitting but admirable, yet among adults who have committed themselves to a specific set of rules and objectives, such extra-ludic impulses almost invariably have a deleterious influence on a game's tone or mood, because they undermine the integrity of its outcome.

Louvre, Paris

Cheating is a more obvious example of the intrusion of life's unruly impulses into the world of gaming, which is orderly and honorable both by definition and by mutual consent. Everyone hates a cheater, and beyond that, feels a certain moral revulsion in the presence of such an individual, as if all of life, and not merely an inconsequential game, had been tainted by such behavior. As indeed it has been.

In George de La Tour's painting "The Cheat with the Ace of Clubs" our attention is divided between a plump baby-faced dandy intent on scrutinizing his hand, and a slightly raffish older man sitting across from him with his face in shadow, who looks toward the viewer as he deftly pulls an ace of clubs (no numbers on these cards!) out of his belt. In the center of the canvas a serving girl pours a drink for a third player, a well-dressed woman with a guarded expression who nevertheless succeeds in passing a sly look to her servant as she accepts the glass. Clearly all three are in on the scam. Our attention returns to the young dandy, as if to alert him to the danger he faces, but everything about him, from his silk brocades to his erect posture and his self-satisfied expression, bespeak an individual of privileged upbringing who could benefit from a slap or two of awakening to the real world, where character is everything, and trust can easily be misplaced. As our gaze returns to the swindlers we begin to admire their delicacy and coordination in spite of ourselves. The poor chump will never know what hit him. This feeling is reinforced by the expression on the cheater's face as he looks in our direction: it is neither sheepish nor conniving, it appeals to neither our forbearance nor our complicity. It is an astute face. It knows what it is about.

La Tour's remarkable handling of the expressions on his protagonists faces, not to mention the stunning treatment of light and shadow for which he is well-known, have made "The Cheat with the Ace of Clubs" one of his most widely admired canvases. But as the title itself should suggest, it's a painting, not about gaming, but about life.

Let me suggest that against the intrusions of life into games that La Tour's "The Cheat with the Ace of Clubs" portrays, we set John Huston's cliché-ridden yet underrated action film *Victory* (1981). This film, (it was called *Escape to Victory* when I saw it) will appeal to anyone who grew up watching afternoon television in the fifties and early sixties, when dramatic works like *Sands of Iowa Jima, Porkchop Hill, The Flying Leathernecks, Guadalcanal Diary, Sink the Bismarck, Merrill's Marauders,* and *The Great Escape* were instructing young men (did young women watch these films too?) to be tough and to hate Nazis. The premise of Huston's film is this: the Nazis plan to stage a soccer game in Paris pitting the best international stars from the concentration camps against the Führer's Aryan finest. It's a propaganda stunt, of course, and the fact that the referees are all Nazis leaves the outcome in little doubt, but the French Underground has devised a plan to free the Allied participants from the locker room at halftime.

As it happens, after a rousing first half, the Allies are only behind by 3 to 1. The fru-fru French emerge on cue from the storm sewers and urge their friends to escape with shouts of "Come on! Come on!" But the Allies, led by Péle and Sylvester Stallone, reply, "Hey! We can win this game!" And they charge back out onto the field to show the Nazis what they're really made of.

The Leonard Maltin film guide gives the film 1/2 star:

> *P O W s get a chance to escape German prison camp but stick around to finish soccer game—just as it would have happened in real life. Only Péle's celebrated kicks save this silly bore from a BOMB rating.*

Do you detect a hint of sarcasm here? "Just like real life?" Then again, there's something about arrogant, supercilious Nazi cheaters that can make a POW's blood boil. I may have neglected to mention that the match is being broadcast worldwide as a test case of racial superiority. Would it be better for Stallone and company to slink away through the sewers of Paris, or to return to the field determined to show the world what the spirit of liberal multi-ethnic free-play can do even against the greatest odds?

In *Victory* play takes the upper hand against "real life" because in some ways games are more real than real life. It would be impossible for our heroes to win the war on any given Sunday...but they just might win the soccer match, and such "hollow" symbolic victories can sometimes have a great effect on the course of events.

It would appear, then, that just as life intrudes in games, so games can take on a significance well beyond the confines within which they operate. But the abiding value of games is most strongly to be felt, I think, at those times when gaming and life sit in easy harmony with one another, a condition exemplified by Cezanne's *The Card-Players*. In this well-known canvas (there are five versions, in fact) we see a room, a table, a bystander, and three players hunched stolidly over their cards. The light is meager; the absorption is complete. Life encompasses the game without subverting it. The game animates the life surrounding it, without striking it down— there is no need. These cronies are comfortable in their game, which they've played many times before and will play again, late into the night, a sacred diversion among relative equals. In Cezanne's vision you don't play in order to win, you win in order to have played. And when you don't win—which is most of the time, perhaps—you accept the necessity of the rules, the fall of the cards, and the glory due to whomever does carve a victory out of the mess that Fate has dealt to him or her. Gaming (and also life) is like that.

And here we come to what is perhaps the most appealing aspect of gaming: the idea of *necessity*. The deal might have been different...yet it wasn't. To enter into the play you must get a hand, and it happens that this is what you've gotten. No reflection on your character, really. It's a matter of chance.

The association of necessity and chance may strike you as a little odd, but the long tradition of associating necessity with "cause and effect" is odder still. Casual principles are conditional, after all: if A, then B. Necessity, on the other hand, presents us with a *fait accompli*. You'll deal with it, because you have to. There is no alternative.

That which IS is necessary, in other words, not because we know its cause, but simply because it IS. Caesar *did* cross the Rubicon, and there is no way to get him back on the other side again, as if it had never happened.

If the word necessity referred to nothing other than the actuality of things at any given time, however, it would not carry such a weight of obscure and portentous meaning. Necessity leans toward the future. The well-known expression, which appears as early as Plato, that "necessity is the mother of invention" suggests that a dire situation calls upon us to produce a remarkable response, rather than merely buckling under its weight or losing ourselves in dreams of what might or ought to have been.

The Greeks remain the masters of facing and even revering that dreadful thing Necessity. They called it *ananke*, which derives from a Semitic root *chananke*, of which some of the meanings are "narrow," "throat," "surround," "embrace," and "strangle." The first (and in the eyes of some, the greatest) masterwork of Western literature, the *Iliad*, is fraught with this constricting weight of necessity. You may be surprised to hear me say this. In the *Iliad* the repeated intervention of the Gods in the unfolding of the Trojan War may seem to give the story an element, not only of unpredictability, but of irrational whim. The caprices of Zeus or Aphrodite would appear to be the opposite of Necessity, which is rooted in the flow of events. But the Greeks knew better. In the *Iliad* the combatants share an unquestioned assumption that what the Gods will is what *must be*, of necessity, and no one, no mortal at any rate, can do anything about it. As a result we find them repeatedly weighing the likelihood that they'll succeed, at last, in taking Troy, against the gnawing suspicion that the Gods, at least for the time being, are NOT ON THEIR SIDE. We hear them time and again rousing themselves to bloody ferocity with valiant declarations of indomitable combat prowess, then adding:

> ...If it is my destiny to die
> there by the ships of the bronze-armored
> Achaians, then I wish that.

Homer's dispassionate descriptions of the various ways that Greeks and Trojans meet their ends in combat ring with grim finality:

> For in his back even as he was turning the
>   spear fixed
> between the shoulders and was driven on
>   through the chest beyond it.
> He fell, thunderously, and his armor
>   clattered upon him.

or:

> Throwing first, he struck the horn of the
>   horse-haired helmet
> and the bronze spear-point fixed in his
>   forehead and drove inward
> through the bone; and a mist of darkness
>   clouded both eyes.

Like the Hebrew God, the Gods of the Greeks are fickle. Both Yahweh and Zeus change their minds, love mortals, play favorites. The difference between the two schemes lies in the far greater emphasis placed in the Judeo-Christian tradition on justice, as opposed to necessity. It's as if a Greek, picking a hand of cards, were to remark, "I've been dealt a bad hand, the Gods are angry or indifferent, or simply having a good time at my expense. Nevertheless they are the Gods, and they're far greater and more brilliant that I am: all I can do is play the hand I've been dealt as well as I can." A Christian or a Jew, picking up the same hand, might say "I got a bad hand...what have I done to deserve this?"

In *The Death of Tragedy* George Steiner writes:

> *The Judaic vision sees in disaster a specific moral fault or failure of understanding. The Greek tragic poets assert that the forces which shape or destroy our lives lie outside the governance of reason or justice. Worse than that: there are around us daemonic energies which prey upon the soul and turn it to madness or which poison our will so that we inflict irreparable outrage upon ourselves and those we love.*

Between the two the Greek vision corresponds more closely to experience, I think, and although it may seem dark, it's also the more life affirming, in so far as it acknowledges that life is composed of several dimensions, only one of which is ethical.

Humans can and often do deal fairly with one another, but life, in its vastness, extends far beyond what any of us would consider just, fitting, agreeable, or even intelligible. That's the scary part, but it also makes life's latent beauty all the more compelling. To extend the boundaries of the domain within which justice *does* prevail; to grope toward a clearer understanding of the gravity and truth of our situation; to expand the reach of our personal warmth and congeniality—are not these things, in the end, forms of playing the game, and even, perhaps, beyond that, of winning?

ROAD MONET: 1995

A rt lovers across the country were captivated by the "once-in-a-lifetime" Monet show assembled last summer by the Art Institute of Chicago. Many people from Minneapolis drove down to see the show, and Hilary and I did too, leaving on a Saturday morning and returning the following afternoon. If it hadn't been Monet, we might not have gone, but the desire to see Chicago again also carried a certain appeal. I must confess that I was also intrigued by the idea of participating, at my advanced age, in one more of those driving marathons that so often punctuate the lives of young college students. "Hey! Let's take Chet's Corvair and drive to New York non-stop! We'd be back in time for the Anthro final!" Chicago isn't that far away–an eight hour freeway drive, nothing more–but we had agreed to go with friends whom we'd known since college, and all four of us seemed to be inspired by the slightly irrational nature of the enterprise: sixteen hours in a car for the sake of two hours in a crowded museum looking at pictures of sailboats and fields, many of which we'd already seen before at other museums. Well, why not?

I was under no illusion that our trip to Chicago would in any way approach the pixilated grandeur of various college cross-country escapades. In fact, in looking forward to the weekend I invariably imagined myself crossing the bucolic Wisconsin countryside asleep in the back seat of our friends' spacious van. It was with some surprise, therefore, that I learned while playing tennis with Tim on the Wednesday before our departure that his vehicle, leased from the dealer, was approaching its mileage limit. "Actually, John, we were hoping we could take your Toyota."

We've known Tim and Carol for most of our adult lives. Hilary and Carol became friends in the ninth grade, and Tim and I met as sophomores in college. I met Hilary as a result of her friendship with Carol, who by this time had formed an attachment with Tim. Summer softball games, water-balloon fights, canoe-trips, volleyball. We married in the Bicentennial year, spring (they) and fall (we). I remember a heated debate in the honeymoon suite of the Sofitel on Tim and Carol's wedding night, he holding forth on the supremacy of the guitar among instruments (it being portable), and I of the piano (the repertoire being infinitely superior). Why neither of us seized upon the accordion can only be attributed to youthful ignorance. And if this seems an odd way for anyone to spend their wedding night, let me add that on *our* wedding night Hilary and I hosted a bingo party in our apartment in Stillwater, for which the grand prize was a copy of Chairman Mao's *Little Red Book*.

Over the years the four of us have spent winter weekends smoking cigars in sub-zero cabins in the North Woods, played enough rounds of bridge to have become much better at the game than we actually are, watched numberless slide shows of European vacations which invariably drive us to fever pitch. We'd always planned to meet under the statue of Henry IV at the point of the Ile de la Cité in Paris someday. So far, it hasn't quite worked out that way.

We've watched their children grow from helpless babes into quite respectable poker players. Meanwhile we exchange dinners, sample unusually good wines, debate the relative merits of Conrad and Ford, of Ravel and Debussy, and fantasize about our perhaps never to be realized week by the pool in a rented villa in rural Provence or Tuscany. Tim, a decent and proper classicist after all, his abiding interest in Slavic folk music notwithstanding, holds to *Don Giovanni* above all other operas, while Carol repeatedly reminds him that the Don was an insufferable JERK, (although no one would refer to Tim in such terms). Meanwhile, Hilary and I hold firm in our devotion to the gushy and (in our view) deeply moving sentiments of Puccini's lush idiom.

You can't say very much about a friendship or a marriage without running the risk of betraying the substance of its active, living core. This explains why so much literature, from the French Fabliaux of the thirteenth century to yesterday's mediocre romance, concerns itself with waywardness, infatuation, adultery, divorce, and domestic disintegration. Who wants to read about someone else's enduring happiness, after all? Indeed, who can write about such a thing without sounding fatuous or smug? And who, reading it, would believe it? Tolstoy's remark in *Anna Karenina* is put exactly backwards, therefore. All unhappy couples experience the same unhappiness: we read, and we relate. It's happiness that's in every case unique and inexplicable. It can neither be described nor shared.

With friendships the situation is much the same, I think. "We were friends." There, you've said it all. I might adapt the remark of Montaigne to the rich and peculiar matrix of relationships I'm attempting to evoke. "It's because we are we, and they are they." At the root of this evasive formula three qualities loom: affection, continuing interest, respect. No doubt each one of us, given the chance, would describe the situation differently, would see different angles of communality and tension. Yet each would also defend the integrity of the relationship, I think, and testify to its abiding personal significance. To Montaigne's remark let me therefore add a second, this from the Italian aphorist Antonio Porchia: "I love you as you are, but do not tell me how that is."

We picked Tim and Carol up at seven A.M. "Oh, you wore that? I should have dressed differently. We made some sandwiches. Did you bring the fruit? A bottle of Scotch? Good idea!" Before long we were commenting on how much more attractive the rolling countryside of Wisconsin was than the flat fields we'd left behind in Minnesota. Vague remarks about "the driftless zone" were bandied about which Tim, a geologist, let pass with noncommittal grunts. We began swapping stories about our hitchhiking days, all of which we'd exchanged many times before. Carol and Hilary hitching across Canada, Tim on his way to British Columbia in the back seat of a Triumph Spitfire driven by a homicidal maniac, my peculiar ride in the cab of a road grader south of Sioux Lookout, Ontario, Hilary's motoring adventures in the precipitous fjord country of Norway.

Once we'd passed Madison the countryside deteriorated, and when we crossed the border into Illinois the funnel-like tollbooths of the turnpike kept us churning toward Chicago with the quiet and ineluctable energy of Harvey's circulatory valves, so that we breezed within sight of the spreading metropolis without having experienced an iota of boredom or fatigue. As we entered into the final stretta section of our dramatic approach to the city, ("A beer to the first one to spot the Standard Oil Building!") negotiating the concrete freeway canals with remarkable aplomb, we removed the tape of Bach violin sonatas we'd been listening to and slammed a rock-n-roll selection indiscriminately into the machine.

The afternoon was bright, cool, and clear. Eager to make the most of it, we parked in the shadow of the Sears Tower, and got out to see the Loop on foot.

Although the Sears Tower is among the tallest buildings in the world, it's never become an icon on the order of the Eiffel Tower, the Leaning Tower of Pisa, the Tower of London, the Empire State Building, or even the World Trade Center. I asked a friend of mine born and raised in Chicago whether this was indeed the case and he became defensive: "I like the Sears Tower, I've always liked it...that's the slim white building that comes to a point at the top. Right?" "No," I corrected him, "You're thinking of the TransAmerica Building. That's in San Francisco."

I like the Sears Tower. The way it rises by irregular slabs that twist off one another remains, I believe, unique. In fact, the building has a slightly chunky and inelegant "build it yourself at home" look that few architects would care to emulate. But this same quality underscores the building's tallness in an entirely unostentatious way. It's as if its designers were making an emphatically American statement: "Yes, we know all about harmony, proportion, and the golden section. We're not interested in these things. What interests us is up, up, up." When you look at the Tower from a distance you keep trying to reassemble it in your mind, making the lower slabs longer and the upper ones shorter, while shifting them all away from their irregular spiral orientation toward a more regular bi-axial one. But it won't be altered, it won't be moved.

The Sears Tower stands a little inland from the heart of the city, a little off by itself. After a heated discussion we decided to ride the elevator to the observation level at the top, but it was a clear cool afternoon and half of Chicago was standing in line in the lobby waiting to make the ascent. Happy to have saved an hour of time, and also a chunk of money (which we could spend again and again in the course of the weekend), we returned to the street and began our peregrinations downtown.

We passed the Rookery Building and ducked into the lobby, which was redesigned by Frank Lloyd Wright in 1905. The delicate wrought iron tracery, painted white and gold, and the wide staircase leading up to a broad mezzanine, struck me as fussy and grandmotherish, although Carol and Hilary were entranced. Two liveried men were setting up tables with white tablecloths and vases of flowers, oblivious to our presence.

"What's going on?" I asked one of them.

"A party," the man said indifferently, though when he saw my eyes light up he condescended to elaborate: "A PRIVATE party."

We looked down a side street toward the Monadnock Building, which is the tallest building in the world made entirely of masonry. It isn't very tall. A few minutes later, following the sounds of an accordion, we came out into the plaza in front of the Berghoff Restaurant, where a large canvas circus tent had been set up. A polka band was playing, people were milling around with beer in plastic glasses and bratwurst dripping with sauerkraut. I looked out at the sea of faces as we entered the plaza and I asked myself, "Why does this look so much like a Chicago crowd, rather than a New York or a Minneapolis crowd?"

That this was not a New York street scene was obvious. Not multi-ethnic enough, not neurotic enough. The contrast between the two corn-belt cities was more subtle, more elusive. Squinting, I summoned all my powers of impressionability and concluded that Chicagoans are more fun-loving, relaxed, and comfortable in their urban identity and stature than Minneapolitans, who tend to be slightly pinched in spirit, self-conscious in their exercise of urbanness, and overly-eager to be taken as cultured cosmopolitans.

Minneapolitans like to think they're more sophisticated than Chicagoans, many of whose enthusiasms (pizza, gangsters, Mayor Daley, Studs Terkel, John Belushi) are low-brow. Chicagoans, on the other hand, have only a vague idea where Minneapolis is, and really don't care.

The facade of the Carson Pirie Scott Building just down the street is frequently cited as one of architect Louis Sullivan's outstanding achievements. The windows are wide and blocky, however, and the ornamental coils of *art nouveau* spider web that have been stuck to the white exterior walls seem both gaudy and out of place in a building designed by the man who said "Form follows function." The technology of modern architecture—the steel beam, that is—is being put to good use here, but the imagination remains enthralled by the musty shadows, curves, and details of the late nineteenth century.

As we approached the Chicago River the skyline of the Near North Side came into view. At the base of the corn-cob towers of Marina City a man was revving the engine of his fifty-foot black and white runabout impatiently; another resident was evidently about to emerge from the building on his or her way downtown by boat for a loaf of bread. The river itself was beautiful: water is always itself—green, wavy, and wet—even when surrounded by concrete walls and soaring glass and limestone buildings.

We re-crossed the river by another bridge upstream, our faces turned now toward the late afternoon sun, and made our way back to the car, but along the way we stopped to take a look at Helmut Jahn's controversial State of Illinois Center. Though it was closed, we could see the yawning 8-million cubic foot atrium through the windows. "The theory," Tim explained, "is that government should be open to the people; therefore, every office opens out onto this atrium." Fine sentiments, I guess. Yet the building itself looks cramped on its site, making the interior space seem illogical and wasteful, and the tiny pillars that run along the exterior facade only add to the clutter and confusion. Meanwhile, the narrow alternating panels of blue, pink, and white with which it's faced give it a tacky carnival air. It would be difficult to imagine a conception further removed from Mies van der Rohe's boxy and austere Federal Center, which stands just a few blocks away to the south.

Our hotel, the Essex, is the cheapest on State Street. I breathed a sign of relief when the receptionist pulled four tickets to the Monet show out of an envelope and handed them to me. Although I'm not much of a worrier, I was subliminally concerned that our weekend excursion would be deprived of its *reason d' etre* through some administrative mischance or oversight. "We're sorry you drove all this way for nothing. Of course we'll refund the price of the tickets. Perhaps you could try again next week."

We sat in our room—Tim and I at the table, Hilary and Carol on the beds—drinking scotch and looking out through the slightly opaque Plexiglas window at the brick wall of the Hilton across the street. From our vantage point on the twelfth floor we could also see both the Sears Tower, standing far off to the west, and the choppy blue-green waters of Lake Michigan to the east. After the long drive and the strenuous walk we were happy to be lounging, shoes off, feet up. We paged through travel guides and local newspapers and settled on a meal in Greek-town. Four blocks of restaurants to choose from and live music if we were lucky.

Thirty seconds west on the Eisenhower Expressway and we were spat off into a sea of parking lots and low-rise brick buildings. We took the last remaining parking meter and, crossing Halsted Street, found ourselves in front of the Pegasus, an attractive white stucco restaurant that was already buzzing with activity. The prospect of bouzouki music kept us moving, however, past the Santorini, the Greek Islands, the

Parthenon, and several other establishments toward the Courtyards of Plaka, which was closed for remodeling. On our way back up Halsted Street we passed men playing backgammon at window tables, vending machines holding Greek language newspapers, and shops selling icons, candles, and cans of aerosol holy water. On second glance the Santorini, famous for its grilled seafood, looked especially inviting, but it also looked expensive. We were weighing the merits of the Pegasus, which appeared to be popular with indigent student types like ourselves, when a man came out the door with a Styrofoam container jammed with *gyros* shavings. "This place is good," he said, "and they give you so much!" Well, that settled it.

It was then, while we were standing on the sidewalk outside the Pegasus, that I saw the clouds. A storm was brewing and a mountain of thunderheads had developed out on the lake beyond the city skyline. The sky was black but the setting sun lit the clouds, and to a lesser extent the buildings below them, in shades of copper, pink, and fiery red. The skyline itself, unobstructed by nearby buildings, was impressive enough—from where we stood, on the far side of the freeway, it has a clear, vigorous, almost two-dimensional sweep that even the skyscrapers of Manhattan can't match. Yet it was dwarfed by the spangled clouds towering motionless in the darkness behind it. I looked and I looked, I had never seen a more spectacular scene. Where is my camera? I thought, but I realized immediately than no photograph would be likely to do justice to such an awesome display of nature's power. Then I noticed, in the middle distance, the tarnished green dome of a church, low to the ground and no bigger than a fingernail, which provided the singular and perfect highlight in the midst of those glowing buildings.

A minute later the sun had set. We were sitting at a table in front of a giant screen TV that was projecting images of

Greek villages, home movies badly edited. The appetizers were tasty, the entrees merely passable, but the bottle of Botari Naussa Reserve was superb. It was then that Hilary noticed she'd lost her silver starfish pin. After dinner we searched up and down Halsted Street in the streetlight glare, but it was not to be found. "We'll just have to go back to Naxos and get you another one," I said lamely. "Ariadne's fate was to be abandoned there, but your fate will be to be brought back there again and again in search of silver starfish."

The neighborhood had come alive with large parties of slightly inebriated men and women, passing from bar to restaurant through the cool autumn evening, but our plan was to return downtown and then venture out on foot to Buddy Guy's Legends, a blues club referred to in several guides as the best in Chicago, which happened to be half a block from our hotel.

The "legend" playing there at the time was one that none of us had heard of. I asked the bouncer at the door if I could go inside and take a look around. He nodded and I entered the small clean club, which had black and white linoleum tiles on the floor, a bar across one side, two violently lit green pool tables in an alcove on the other, and a stage projecting out from the front wall. There weren't many people inside. The band was just beginning to set up. Returning to the door I asked the bouncer, a tall, bald, black man with a child-like face, who this so-and-so was that we were going to hear.

"You see The Blues Brothers?" he asked me.

"Yeah," I said. (I lied. But if I'd said "No," the conversation would have been at an end.)

"Well, did you like it?"

"It was great!" I said.

"Well, that's him."

I took this to mean that the band playing behind Ackroyd and Belushi in the film was the one performing at Buddy Guy's tonight.

"I'll go tell my friends," I said.

Our next stop was the Blackstone Hotel, where jazz trumpeter Maynard Fergusson was scheduled to appear. When we entered the lobby of that venerable hotel Maynard and his big band were, in fact, standing near the door to the nightclub, waiting to make their entrance. "The first set is sold out," the doorman told us, "but wait, I'll see if I can find you some space at the bar," and he rushed off before I had the time to tell him we had no intention of seeing the show. Meanwhile, the band members entered the darkly lit club one after the other, leaving no one in the lobby but Maynard and ourselves. Looking for all the world like "the captain" on Gilligan's Island, his shiny gray suit notwithstanding, he practiced his chops, pedaled the keys in pantomime, crouched, then reached for a high note, but without ever actually blowing through the horn. A minute later he was up on stage, squealing in his characteristic way, and we were back out on the street.

We stopped at a used bookstore, enticed by the multicolored bindings and the golden light inside. Then we walked back to our hotel past the Auditorium Theatre, where the gala opening of an opera or an orchestra season was in progress. Under the awning men in tuxedos were pulling on cigarettes, women in fine dresses were holding drinks close to their faces, they stood together in small groups, men and women, discussing what? The cost of college education? The stock market? Classical music? The waves on the lake?

Our only issue was deciding whether or not to return to the blues club, and in this there was really very little to consider. We were all dead tired, and Carol alone made a plea for continuing further with what had already been a fairly long day. No one was surprised by this. Of the four of us Carol undoubtedly has the greatest capacity for slightly frazzled fun. In fact, I remember a bitterly cold evening many years ago when we four decided to take a psychological profile test together as a kind of parlor game. Our scores were similar in many ways, but on one of the scales Carol scored very high where the rest of us scored very low: Having Fun. "You guys are lying," she shouted defensively, "You like to have fun as much as I do, you're just ashamed to admit it."

For one day, at any rate, the fun was at an end.

∽

Sunday morning. Breakfast in the cafe adjoining the hotel. Back into the car. South to Hyde Park and the University of Chicago.

Before having seen the University of Chicago, I imagined it as a single modern office tower of the boxy Mies van der Rohe type with Milton Friedman, Alan Bloom, and Saul Bellow sitting in the top of it, surrounded by an array of lower red-brick buildings, then a patch of grass, and then the slums of South Chicago. I had never thought about the matter seriously, as you may surmise, but at no time did it occur to me that the University of Chicago might look like Cambridge. Yet it does, and it's supposed to. In fact, unlike almost all *faux* Gothic buildings in the Western Hemisphere, the buildings that make up the University of Chicago actually look old. The stones are weathered and the glass has been specially designed to resemble old English glass. It's all very nice. As you approach the campus along shaded boulevards you pass a sign that says: "Welcome to the first stable racially integrated neighborhood in the United States," and that, too, is very nice.

During our whirlwind tour of the neighborhood we made sure to pass the Robie House, one of Frank Lloyd Wright's most renowned residential creations. It sits on a long narrow corner lot on a quiet shady street. No tours were being offered that Sunday morning, but we did take the opportunity to peer through every window we could as we scrambled through the bushes, up and down the stairs, and around the house.

At this point I ought to mention that I consider myself unusually well qualified to evaluate the works of FLW. I spent my early childhood in Bartlesville, Oklahoma, the home of the only skyscraper that Wright designed—I passed it every day on my way to kindergarten; and during the course of my adolescent years my family stopped on more than a few occasions at the Phillips 66 station in Cloquet, Minnesota, which happens to be the only gas station in the world to carry the FLW stamp. Art galleries, dentist offices, churches—I've visited Wright buildings of every stripe, and I have found each one to be strikingly idiosyncratic, stimulating, original...and yet often unsatisfying from the aesthetic point of view. While it would be difficult to admire too much the graceful lines, the splendid use of materials, the cantilevered roofs, the intriguing angles and cruxes, the various built-in cupboards and trap-doors, and the stylish windows and molding details, to my mind the cumulative effect is that of a precocious adolescent doodler who does not know when to stop. In the end the eaves stick out *too* far, the ceilings are *too* low, the detailing becomes merely fussy, while the free-standing furniture is both ghastly and uncomfortable. The entire building begins to shout "Frank Lloyd Wright!" a mantra which I'm not sure many homeowners would care to be subjected to day in and day out.

In saying this I don't mean to belittle the unparalleled influence that Wright's designs have exerted on residental architecture in our century: Most suburban ramblers and split-levels are FLW knock-downs after all. Nor do I mean to suggest that Wright's buildings lack character or interest. To argue either point would be ridiculous. I only mean to suggest that it is easy to have too much of a good thing, that Wright's ingenuity almost invariably ran well ahead of his sense of taste and proportion, and that the best examples of organic "Prairie School" architecture are to be found in modest homes designed by little-known architects following in Wright's footsteps with less brilliance but greater concern for the interests of the women and men who were going to dwell inside and to decorate them. In a word, the works of the Master himself are mannered.

Take the Robie House itself. A long heavy brick structure, it presents us with a rectangular fortress-like facade full of wall-sections and overhanging eaves. The home is anchored by a short, stout, central cross-section, which is, in fact, the fireplace chimney. The entrance is around the back, allowing the facade to remain unbroken; while a massive window-well extends out toward the sidewalk under the main battery of heavily outlined and ornamented windows, giving the home a hieratic, three-tiered, almost Ziggurat-like appearance.

Discussing the Robie House, one critic has remarked:

> Entrance is at the rear, so that the whole composition toward the street can remain one of pure and unbroken horizontals rising in tiers. The meaning embodied by them would seem again to be double: it is first of the earth, with its clefts, hollows and climactic masses, felt as full of life, always moving and lifting itself like some great beast, as Cézanne saw it. The second meaning grows out of the first. As the earth and objects upon the earth are pulled into the rhythm of flux and change, it and they fragment into their components, which then oscillate around each other in an "eternal becoming." This is the world as the Cubists saw it. The Robie House thus combines Cézanne's reverence for the majesty of solid things and his recognition of the forces that

*pull at them with Picasso's and Braque's fragmentation of
solids into planes which move continuously through space.*

What this viewer seems not to have noticed is that the Robie
House is made up almost exclusive of blocks and rectangles
set parallel with or at right angles to one another. Because of
this fact, comparison between Wright's work and that of
Cézanne and the cubists, interesting though it may be,
nevertheless leads us to quite a different conclusion than the
one proposed. What makes Cézanne's work compelling is the
unresolved tension between the curving and irregular shape of
natural objects—Mont Sainte Victoire, for example—and
Cézanne's inner need to give forms rigidity and substance.
This tension gives his best works a bizarre and fascinating
gravity and distortion. The cubists were working in precisely
the opposite direction, seeking to explode forms into a
cacophony of conflicting views. The tension and interest
offered by *their* works arises as a result of the mind's natural
tendency to group and organize images, even the most
fragmentary, coupled with the fact that the images themselves
are almost invariably not only familiar but agreeable—guitars,
cigarette packages, vases, flowers, etc. The end result is an
atmospheric haze, urban or domestic, which allows us to take
pleasure in simple scenes and objects once again by returning
them to us in an artfully confused and challenging hodgepodge, bit by bit.

Both Cézanne's and the cubists' approaches, in short, draw
on a tension between the curved and the straight, the orderly
and the disorderly, the natural and the conceptual. Wright's
work, on the other hand, and the Robie House in particular, is
made up almost exclusively of the orderly, the conceptual,
and the straight. It reeks of the blueprint and the drawing
board. In more general terms, it would almost be fair to say
that as the Richardsonian element in Wright's work diminishes, the Mussolini touch becomes ever more pronounced.

All the same, I enjoyed poking around the grounds of the Robie House, admiring the guarded banks of windows, the inaccessible balconies, the interplay of over-extended rooflines and the elegant stained glass. In fact, I wouldn't at all mind living in the Robie House for a few months or years, just to get the feel of the place. I could take some classes at the U.

◈

From Hyde Park we returned to Lake Shore Drive and sped north along the lake, where the waves were crashing vehemently against the deserted beaches. The water was a stunning blue-green which reminded me—I'm not making this up—of Monet's early seascape *The Beach at Sainte-Adresse* (1867, Chicago). We passed museums, apartment towers, gardens, and playgrounds, veered briefly out onto the amusement park on Navy Pier, and continued north past the Drake Hotel, the Gold Coast hotels and apartments, and Lincoln Park. Hospitals, campuses, private homes, the city goes on and on, with broad swards of green grass and trees along either side of the highway, runners and dog-walkers everywhere, and the dazzling aquamarine waves pounding ceaselessly beyond the breakwater out to the east.

After a few miles and a few jogs in the road, we turned west onto Devon Avenue where, we'd been told, ethnic enclaves abounded. The first mile seemed indistinguishable to me from West Broadway in North Minneapolis, and I was beginning to think we'd made a mistake coming so far north, when distinctive signs of exotica began to appear. First it was India, with three saree shops on the same block. We parked and went into the East India Trading Company, where canned goods, dry goods, fabrics, and kitchen utensils, along with numberless spices, canned and bagged, were arranged neatly on white wooden shelves, or stacked, or binned. Barrels of beans, nuts, and figs were arranged along one wall. The air was heavy with sweet, unidentifiable, almost overpowering odors. Most of the people in the store were draped in flowing white or brightly colored garments. Momentarily stunned by the luscious fragrance and the (to my eyes) unusual mode of dress, I had the feeling I'd stepped into a novel by Conrad.

A few blocks down the street we entered and browsed through a Russian bookstore; unfortunately (for everyone but Carol, who speaks Russian), all the books in the shop were *in* Russian. Then it was a Korean variety store (where the merchandise was too cheap), then a Jewish bakery (where the line was too long). Many of the shops and restaurants were closed, it being Sunday morning, and it was probably just as well, for we were getting anxious to get back downtown to see the show.

By the time we got back down to the Loop a crowd of people had formed in the plaza in front of the Museum. We dropped off our friends so they could get in line, (if there happened to be a line) and returned to the hotel to park the car, making our way back on foot through the gardens along State Street. In the meantime our friends had gone across the street to buy a cup of coffee; they sat on the steps passing it back and forth, it was still too hot to drink, and it was enormous, so I suggested that Hilary and I might go on ahead, which we did. We gave our tickets to a woman inside the door, who lead us to another woman, who led us down a hall past some Chinese statuary, while other visitors were being shunted in other directions, down corridors and along drooping velvet ropes. Eventually we went up a stairway and turned a corner, and there we met up with our first real line. It wasn't a long line–the line to the observation deck of the Sears Tower had been ten times longer. We almost immediately found ourselves inside the first room of the exhibit itself. It was thick with people. But we were elated. We'd made it! We were there!

Standing in front of the first exhibit, a series of caricatures that date from Monet's teenage years, I said to myself defiantly, "I paid good money to get into this show, and I'm going to see every bit of it." Five minutes later I was still standing in front of *Caricature of Léon Machon,* and I said to myself defiantly, "I'm not going to waste any more time on this juvenilia." I glanced briefly in every direction without seeing anything but people's heads and picture frames, and proceeded to the second room.

Here the masterpieces began to appear with startling frequency, like shooting stars at the peak of a meteor shower. *The River, The Magpie, La Grenouillére*, bing, bing, bing, and down the way *Boulevard des Capucines,* with the unearthly subtlety of its pink balloons and wintry trees, and across from it *The Highway Bridge at Argenteuil,* bristling with heat and summer pleasure. To be honest, I hardly glanced at these great and eternally fresh creations. I'd seen them too many times before, in person or in books, and it grieved me slightly to note once again how similar the originals are to the reproductions. This is a good thing, of course, when you're at home looking at a poster, a postcard, or an illustration in a book. But face to face with the original it's only natural to expect to be more deeply moved, yet that effect is not always forthcoming. Yes, there is the sudden awesome realization, that This is It, the one and only, and you happen to be the only person in the *world* standing in front of it at the moment. But other viewers are crowding in on either side of you, distracting you and occluding your vision. What you'd hoped would be an extended and deeply personal *téte-á-téte* has become a committee meeting, and you'd rather not have seen your beloved at all, than have been in her presence without being able to make contact on that intimate level which is so singularly rich and satisfying. Meanwhile, canvases on either side of your peripheral vision are tugging you away. "Remember me, remember how you used to swoon over me, why are you staring so long at that shallow hussy, with her clichéd clouds and her cheap river effects."

Yes, there's a good deal to be said for reproductions. In fact, it has even occurred to me that strange as it may seem, in some cases the reproductions look better than the originals. The reproductive process removes the oily glare from a painting's surface while at the same time making it smaller, so that the colors are intensified. Meanwhile, the fact that you're viewing a reproduction from the depths of an overstuffed chair in the comfort of your own home, rather than standing in a hot room crowded with strangers like a herd of cattle at the end of a very long cattle drive, also has its effect. But I'm overstating the case. In the end, time spent in front of an original will almost invariably be rewarded well beyond anything to be got from the plates of a book. And no reproduction, even the very best, can even begin to convey the role texture plays in Monet's later work.

All the same, I must confess that the paintings I took the greatest pleasure in, in the early rooms of the Monet exhibit, were those of his works I hadn't seen, or hadn't noticed, before. Two in particular stand out in my mind: *Breakwater at Trouville, Low Tide* (1870, Budapest) and *Sailboat at Le Petit Gennevilliers* (1874, private collection). Both paintings have an unusually pink or peachy sky. Both, at first glance, look "unrealistic." This fact also pained me a little. Had I reached the point where realism, impressionism, the quest for verisimilitude, and the authentic interplay of land, wave, leaf, light, and eye, was giving way, once and for all, to Fauvist extravagance and the unbridled exuberance of the giddy soul? For shame!

∾

For well over a century art critics have been struggling to escape from the horns of a dilemma brought about by the fact that the art form most widely esteemed by the public– Impressionism–stands diametrically opposed, in both conception and execution, to the guiding aesthetic of our time. Art historians relate the development of modern art in terms of a liberation from the constraints of represent-ationalism, yet Impressionist art is, more than that of any other modern school, representational in character. In order to escape this dilemma historians and critics have repeatedly struggled to construe the Impressionist aesthetic as one that eschews mere representationalism in the interests of "pure form" or of "light itself," evidently oblivious to the fact that "pure form" is a meaningless abstraction, that "light itself", even if it comes directly from the sun, is always "light that has been refracted off and altered by *things*." In the process these observers have denied or belittled the genuine spiritual character of the Impressionist revolution, which lies in an unabashed recognition of the power of nature, of things, of life itself, both to engage and to move us. Every painting in the Monet exhibit, for example, has the same meaning, the same message: NATURE IS BEAUTIFUL. No one who has gone on a walk at dawn can be unaware of this fact. For a painter the difficulty lies in capturing the truth and the effect, once and for all, in light, in form, in images.

Monet was far from being the first to succeed in his endeavor to "capture" nature, but it may be argued than in the long history of landscape art, he has been the most wide-rangingly effective. It might also be suggested that his work, more than that of any other painter, reflects an effort to escape from the tyranny of what things are conventionally *thought* to look like, beautiful or not, toward a more accurate, and hence a more moving, rendering of how an entire scene actually affects the eye. His own description of the method is revealing:

Do you really think that the excitement and ecstasy with which I express and fulfill my passion for nature simply leads to a fairyland?... The truth is simpler; the only virtue in me is my submission to instinct; it is because I rediscovered and allowed intuitive and secret forces to predominate that I was able to identify with creation and become absorbed in it. My art is an act of faith, an act of love and humility.

In his efforts to transfer this act of identification, and hence the excitement and even ecstasy associated with it, Monet struggled early in his career to establish tones on the canvas that would match the subtle interrelations brought about by the presence of a given caste of light in the field. Critics at the time were quick to note his sensitivity to such nuances. His early mentor Boudin, for example, remarks in a letter:

I met Monet in the Salon. He has set an example to us all by his faith to his principles. One of his canvases has been exhibited, thus scandalizing a number of people; they are wrong, for this painting does display a praiseworthy research into "true tone" which everyone is beginning to value.

Certainly "true tone" was not a new idea at the time. A generation earlier Corot had been counseling his students "...in nature seek first of all for form; then for the value or relationship between tints..." Monet is reported to have referred to Corot as "the greatest landscape painter who has ever lived," and it isn't hard to see why. The best of Corot's landscapes have the same uniformity of light, brought about by the same careful interrelation of tones, that Monet's early seascapes possess. In 1873–that is to say, long after the Impressionist revolution had gotten underway–the Durand-Ruel catalog could still report, with respect to Monet's work:

That which immediately strikes one when looking at this painting is the caress the eye receives—it is harmonious above all. What finally distinguishes it is the simplicity of means in achieving this harmony. One quickly discovers, in effect, that the secret is based completely on a very fine and very exact observation of the relation of one tone to another.

It was not long before Monet brought texture into play alongside tone as a means of evoking nature's power to absorb and excite—the intricate play of light on fields, trees, rippling water, and even architectural facades. Yet it strikes me that some of his early works have a beauty, simplicity, and freshness that few, if any, of his later works can match.

Passing from room to room in the enormous exhibit I found myself drawn to paintings I'd previously found too dull, and to others that had once seemed too flamboyant and extreme. Reproductions of the huge *Floating Ice* (1880) for example, the last work Monet submitted to the Salon before abandoning all hope of conventional success, had always struck me as slightly vapid, but standing in front of the original for the first time—it's much larger than I'd imagined—I was enthralled. But this could be said of any number of Monet's later works. You don't see what you're supposed to see until you stop looking, relax, and let the vision "come in." Your submission to instinct in viewing the painting must approach Monet's own in executing it.

How often the viewer, moving from room to room, can summon the mental energy to generate such an effect, varies widely among individuals. Hilary did a better job of it than I did, I'm sure, for I was repeatedly circling back to see what was taking her so long, only to find her transfixed in front of a canvas I'd dismissed with hardly a glance. Forced to linger and to look again, I would begin to "see." We came to agree that the filmy gray *Branch of the Seine near Giverny* (Mist) (1897, Chicago) and also the hot, dry *Bend in the River Epte* (1888,

Philadelphia) were masterpieces of staggering subtly and perfection, as well as the wispy, minty *Val-Saint-Nicholas, near Dieppe, Morning* (1896-97). I spent a good five minutes in front of *Vétheuil in Summer,* 1880; I drew in the sweetness of the poplars, the cathedral tower, the village, the clouds, and the shimmering water, all of which were rendered with precisely the degree of detail to suggest the slightest afternoon haze; and I revelled in the genuine "true tone" which gave the entire scene a single unified effect, like a childhood memory ripe with love and nostalgia. But this took time. And we were running out of time.

For me the big disappointment of the show was that only three of Monet's series were represented: the Haystacks, the Waterlilies, and the Houses of Parliament. It was pointed out in the text that the Institute had mounted a show called "Monet in the 90s" which largely covered that body of work just a few years earlier. Yes, but what about me? I had come to Chicago expressly to see the Poplars series, the Garden Path series, and the Rouen Cathedral series. "Sorry, buddy, you're five years too late."

After that blow, my attention waned considerably. Viewing the Houses of Parliament, I couldn't help thinking of Andre Derain's far more colorful and primitive renderings of the Thames, while many of the Waterlilies paintings, of which there were a great number on display, reminded me of the dull silvery sides of beat-up aluminum canoes. On the other hand the garish colors of the Mediterranean paintings like *Coastal Road at Cap Martin, near Menton* (1884), which looks like a romanticized postcard in reproduction, pleased me considerably, and I was also struck by the messy purples and pinks of the massive diptych *Wisteria* (1919, private collection) which I'd never seen before. This immense work might easily be taken for an Expressionist abstraction, except that the pastel colors resemble the colors of wisteria, leaf and flower, while the swoops and rings of hastily applied paint swing and drop like a clinging vine. It isn't a painting you'd care to examine at length—it lacks specific detail. Monet was practically blind when he painted it. But I can think of no mural better suited to decorate the rear wall of a cozy and affordable French bistro.

You may accuse me of damning with faint praise here, in thus reducing a work of the greatest Impressionist master, and indeed one of the most remarkable and sensitive poets in the entire history of the West, worthy to stand with Bruegel and Goya, with Tu Fu and Faure, with Machado and Montaigne, to the level of restaurant decoration. I'm not sure Monet himself would agree. Decorative and fine art were not as widely separated in Monet's day as they have since become, and he himself referred to a number of his canvases as "decorations." If the motive underlying his seemingly inexhaustible efforts to paint nature in its sundry manifestations was to identify with and become absorbed by it, then it would be reasonable to suggest that he desired that same communion to be extended to anyone who subsequently viewed the work. A museum is not necessarily the best place to establish such a connection, however. A home is a better one, I think, although a restaurant will also do nicely, especially if the food is fresh and good, the music inspired, the conversation lively... and if the walls never let us forget that wherever we go, we're still in the midst of life's sublime flux and glory.

Following our two-hour journey through the sixty-year career of Claude Monet, we stopped briefly in the gift shop, but neither the Monet T-shirts nor the Monet coffee mugs appealed to me much. Later, having freed our car once and for all from the confines of the Hotel Essex garage, we drove out to the Shedd Planitarium, where the wind from the lake was blowing fiercely. We'd planned to have a picnic lunch looking north across the bay toward the skyscrapers downtown, but we ended up on a broken slab of concrete looking east toward the smokestacks of Gary, Indiana. Still, the sun was dazzlingly bright, the sea was green, the clouds were enormous, and the food we'd picked up at the East Indian Trading Company was very tasty. We had our little *Dejeuner sur l'Herbe,* the four of us—neither the first, nor, I trust, the last.

And then we drove home.

Even the Darkness is Light

As I sat in the darkness I could see the chair through the glass of the sliding doors. It was a luminescent purple in the pre-dawn shadows of the deck. I watched it becoming light. Or white. (But the chair has always been white!) And a single bird began to chirp.

The mind moves slowly, half-awake, asking itself from one moment to the next, *Is it lighter now than it was a moment ago?*

You can't see light come, however. You simply notice that it has come. If you look away, more of it will come.

Meanwhile, a second cup of coffee brings a degree of light to those inner reaches where memories and sensations meet and mingle and combine into simpler or more sophisticated forms. There is something almost divine about the bitter edge of a cup of dark coffee in those moments between darkness and daylight, when everything is purple or pink or blue, and everything is wet; when the mind has not yet begun to refill itself in a sort of panic, as if it feared it was about to disappear; when nothing is planned, nothing is required, and the single, sharp report of the unseen bird—simultaneously an exclamation and a threat—tells the story of the entire universe.

The first thought to surface from the mists of my crepuscular delight on that quiet autumn morning was: "That chair has really held up well." How banal! But there's a story behind this rudimentary observation, and I think I ought to tell it. A decade ago a local department store brought out a line of outdoor furniture, manufactured in Taiwan out of bent metal tubing and wire mesh. The chairs were inexpensive and they were also poorly made. The paint cracked and flaked; the welds weakened and eventually snapped. If you got two summers of use out of them you considered yourself lucky.

Hilary and I bought a few of these chairs, wore them out, and discarded them. We were on the lookout for something better when we came upon a set of four chairs shaped exactly like the ones from Taiwan, except that the seats and backs were made of solid plastic ribbing. This set was made in Italy, and it cost a good deal more. We bought it. The parasol has long since deteriorated, the underside of the table has patches of rust, but after years of weathering the chairs themselves are absolutely pristine—not a single chip, crack, or flake anywhere—as if they'd been immersed, like Achilles, in the river Styx.

Not such an exciting tale, perhaps. But as I looked out at that chair glowing purple-white in the dark, the image of another white chair—cracked, rusted, broken, parked beside the garbage can in the alley behind our house back in the days of Haley's Comet—surfaced, and I was filled with a kind of moronic wonder at the enduring material integrity of the piece of simple furniture that stood in the pre-dawn light beyond the window glass. And, although the thought may strike you as absurdly consumerist in orientation— "Those chairs have really held up well"—I was not vainly priding my-self on my shrewdness in having bought them. Nor did it occur to me that a scientist in a plastics laboratory at Du Pont or an industrial designer in Milan was due for a hearty round of applause. It was the chair itself, looming silent and self-assured in the darkness, which filled me with admiration and even a touch of stupefied reverence.

The second thought to surface on that pre-dawn morning was equally primitive: "God is light." This passage appears in the Bible, probably more than once or twice, but every time I hear it I'm reminded of the use that medieval philosophers and theologians have made of it. In scripture the phrase "God is light" is fraught with spiritual connotations. On the other hand, in his little tract *On Light* (c.1229) Robert Grosseteste describes light as the first *form*, which stretches itself instantly in every direction, drawing matter along with it to create the *machina mundi* or world-machine in which we live. He doesn't go so far as to say that this light is God. To do so would be to deny that God is active (light doesn't generate itself); wise (light knows nothing); or even good (light is indiscriminate, it lacks an ethical dimension). You light a candle, you turn on a lamp, and what issues forth is...God? I don't think so. Nevertheless a creeping sense pervades the literature of that rather dark period that the spread of light and the spread of, say, divine love, are inextricably intertwined. At one point in his *Divisions of Nature* (c.850), for example, John Scotus Erigena observes "Will, love, delight, sight, desire, and motion are, when predicated of God, to be taken as suggesting one and the same thing to us."

As I pondered this odd association–that God's love and the spread of light are actually one and the same thing–a second note introduced itself to my reverie, "the envelope of light." This expression, widely quoted in museum catalogues and monographs, appears in a letter the painter Claude Monet sent to a friend at a particularly challenging moment in his career. The text, in part, reads as follows:

> *I am working away. I am set on a series of different effects, but at this time of year the sun goes down so quickly that I cannot follow it... I am working at a desperately slow pace, but the further I go, the more I see that I have to work a lot in order to manage to convey what I am seeking: "instantaneity," above all, the envelopment, the same light spread over everywhere; and more than ever, easy things achieved at one stroke disgust me. Finally, I am more and more maddened by the need to convey what I experience and I vow to go on living not too much an invalid, because it seems to me I am making progress.*

It was a single phrase, however, which returned to me that morning as I stared out the window at the glowing white chair, the nascent pink clouds, the bushes and the trees looming in the shadows of the back yard. "The envelope of light, spreading everywhere."

While these two random and isolated thoughts jangled in my mind for equal time like distant radio stations on a cloudy night, a third appeared abruptly. It was a line from a Psalm: *Lord, to you even the darkness is light.*

It seems to me that this is one of the greatest lines ever uttered by woman or man. (Did a woman or a man write the Psalms? No one knows.) It may be difficult for those of us who don't know Hebrew to tell exactly what the tone of the line is, however. Another translator (less compellingly, I think) gives it as

> *In your tender sight*
> *black and white*
> *are one—all light*

I prefer the first of these renderings, because it conveys a reverence and awe toward the creator, whose loftiness is irreproachable and sublime, notwithstanding the fact that to us mortals his creation falls painfully short of perfection. The second version suggests a deity who is merely sentimental and undiscriminating—not, I think, what the author of the Psalm intended. In either case, the line takes us a long way beyond the facile logic of Robert Browning's famous "God's in his heaven, and all's right with the world," as well as the somewhat more sophisticated formula of Leibnitz, cattily ridiculed by Voltaire in *Candide*, "It's the best of all possible worlds." The Psalmist acknowledges, against Browning's ungrounded optimism, that all is not right in the world—there's still a great deal of darkness in it. Our existence may well be, as Leibnitz suggests, the best that could have been devised under the circumstances, but the Psalmist is directing our attention out beyond our personal circumstances toward that being who underlies and animates *all* circumstances, both the ones that suit us and the ones that run counter to our interests. Whether it's the best or the worst of all worlds, it's the *only* world, and to find ourselves in the midst of it is a remarkable thing. There may be exasperation, resignation, humor, or bitterness, in our realization that the circumstances of life are largely beyond our control. Yet on those rare occasions when we palpably sense the ubiquitous presence of that Spirit who, through Providence or Love or Whimsy or Necessity, generates and sustains it all, the particulars of our personal fortune, both light and dark, fade to insignificance.

A famous passage in Greek literature conveys something of the same attitude toward this issue of divinity and darkness. I'm thinking of the moment when Odysseus, having been shipwrecked and tossed up naked on a beach, encounters the beautiful young princess Nausiccia. She asks him who he is, he tells her of the misfortunes that have befallen him, and she replies, rather cavalierly:

> *friend, you're hardly a wicked man, and no fool, I'd say—*
> *it's Olympian Zeus himself who hands our fortunes out,*
> *to each of us in turn, to the good and bad,*
> *however Zeus prefers...*
> *He gave you pain, it seems. You simply have to bear it.*

To me there is something both beautiful and comical about a young and inexperienced princess giving the great Odysseus, the "man of pain," who has been through *everything,* casual advice about how to handle adversity. She doesn't know she's speaking to the great hero, of course. All the same...

Another translator renders the same scene as follows:

> *Stranger, there is no quirk or evil in you*
> *that I can see. You know Zeus metes out fortune*
> *to good and bad men as it pleases him.*
> *Hardship he sent to you, and you must bear it.*

Once again I prefer the first rendering to the second. What distinguishes the two, and gives the first an almost shocking insouciance, are, first, the phrase "it seems," (as if Odysseus might merely be spinning yarns) and then the single word "simply" inserted soon after.

He gave you pain, it seems. You simply have to bear it.

Is that so, young lady?

⤐

These are autumn thoughts, brought on by the chilly air and the increasing darkness of the morning. Light becomes precious, and growing things take on a new beauty and poignancy. I'm not a morbid soul, but low light and dusky colors appeal to me. I dislike overhead lighting, and it makes me a little uneasy that the sun takes so long to set in the summertime. Fall light is dense and inescapable, and it brings with it a melancholy that I find luxurious. Sitting in the half light, staring out the window at a white metal chair, with the purple chrysanthemums blooming in the garden below, I feel that I'm being drawn along with the movement of the stars, or worse yet, with the terrifying and ineluctable tidal ooze of all things toward and against one another; and a famous line from Leopardi's poem "The Infinite" appears out of nowhere, as if to cap my early morning reverie:

...and sweet to me, being shipwrecked in that sea.

Darkness? Shipwreck? Few of us, after all, seek out such things. All the same, the moods I'm describing are in perfect accord with the latest scientific research. The biologist René Dubos, for example, writes:

On the one hand, the external manifestations of human existence change continuously and at an increasing rate under the influence of social and technological innovations. On the

other hand, man's anatomical structures, physiological pro-
cesses, and psychological urges remain in phase with the
cosmic conditions that prevailed when Homo sapiens
acquired his biological identity.

Though we may live in cities, in other words, we respond to
changes in our environment the same way the Neanderthals
did. Nor, in Dubos's view, are our seasonal moods driven
entirely by changes in light.

The behavioral patterns associated with the seasons cannot
entirely be accounted for by changes in temperature or in the
luminosity of sky. They have their seat in the genetic consti-
tution and originate from a time in the evolutionary past
when man lived in such direct contact with nature that he
could survive only if his bodily functions and his mental
responses were precisely geared to the seasonal rhythms of
nature and the availability of resources.

I don't see how genetics can entirely account for the
immediate emotional impact of mercurial fluctuations in air
pressure, cloud cover, temperature, or light, however. When I
step out onto the deck on a cool autumn morning, sights,
sounds, and smells that weren't there even a few days ago
incite me to rhapsodize. Lower light, dew in the long pale
grass, and the chrysanthemums, which the Chinese associate
with the beauty and melancholy of the season:

I remember, when I was young,
How easily my mood changed from sad to gay.
If I saw wine, no matter the season,
Before I drank it, my heart was already glad.
*   But now that age comes,*
A moment of joy is harder and harder to get.

And always I fear that when I am quite old
The strongest liquor will leave me comfortless.
Therefore I ask you, late chrysanthemum-flower,
At this sad season why do you bloom alone?
Though well I know that it was not for my sake,
Taught by you, for a while I will open my face.

—Po Chü-i, (812)

The penultimate line of this little gem, in which the poet acknowledges the radical separation between his fate and the ebb and flow of circumstances that surround him, seals its modest beauty.

I sometimes wonder if the sensual pleasures of autumn, with its low light, brisk air, and vanishing vigor, are heightened by the realization that outdoor work is finally at an end. Unfortunately this pleasant thought is often accompanied by the nagging sense that we've somehow failed to fulfill the promise of the summer that's now lost to us. It's a sweet feeling, but there's an element of pain in it as well: summer heat and light and vegetation, which until very recently surrounded us on all sides, now lie beyond our capacity to seize or to make use of fully. As the darkness and the cold encroach we look back nostalgically to summer because we know things are going to get a lot worse for us before they get better. The eye needs light, the body needs activity, the tongue needs fresh summer tastes, the awakened ear needs the sounds of the morning, the olfactory unit longs for an escape from furnace dust. Some of these things can be arranged, of course. What seems never to have the desired effect is to return to summer by means of images. If it isn't palpably present in one form or another—canned pimentos or a vacation in sunny Zihuatenejo—summer no longer exists.

As a means of testing this theory, I just now opened one of my summer journals more or less at random. Here's the passage I hit upon:

> *O Perfectness! Whatever surpasses me,*
> *Lying beyond me, sustains me:*
> *I depend on the things of this world!*
> *On all that has being, that lives,*
>
> *And that is not myself: that goes on propounding*
> *A volume undreamt of by hands,*
> *Intent on the bliss of an unforeseen*
> *Wonder, resolved in an act!*

These lines are by the Spanish poet Jorge Guillén. They're followed by what seems to be a ragged attempt on my part to sustain the mood, or to exemplify the message.

> *Feet in the water, wine in the glass.*
> *Three men fish from a boat.*
> *A mallard glides by heading toward the sun.*
>
> *The white foam on the beach.*
> *The pink and white striped sails.*
> *August is summer taking itself for granted.*
>
> *43, and do we call this living?*
> *It's nice to see so much of the sky.*
> *Gulls coming in from overhead like a*
>   *Japanese print.*
>
> *"When we say that the spirit does not exist,"*
>   *Alain writes,*
> *"we mean that it is more than existence. This*

simple description goes beyond all the
    hyperboles of theology."

Bigger waves. A woman in an inner tube.
Guillén's Cantico.
Tonight is the night to get to know it.

(To me a floating leaf is a miracle of substance.
Yet I don't connect well with people, Or,
I connect very well with people—which is it?)

The swim was short, refreshing.
The suit dries slowly, however.
Discarding the wine, I turn to bottled water.

Many sailboats now, with white sails.
The sun has half an hour of life at least.
It's a race! I see the boats rounding the buoy.

"There's somebody at our beach," the boy
    cries from
the path in a high-pitched voice.
"Can we still swim here?"

The same tall man, with his two sons, came
    to swim
When Hilary and I were here a few weeks
    ago.
His speech sounds vaguely Scandinavian.

He plays with the children at great length, tirelessly.
The mother, who sat alone in the sand last
    time, does not appear.

A white feather floats on the surface of the water.

When the fog is in the pines and the warblers have long since passed through on their long journey south, scenes like this one sound altogether too colorful and poetic. And yet I must admit, reading over it at this distance, I'm equally struck by the elements of negativity contained in it—that the sun drops in the sky, that someone else (namely me) has occupied the boy's beach, that the mother has not returned. Wine poured into the sand reminds me of the ancient Greek practice of feeding the ancestors buried in the back of the house, while the white feather calls to mind the passing bird.

In any case, the distinctly summery elements of the canvas—the sailboats, the gulls, the foam on the beach—have little power to warm us. At best they're an irrelevancy, at worst they're an insult to the gravity of our condition. The moment will arrive when, looking forward to a new year, we revive our memories of summer sunlight in an anticipatory spirit, but that moment is still a long ways off. For now, we wallow in the dimming light, in the sweetness of things that have ripened, fallen, lost their luster, or collapsed.

Things that vanish. Outlines, distinctions, gaps. To *discern* is to "sift apart," and it's often been said that we seldom fully recognize the value of anything until we've become removed from it somehow. I don't think this is true, yet there's often a painful wholeness to those experiences we no longer find ourselves in the midst of, and this can be a source of nostalgia or a spur to art.

The Japanese have elevated the appreciation of things that vanish to a high art; they have a word for ephemeral beauty, in fact, "aware." The monk Kenko explored this issue at length in his classic *Essays in Idleness* (1332):

> *Are we to look at cherry blossoms only in full bloom, the moon*
> *only when it is cloudless?... People commonly regret that the*
> *cherry blossoms scatter or that the moon sinks in the sky, and*
> *this is natural; but only an exceptionally insensitive man*
> *would say, "This branch and that branch have lost their*
> *blossoms. There is nothing worth seeing now."*

An obvious point, perhaps. What needs to be more adequately explored, I think—and here, perhaps, is the idea toward which these seemingly random reflections have been groping—is the notion that the things we value most highly have somehow integrated or absorbed a degree of this absence or "negativity" into themselves. Kenko seems to be suggesting something on this order when, further on in his essay, he asserts that only the individual who has lost that which he cherishes can fully know its value.

> *Does the love between men and women refer only to the*
> *moments when they are in each other's arms? The man who*
> *grieves over a love affair broken off before it was fulfilled, who*
> *bewails empty vows, who spends long autumn nights alone,*
> *who lets his thoughts wander to distant skies, who yearns for*
> *the past in a dilapidated house—such a man truly knows*
> *what love means.*

Although I like the phrase "dilapidated house," this turn of the argument strikes me as more than a little absurd.

It may be true, in some abstract or Hegelian sense, that absence illuminates being. Yet it's also worth considering whether, beyond the cycle of love and loss, of enthusiasm and disillusionment, there is a realm of experience in which the energy and presence of being (which inspires us with love) carries an element of finitude, depth, and darkness *within it*. I might even go so far as to suggest that these elements underlie the abiding appeal of those beings to which we become seriously attached.

Kenko is certainly right to suggest that the beauty of cherry-blossoms becomes more precious to us once we've seen how fragile and short-lived they really are. (The leaves on the maple in my back yard have a translucent hue this morning that's neither yellow nor green. I'm tempted to say it's the most beautiful color on earth.) But the blossoms themselves are nevertheless more beautiful, in their pink transience and fragility, than are the naked branches that remain once the blossoms have fallen. And the best view of all may well be the one that reveals the structure of the branches through the gaps where the delicate blossoms have already begun to fall!

Kenko goes too far, therefore, when he asserts:

Are we to look at the moon and the cherry blossoms with our eyes alone? How much more evocative and pleasing it is to think about the spring without stirring from the house, to dream of the moonlit night though we remain in our room!

This form of romanticism exhausts itself in memories and dreams; to think about the spring presupposes a familiarity with the spring, after all, and if this familiarity brings with it a recognition of both the beauty and the transience of the season, that is no reason for us to attenuate our exposure to it on that account. A true knowledge of *anything*, I think, involves a recognition and acceptance of this element of transience. The Psalmist exempts his Lord and creator from such troublesome realities—the Lord draws all things together, the light and the dark alike, into a pleasing and incandescent self-regard that's not egotistical, because it extends outward to encompass everything. The exception merely proves the rule, however. Even in our finest moments we have far more in common with Odysseus standing naked on the beach; we've been through hell and now we're being lectured to by a Princess who has never really *lived*. Perhaps we may soon be invited into the palace, as Odysseus was, and lavishly clothed, and wined and dined, and invited to tell our sorry tale for the amusement of the nobles who have gathered there to be entertained. Then again, perhaps not. In any case, this is our lot, and it isn't simply resignation that drives us to embrace and to love it for what it is, but a gleeful recognition that only the emptiness between things gives us space to approach and to familiarize ourselves with them.

The Spaniard Guillén's ecstatic love for the things of this world—

> *O Perfectness! Whatever surpasses me,*
> *Lying beyond me, sustains me:*
> *I depend on the things of this world!*

—may sound glib, but it rises from a deeper source, I think, than the tears shed by a jilted lover moping around in a bamboo shack. For it does happen that, in the constitutional alienation, the negativity, and the spiritual exile of our self-conscious reserve, we may occasionally be surprised to find ourselves entirely "at home." The stars continue to shine, the mist rises from the bay, the poem strikes a chord, the beloved smiles. There is value everywhere, in fact, as well as a measure of emptiness. The mix of the two—the value, the lack—is never the same, from moment to moment, person to person, place to place. The slow movement of a Bach violin partita pulls at us in a very different way than does a fiery flamenco cante, but they both hurt...and they both shine.

MOUNTAIN
UPSIDE DOWN

I enjoy the sight of camping gear strewn haphazardly across the living-room floor. Whether I'm packing it or unpacking it, I find the unintended clash in life-ways both attractive and stimulating. The bright blue tent, the rumpled sleeping bags, the plastic plates, the water filter, maps, and tiny stove, sit on the thick carpet beside the couch, or on the coffee table, or over by the piano, or in front of the stereo, all of which furnishings and accoutrements bespeak an entirely different and far more complicated way of life. The one supports, the other liberates, perhaps, although neither, I think, is entirely satisfying or sufficient unto itself. The one grows by accretion and sometimes takes on monstrous forms. The other strips and simplifies, to the point where there is almost nothing there. Yet this "almost nothing" opens the door to shadowed paths along mountain creeks and long dry trails through dusty canyons; it brings us close to the sounds of the night, the arrangement of the stars, the smell of wood-smoke, and the heightened appeal of simple food to the tired and hungry body.

As I write these words I'm unpacking, as it happens, having just returned from a ten-day trip to the Southwest. Memories of mesas, canyon creeks, billowing clouds, and endless vistas struggle against the encroachment of newspaper headlines, credit card bills, and incipient thoughts of what lies ahead at work. It's a pleasant turmoil, although at this point the weight of emphasis remains on the memory of the extraordinary places I've just visited. I'm thinking in particular of the inner reaches of the Grand Canyon.

Everyone knows that the Grand Canyon is both a geological anomaly and a tourist cliché, and everyone knows what it looks like, more or less. It may be difficult, if not impossible, for those who haven't actually *seen* the Canyon to comprehend what an extraordinary aesthetic (and metaphysical!) phenomenon it is. We've all seen colorful pictures taken from various angles and overlooks, but no picture can begin to suggest how the canyon falls away and spreads in every direction to fill the eye with form, shadow, texture, and light. There is an unbelievable and joyous beauty and barrenness to its contours, which the thirsty eye laps up like precious spring water, and cannot get enough of.

A hodgepodge of hotels, restaurants, and gift shops, some modern, some rustic, sits on the south rim at Grand Canyon

Village. (Passing a few minutes' time in one or another of these shops at various times, I've found it impossible to resist purchasing a deck of Grand Canyon playing cards, a tape by the Navaho flutist R. Carlos Nakai, a box of piñon incense, and a ceramic mug that identifies the twelve major layers of sediment through which the Colorado has cut in the last six million years.) A flagstone patio stretches along the rim for several hundred yards between this string of buildings and the edge of the canyon, with a low rock wall to prevent tourists from inadvertently tumbling down into it. Crows sit in the branches of trees that dot the escarpment below the terrace, scrutinizing passing humans with icy glee before lifting themselves up and out and down into the yawning abyss.

A footpath leads beyond the village to the west toward the promontories that provide many of the breath-taking views we so often see reproduced in magazines and travel brochures. These overlooks can also be reached by car or shuttle, and they usually are, I think, judging by the fact that Hilary and I met no one on the evening we hiked out that way. As night descends tourists, many of them speaking German or French, gather at these overlooks. Conversation is muted and intermittent, in part because so many people are taking pictures, in part because the intensifying beauty of the vistas drives onlookers into a state of stupefied awe. In fact, the word *tourist* doesn't adequately convey the spirit of those individuals and families who have traveled great distances and arranged for accommodations, with no other thought in mind but to see this remarkable transformation of the canyon into night. The word *pilgrim* would be more apt.

And the scene changes. From Grand View, on the eastern end of the southern highway approach, the Canyon looks broad, intricate, and yet somehow *manageable,* as you look north toward Marble Canyon and the Vermillion Cliffs. Turn your head west, however, and a more intractable landscape presents itself. The river has cut deeper here, and the canyon rises to a point where you can no longer see what lies beyond the rim; the buttes, side canyons, plateaus, and pinnacles stretch to the horizon, a vast array of jagged and elegant forms with no point of reference outside of or beyond itself. As you travel west by car along the rim road this effect increases, and the fact that the northern rim lies a thousand feet above where you stand only adds to the all-encompassing fullness and intricacy of the scene. Every turnout and viewpoint offers differing angles and perspectives on a collection of buttes and spires bearing odd and seemingly arbitrary names like Brahman Temple and Cheops Pyramid. Once you've deposited yourself at one or another South Rim Lodge (and you'd better have reservations!), you can make your way out on foot across a two-mile trail to Hopi Point, where a new and entirely different section of the canyon reveals itself.

From the North Rim Lodge—18 miles as the crow flies, 200 miles by road—the canyon looks larger, but also less coherent. You're looking out across ten miles of side canyons toward the enormous bowl of the main canyon, which largely escapes your view. The views are stunning, but also fractured and incomplete.

The canyon is at no place more dramatic, perhaps, than at Toroweap, an overlook reached by traversing a sixty-mile gravel road an hour west of the main north entrance. The drop is sheer at this point, but it's only 3,00 feet (only?), because a thousand feet of the canyon's depth has by this time been converted to graceful ridges rising behind and above the point where you stand.

The Native Americans called the Canyon Toroweap, which means "mountain upside down." This is an apt and poetic description, I think. On the other hand, a mountain looks both more majestic and less detailed, the farther away you get. The Grand Canyon remains invisible, hidden in the flat and nondescript scrub of the Kaibab Plateau, until the moment you come upon it, at which point it curls up toward you to expose both its inimitable expanse and its every detail to view with startling immediacy. Because of its enormous size and length—from Lee's Ferry to Lake Mead the Grand Canyon is 277 miles long—it would clearly take a long time for anyone to become even remotely familiar with it. On the other hand, a single glance from the South Rim puts us face to face with a concatenation of beauty, grandeur, intricacy, and danger that I suspect has no parallel on this earth. We look again and again in the changing light, as if some clue to the ultimate mystery of existence were hidden in its shadows and contours.

The Canyon's sinister aspect presents itself the moment it occurs to you that wherever your eyes take you along the seemingly endless ridges and ravines, you will, in all likelihood, be looking at a spot where no one has been and no one will ever be. This combination of brash visibility and utter inaccessibility is both tantalizing and unnerving. "If I were right *there,*" you say to yourself, "I would be dead before long. If I fell in over *there,* there is no way they could get to me, even if I survived the fall." This strange overtone of shrinking dread, in the midst of an experience of all-encompassing beauty, brings to the Canyon an element that the German Romantics would have referred to as *sublime.*

Once you've stared down into the canyon for a while, moving from point to point along the rim, the urge grows to act on the affection you feel. You want to take hold, somehow, of the wild and powerful beauty both within and in front of you. It gnaws at you—you want to *go down into* the Canyon. And why not? Nothing could be easier. You'll find the trailhead to the Bright Angel Trail behind the Kolb Studio, just a few feet from the popular lodges on the South Rim. Every day thousands of tourists walk down a few hundred yards or even a few miles. Unfortunately, the views along the upper reaches of this trail are largely blocked by encroaching canyon walls. It would be better to take the shuttle to Yaki Point, eleven miles to the east along the rim, where the South Kaibab Trail takes you down along the top of a naked ridge into the heart of the Canyon with spectacular views on either side.

Hilary and I did this on our first visit to the canyon. In those days you could drive out to Yaki Point. Although I thought we'd gotten an early start, when we arrived at the trailhead the parking lot was full and there were cars parked in the ditches up and down the roadside as well. (I guess this is why you can no longer drive to Yaki Point.) We started down in the company of other day-trippers–the back-packers had gotten an earlier start, no doubt–and as we descended we met several ascending hikers who'd gone down early to photograph the sunrise. The trail is well maintained, wide, and not too steep. It isn't likely you're going to fall off. Yet the minute you drop into the shadows of the canyon basin, with crows soaring hundreds of feet *below* you across the snow-dusted pines on the steep upper escarpment, you feel the excitement that comes with the realization that you've entered a different world.

Before long the switchbacks brought us out into the full glare of morning sun. We'd made our way through the steep Kaibab, Toroweap, and Coconino layers, at which point the Canyon opens out onto the gentler slopes of Hermit Shale. Bright red dust pounded by a thousand heavy footsteps caught the early morning sun from the east, and the pale green sheen of the Tonto Plateau far below had become a forest of tiny stunted shrubs. One woman we passed along the way was wailing, "My knees are shaking! My knees are shaking!" to which her husband replied, "Get a grip on yourself. We've been on more strenuous hikes than this back in Seattle." But the knees do suffer relentless pounding as you step down and down the rocky trail–the knees and the toes–and the act itself of descending, in the growing heat of the sun, into an untamed landscape where (as everyone knows) many people have died, past cautionary signs about carrying plenty of water, surrounded above, below, and on all sides by bristling desert vegetation, precipitous drop-offs, and harsh, craggy, lifeless rocks, can easily turn what had been a giddy thrill into a kind of irrational panic.

By the time we reached Cedar Mesa, a relatively level spot a mile and a half in, small groups of hikers were admiring the vistas, nursing their precious water, squatting in the shade of the scraggly cedar that gives the spot its name, or waiting in line to use the outhouse. This is the turn-around point for many parties, and it's a good one. You've dropped more that a thousand feet into the canyon, and it will never again be something merely to look down into. You've become acquainted with it, you've gotten to know it a little, and it seems both more all-encompassingly beautiful, and also more intimate and friendly, from this new perspective. The hike has been exhilarating and also relatively easy. On the other hand, because the canyon is all around you now, rather than entirely below you, it seems somehow smaller, or at any rate less formidable and mysterious, and it's likely that as you move farther down the trail this effect will increase.

All the same, Hilary and I wanted to see the famous river that lurks hidden in the depths of the inner canyon, so we continued down in the mid-morning sun along the flank of O'Brien Butte. We were excited but also anxiously aware that every step we took would have to be retraced in the heat of the day with the force of gravity against us. The stream of hikers had thinned. Several back-packers passed us headed for Bright Angel Campground on the river bottom, and a number of carefree hikers we met had astutely arranged to spend the night at Phantom Ranch.

Our plan was to hike out at least to Skeleton Point, where the trail takes a sudden and precipitous drop to the east, and then re-evaluate our position. Before long we'd reached and skirted the end of that point, and sat dangling our legs over the edge of the canyon wall, out of sight and hearing from the hikers passing at intervals on their way into and out from the depths of the inner canyon. The green stubbly sward of the Tonto Plateau spread itself below us, and in the distance we could see the trail to Plateau Point, draped like a piece of thin white thread across the canyon's sloping surface. Below us in the distance the trail we'd been following reappeared from amid the layers of rock perhaps an hour of hiking away. From that point, we guessed, it would be possible to look directly down into the dark and forbidding schists of the steep inner gorge. Looking back at where we'd come from on the rim, it seemed we'd hardly begun to enter the canyon! But from our vantage point we could, for the first time, see a ribbon of brown water through a break in the ridges and waves of canyon rock below—the mighty Colorado itself! We sat, and gazed, and sat some more in the brilliant sunlight, surrounded by energy and color and light and space and peace, staring off and down at places we wanted to get to, but could not; three rubber rafts drifted into view in the silence a thousand feet below us, the size of grains of rice, and then disappeared again into the rocks.

᳕

Two years ago a friend of ours, with whom we'd been camping in the desert more than once, came up with the wild idea that we visit the bottom of the canyon along with two other old friends to celebrate our 50th birthdays together. He made the reservations soon afterward—with a group of this size you almost have to—and so it happened that, after two years of simmering anticipation, and a month or two of sporadic conversation and planning, we found ourselves once again heading down into the canyon on the South Kaibab Trail.

The trail hadn't changed; it was still stunningly beautiful. We began the descent in the company of a troop of young boys and several groups of heavily laden backpackers that had crowded onto the shuttle-bus alongside us at the backcountry office. The air was cool in the shade of the switchbacks that lead out onto the ridge. Early April, snow in the shadows, crows in the trees, bright sun out in the canyon and a beautifully contoured path leading down toward it. The exhilaration was intense. We were with our friends, and we were also free of the anxieties associated with deciding when to turn back. We weren't going to turn back.

We looked east from Cedar Ridge toward a mid-morning sun that was glaring off a thousand spires and crevices, north into the shadows of the canyon of Bright Angel Creek, or back toward the graceful curves of the upper canyon wall we'd just descended; with each switchback the vision changed, and we stopped frequently to converse and to enjoy the unfolding panorama. When we reached Skeleton

Point we paused once again, to take in the sudden appearance of the distant river below us, and then we continued light-heartedly down the steep switchbacks that would take us to the Tonto Plateau, Panorama Point, and the inner gorge.

The Canyon is an oven; it may be twenty or thirty degrees hotter at the river than it is on the rim at any given time, and we felt the thickening of the atmosphere as we descended. The day itself was heating up as well. The light grew harsher, and those hikers we met on the trail often looked tired, as I'm sure we did too. On the other hand, four miles in a man passed us accompanied by his teen-aged daughter. She was wearing a bikini and carrying a tiny plastic purse! They passed us again later coming out, and it seemed to me they had a long way to go before they reached the top.

Knee and blister problems were beginning to present themselves to several members of our group. Pack trains of mules carrying duffle bags or people passed us, kicking up dust and depositing their own soil. We sat for half an hour in the shadow of a rock and nibbled on the rations we'd brought along. We were tired, but we knew we didn't have far left to go. And, as we continued on our way through light and shadow down endless switchbacks into the dramatic V of the dark inner gorge, lifting our feet painfully over the wooden edges of terraced steps, before dropping them down brutally onto the step below, the bright turquoise blue of the river became a source of relief.

Then the bridge came into view. The trail became steeper yet as we hobbled down to the entrance of the tunnel that leads out onto it. People were playing on a white sandy beach on the far side of the river, throwing a frisby and splashing hesitantly in the frigid water. We stood on the bridge looking out through the wire mesh at the powerful but inconspicuous currents of the river, the sculpted beauty of the inner gorge, and the pale parfait of the now distant and irrelevant strata near the rim.

We had reached the bottom! Nothing remained but to slog the final half-mile under the glaring sun alongside the Colorado past the beach, and then up the semi-shaded valley of Bright Angel Creek past the mule corral, the modest campground, the amphitheater, and the cottages scattered here and there among the cottonwoods, on our way to the office of Phantom Ranch.

Phantom Ranch is neither a ranch, nor a resort, properly speaking, but a summer camp for adults. It has private cabins, bunkhouses, rules, a mess hall, daily educational programs, and assigned seating at meals. The meals are served at set times, family style, and if you miss your seating by even a few minutes you'll miss the meal. So I was told, although no one missed a meal while we were there so I have no way of verifying this. Everyone's hot and tired and sore, but also hungry, so a crowd gathers in front of the mess hall during the period just before they unlock the doors to let you in for dinner.

We reached the Ranch at 2:30 and were assigned to our bunkhouses. After claiming a bed by tossing a water bottle or a pair of socks onto it, and examining the plumbing arrangements, we returned to the mess hall, which was set to close for the afternoon at 4:00. This gave us time to enjoy a beer together in the relative coolness of the large log structure. We sat on the uncomfortable straight-backed chairs and felt good. We felt like we'd done something. It was a simple and unadulterated pleasure. Hey! We're here! And when they kick us out at four to begin preparations for dinner we can go listen to the ranger talk about the return of the California Condor. How civilized. How genteel!

We spent the following day down in the canyon, hiking a few miles up the North Kaibab Trail in the morning, relaxing on benches or playing cards in the mess hall during the heat of the afternoon. When the hall closed we all went down to the river again, though the wading was brief and fitful. We talked with other hikers we met along the trail and at meals, and it was always pretty much the same. Where are you from, which trail did you take down, when did you get your reservation, where else have you been hiking? There were hikers of all ages in the mix, and several families with teenaged children.

On our morning foray up the North Kaibab we met a couple coming down from the Cold Creek trail; we'd seen their tent the previous afternoon, a blue dot impossibly high up on the cliffs on the far side of the river. "Were you on the South Kaibab yesterday?" the man asked. He was wearing a cowboy hat and army fatigues, and both he and his female companion wore the easy grins of outdoor people who are ruggedly extending themselves with no sense of rivalry or pretense. "We saw a helicopter make a rescue near the Tip-Off," and we wondered whether an elderly woman, leaning flushed and tired against the rocks, waiting for her companions, that several of our party had passed and inquired after, had been more seriously stricken than we thought.

My calves were painfully tight the entire day: I was walking around like a clown on stilts. We skipped the evening ranger talk on John Wesley Powell and sat on a bench near the creek drinking a bottle of wine that one of our group had lugged down the trail and stashed in the reeds alongside the stream to cool, in order to properly celebrate the collective birthday. We looked up past the jagged hummocks of schist that form the valley walls surrounding the Ranch and watched the horns of Taurus sink little by little from view, while small chubby bats skittered past us in the dark.

The wake-up call came at 4:30 the next morning. Breakfast was served at 5:00 and before long we were on the trail again.

For me this was the most beautiful part of the trip, perhaps because it was both new and cool. We crossed the river on a second bridge, and then followed the south side of the steep inner canyon for a mile or more. In the early morning shadows and stillness the gorge seemed as powerful and mysterious as it does looking down from the rim, and far more immediate.

At Pipe Creek the trail leaves the river, turning inland up the valley toward the sheer rock cliffs of the upper strata, which we could see above us from time to time between the towering masses of schist. The trail up the valley of Pipe Creek climbed steadily, but not steeply; we passed the "Devil's Corkscrew" without really noticing it, and as the morning light spread across the canyon floor we reached a nameless Eden-like region with murmuring water, verdant river grasses, and the radiant purple blooms of redbud trees.

We were resting along this lovely stretch in the shade of a gigantic boulder when the first group passed us going down to the ranch, and they informed us that Indian Garden was a mere half-hour away. Hey! This is easy, going *up* the canyon. We're practically halfway out.

Indian Garden is the campground you can see from the rim. It lies four and a half miles down the Bright Angel Trail, and the same distance from the river, more or less. There's a source of drinking water there, and as far as I can tell, this is its chief virtue. At Indian Garden you enter the mouth of a box canyon, and from that point on the ascent is little more than a succession of hot, dry, switchbacks with little change of scenery. During this final section of the trail you're also likely to be beset with the recurrent thought that you're *virtually* back on the top—the rim you see above you is the one you were standing on outside your hotel room two days ago—while *actually* you're still three miles and 2000 feet below it. The agony is compounded by the fact that as you ascend the trail you encounter increasing numbers of day-trippers who've come down a mile or two on a lark. No one can blame them for doing this, that's what the trail is for, but it demystifies the finale to your own seemingly Herculean adventure.

In the course of this final stretch, (which would actually be exhilarating on a cool morning), we had episodes of lost cameras, fainting spells, and elusive petroglyphs, as well as more than one encounter with hikers who appeared to be succumbing to the afternoon heat, but in the end we put the ten miles and 5000 vertical feet behind us, and that's the important part of the story. Gayle Anderson (she of the short legs), Keith Kroschel (intrepid planner and venerable sage–he turned 50 last year!) Tim Wahl (resident geologist and wine-carrier) and his wife Carol, along with Hilary and I, will not go down in history, but we sat together at a table in the Bright Angel Restaurant that night–our reservation at the ritzy El Tovar had mysteriously disappeared–feeling good about ourselves, and saying little about our pains or our accomplishment. Of course we'd done it. One or two helicopter rides excepted, everyone who goes down to the bottom comes back up under his or her own power. We offered a few toasts to one another, rehashed the habits and oddities of our fellow travelers and bunkmates at Phantom Ranch, and discussed where we all planned to go next.

The next morning we went our separate ways. The good-byes were perfunctory: we'd be meeting up again in a few days in Santa Fe for dinner at Pasquale's and a hot-tub at the El Rey Motel. Gayle and Keith headed off to the Goosenecks of the San Juan, Tim and Carol to Monument Valley and Mesa Verde, while Hilary and I lingered at the Canyon.

We were just leaving a gift shop on the rim when California condor number 48 (every condor has a number and a radio antenna on his wings–we're worried about these birds!) swooped in on its nine foot wings and came to rest on a ledge a few feet below an observation platform. In my haste to reload my camera with film I left all my shots of the inner canyon sitting on a bench somewhere.

I try to tell myself it's all for the best. The inner gorge will remain forever hidden from casual view, as perhaps it should. But I'll always remember what I saw, and now that I've been *down there*, my feeling for the canyon has changed a little. It remains unspeakably dramatic and beautiful, but it seems slightly less expansive and unfathomable than it used to. Times and distances have become clearer.

This newfound familiarity is largely a conceit, of course. Shift your gaze 15 degrees in any direction and you'll once again be confronting a scene of incomprehensible foreignness. The canyon cannot be tamed, conquered, or come to grips with. Colors, shapes, and distances fuse into a mind-numbing mandala that will draw us back again and again.

Blueberry Lake

Rain on the roof, Wednesday afternoon at the lake, napping on the couch on the last summer of the century. I hear an ovenbird (teacher-teacher-teacher), and now a yellowthroat (witchity-witch), chattering in the woods. Something about the simplicity of woodland life–this isn't a life, of course, but only a vacation–whets the appetite for good meals, long walks in the woods... and metaphysics. This may be because metaphysics, which seems deep and redolent of exotic realms of experience, is, in fact, rather "vacant." The smell of wet leaves on the forest floor is the smell of good German metaphysics.

I've just finished reading a pamphlet by the eminent German philosopher Martin Heidegger called "What is Philosophy?" It's based on a lecture Heidegger gave late in life, and it's described by the man who translated it into English as the best introduction to the great man's work. I rather doubt that it is, but the argument suits the mood of my midsummer northwoods reverie.

In this little essay Heidegger is trying to tell us, I think, that philosophy is first and foremost a yearning toward a return to a harmony with Being. He arrives at this position by way of an approach that's distinctly and deliberately Greek. Why Greek? Because in Heidegger's view the term *philosophia* was coined by the pre-Socratic Greek thinkers. Therefore they, of all people, ought to know what it is. (Strange as it may seem, while I was reading this slim volume I was reminded repeatedly of the works of Confucius, who was not, I think, a Greek.)

Heidegger observes that the word 'philosophy' was coined by the pre-Socratic philosopher Heraclitus to signify the man who loves *sophron*, or wisdom. He goes further to suggest (somewhat simple-mindedly, perhaps) that for Heraclitus wisdom was specifically the knowledge that "One is All."

At this point in the argument the thought crossed my mind (although Heidegger doesn't mention the fact) that many sayings have been attributed to Heraclitus, and not merely the somewhat vague, and perhaps even sophomoric, "One (is) All." Let me give you some examples:

The sun is the width of a man's foot.

The fire, in its advance, will consume all things.

He who would be wise must acquaint himself with a great many particulars.

You never step into the same river twice.

All things come to pass through the compulsion of strife.

Several of these remarks are both more poetic and more "wise" than the rudimentary "One is all," it seems to me. In fact, the vision that Heraclitus gives us in most of his sayings, and the one that he's famous for, is not a vision of static unity, as Heidegger seems to be suggesting, but of violence, flux, and the continual "coming forth" of a divine immanence. Even the statement chosen by Heidegger as pre-eminently wise supports this inference. When rendered in full, it reads as follows:

> *Combinations—wholes and not wholes, concurring differing, concordant discordant, from all things one and from one all things.*

In short, little of the dynamic flux for which Heraclitus is well known is conveyed by the simple phrase Heidegger has seized upon to characterize his position, and the distortion is heightened when, a little further along in the essay, he reshapes that simple remark "One (is) all" to better suit his personal interest: "all being is united in Being."

As I lay on the couch listening to the chirping of woodland birds, I struggled to follow the twists and turns of Heidegger's train of thought. I couldn't help thinking, in the end, that the position he was advancing was neither historically accurate nor logically sound. Heraclitus associates the "one" and the "all" with a matrix of tension and harmony between individual and universal; Heidegger's phrase obliterates this crux of meaning by insinuating the same word, "being," into both the subject and the predicate of the remark. "All being is united in Being." I'm not sure this means anything at all.

✧

The sky clears, I sit on the deck, looking out at the patterns formed by the wind on the blue and gray surfaces of the lake, and it occurs to me that one part of Heidegger's essay carries a nagging interest. This is the part that describes how, through philosophy, the thinker "attunes" himself to

Being. What makes this section suddenly come alive, after so much unenlightened rhetoric, is that it presents us with a distinct and concrete philosophical problem. In fact, it is perhaps *the* distinct and concrete philosophical problem: The one, the many. Individuality, universality. ME, the universe. How are they to be integrated, harmonized, set in a meaningful relation with one another? This problem presents itself to anyone who "loves" nature, for example, but finds it difficult to establish or sustain that sense of communion with the "wild" for which he or she is longing.

Pursuing this issue, Heidegger suggests that Heraclitus himself was not a philosopher at all. He had no need of philosophy because he was already attuned to the "One is all."

His work is more poetical than conceptual, in other words. Coming later, Plato has his world of Ideas, to which he attempts to attune himself through Eros or "divine mania." Aristotle, in turn, has his speculative competence; much later, Descartes comes forth with his cognitive certainty. These remarks are attractive and intriguing because they focus our attention on the way disparate thinkers respond to a single important issue: how are we to orient ourselves toward Being. On his own behalf Heidegger suggests—and I think this is significant—that however we approach this issue of "attuning" ourselves, success will come only as the result of a more or less passive "listening" to the voice of the "being of Being," and not through a well engineered and energetic scramble up the talus slopes of its unstable and dangerous logic. In the end, Heidegger seems to distrust, and even perhaps to dislike, thinking itself. Or, as he himself puts it in his own lovably awkward way:

> *'Philosophia' is the expressly accomplished correspondence (tuning) which speaks in so far as it considers the appeal of the Being of being.*

Although the issue of "tuning" is an attractive one, it exposes the latent weakness of Heidegger's focus on Being *per se*, to the exclusion of individual *beings*. After all, "tuning" is a meaningless notion outside the context of notes, keys, harmony and discord, and music generally, and music—as opposed to monotony or cacophony—is a matter of differentiation, gradation, consonance and dissonance, relationships and proportions, all of which involve a degree of interplay between particular concrete elements or "beings." In short, "attuning" is only possible where Being has individuality, multiplicity, diversity, and nuance.

It strikes me that, in the end, the being of Being is not something that we can passively attune ourselves to. Being may be momentarily staggering to contemplate, and poetic insight may even come of the encounter, but the effect is static and short-lived. When, on the other hand, we turn our attention to the flux of living (if I may be allowed to use that Heraclitean expression), we find that the Being to which we attune ourselves is the one that we participate in, and even shape to some degree. Philosophy begins at the point where the astonishment we feel in the face of Being gives way to, (but without ceasing to provide the frame of reference for) the practical, moral, and aesthetic challenges of authentic living.

❦

The day is heating up. A walk down to the highway. The strawberries are almost ripe. A young deer by the side of the road. A chestnut-sided warbler. Then a refreshing swim. Poulenc piano music. A musty Chardonnay from Australia. And on to Ortega y Gasset's longer and far more interesting lecture series with the same title *What is Philosophy?* Everything Heidegger said, Ortega said first. This can be proven, perhaps, but in the end, who cares? Ortega is a charming and vivacious Spanish genius, Heidegger is a ponderous and relentless German organ-grinder. Take your pick.

We read on page 149 of Ortega's little book:

> *...the failure to understand [the idea of subjectivity] is one of the reasons why the Mediterranean peoples have never become completely modern... The modern type of life is one which does not interest them, does not suit them. There is no way of fighting against it; the only thing to do is to wait until it passes.*

Morning. Golden sun. Green grass. A heron on the lawn hunting for chipmunks.

Brisk morning swim. Smell of the water. Snail floating by, washed out to sea by yesterday's rain, maybe, or dislodged from the bottom. (Where do snails live?) An outboard motor revs up in the distance. Fishermen talking. A yellowthroat down by the bocce-ball court. Also, a red-eyed vireo. Paradise, in short, and the coffee is also good. Hilary is luxuriating in dreamland, and I'm thinking to myself, "four more days of this." Well-stocked with wine, including a half-decent white Burgundy and a twelve-year-old Cabernet.

On the other hand, I don't feel myself to be entirely immersed in the day, to the point of poetic saturation. There is still the thought—"I've got to clarify Ortega's remark about the necessary contributions of both ancient skepticism and Christianity to Descartes' revolution of 'radical solitude.'"

Then I think: Among the many defects of Heidegger's essay one could track down—at the risk of beating a dead horse—is this one: he first defines the origin and ethos of philosophy to be astonishment, and then tacks on his own pet phrase "the being of Being." But before long he's suggesting that philosophy develops as a result, not of astonishment, but of a "yearning" for a return to an original harmony and correspondence with "the being of Being" which has somehow been lost. But it must be asked at this point, "Are we yearning for the astonishment in the face of Being, or for the attunement (or *harmonia*) with the being of Being?" In either case, what we're striving for is not philosophy. We are, on the contrary, in pursuit of some sort of mystical union, or else for an ethical orientation of behavior along the lines of Aristotle's *ethos* or Confucius' Way. Well, mysticism is not philosophy. And an ethical *harmonia* would require that we attune ourselves, not to the "being of Being," but to the "goodness of Being." Or better yet, to the "Being of goodness."

While this is an excellent idea, I think, Heidegger himself makes no reference to the notion of Goodness. St. Augustine's remark that in so far as a thing *is*, it is good, would be to the point here. And I also recall the French philosopher Gabriel Marcel's suggestion that the proper approach to ontology may well be through a consideration of sanctity.

∽

A beautiful drive up to Bayfield, then on to Cornucopia. Lunch at Maggie's, a walk out to the pier to visit our old friend Rainbow, a thirty-foot sailboat we inadvertently beached out in the Apostle Islands last year with some friends. There it sits, floating serenely in its slip. A glorious day, wildflowers everywhere, and we ask ourselves why we don't travel more in the summertime.

A lengthy and animated discussion of "ways of knowing" on the drive up. Intuition, logic, male, female. The essence of philosophy.

Love seeks so that understanding may find.

Ortega differs from Heidegger not only in the fire and brilliance of his attack, but also in the focus of his attentions. In Heidegger's remarks we sense a deep-rooted desire to escape from thought entirely, by recourse to a passive attunement to Being. Ortega embraces the dialectic interplay of act and thought heartily, while promoting at the same time a unifying emphasis on individual beings who live and seek and love in the midst of circumstances they neither chose nor entirely accept. Being and thought, real and ideal, come together at this point of solitary consciousness.

To seek is to anticipate a reality which is non-existent.

Once awakened, love consists in the constant beaming forth of a favorable atmosphere, a loyal and affectionate light in which we envelop the beloved being, so that all her other qualities and perfections can reveal themselves, make themselves manifest, and we will recognize them… Love pre-arranges and prepares the possible perfections of the beloved. Hence it enriches us by making us see what we would not see without it.

Christianity is the discoverer of solitude as the substance of the soul.

All innocence is paradisiac. Because the innocent, he who neither doubts, distrusts, nor suspects, finds himself in the

> *position of ancient and primitive man, surrounded by nature,*
> *a cosmic landscape, a garden—and this is Paradise.*

I don't know about innocence, but I know something about paradise. Lakeside evening, sipping a cheap white Bordeaux, reading Ortega. Hilary is down by the dock sketching. Blue sky, white cloud, green tree.

> *The modern age is melancholic, and the whole of it is more or*
> *less romantic.*

∽

Friday morning. Smells of dew and earth and conifer sap, smells that remind me of the freshness of camping in Colorado. The sun is three hands high coming in across the lake, and the green grasses on the far side of the lagoon are lit from within. This is a giddy pleasure I'm experiencing. Fleeting, precious moments of clarity, of poetry, of involvement, of memory. The mind is blank—or, it only wants to seize and preserve this pleasure it has at being wrapped up in the smells of the morning. Can't be done. The toast is up. Hilary is up. I woke her up, because I wanted to share this pristine interlude with her.

The movement of water projects onto the underside of the leaves high up in the trees. Grackles squawk, and the heron lands near shore, quietly, out for chipmunks again. Sounds from the campground a hundred yards up the lake. Hilary, seated now at the table here on the deck, is eating a bowl of raisin bran. Shall we say, "A god is present," to suggest how lovable the moment is?

I'm preparing myself to say, "The spell is broken," but it seems to me that it may go on all day. Nothing will crowd in, no one will call unexpectedly. It's only a matter of not making plans.

Finish Ortega? Later perhaps. Better a book of European poetry, or Wallace Fowlie's study of Surrealism that I picked up at a dank used-book store on the waterfront in Cornucopia yesterday. Or how about *The Greeks and their Gods* by W.K.C. Guthrie, another Cornucopia find? Dreams and Gods.

What happens is not merely that the morning loses its bloom, but also, that the olfactory sense becomes desensitized through continued exposure to a given smell. This is true of the mind as well. It can nurture a feeling for only so long. Delving into an essay or a poem we re-emerge and feel the impact of the morning all over again.

A desultory walk down the logging road. Slow, the blackberries will be good this year. Bindweed, pale pink and white, running out to the sunlight on the stalks of less glamorous plants. Also, daisies and yarrow. Male and female redstarts in the thick of the branches above our heads. Deer tracks in the sand.

The day heats up, and a pine warbler (?) lands in a tree here above the deck. Back to Ortega:

> *Idealism's error was to convert itself into subjectivism, by emphasizing the dependence of things on the one who thinks them...without noticing at the same time that my subjectivity also depends on the existence of objects. The error lay in making me swallow the world, in place of leaving us both inseparable, immediate, and together, but at the same time distinct and different.*

> *I am myself precisely when I am taking account of things, of the world.*

> *Far from the self being closed, it is 'par excellence' the open being.*

'My life' is given to me, and my life is primarily a finding of myself in the world...

To be is to need.

Fundamentally, life is always un-foreseen.

Life is an activity executed in relation to the future; we find the present of the past afterwards, in relation to that future. Life is what comes next, what has not yet come to pass.

To think is to make, for example, to create truth, to make a philosophy.

Theory, and its extreme form, philosophy, are the attempt which life makes to transcend itself; it is to de-occupy oneself, to de-live, to cease to be interested in things. But this dis-interesting of oneself is not a passive process...to be dis-interested is to be interested in the inner self of each individual thing, to dower it with independence, with substance, one might almost say with personality—put myself in a position to look at it from within its own point of view, not from mine. Contemplation is an attempt at transmigration... But to seek in a thing what it has of the absolute...to serve it so that it may see itself...is this not love?

Swimming, and a faint smell of salt-water drifts up from the diving mask as I remove it. As it happens, we've been cooking up a *recado* made of anchos, chipoltes, and other chilies, along with garlic, allspice, cloves, sugar—a Mexican barbecue sauce.

As usual, Ortega's book ends without any dramatic or even significant conclusion beyond that of defining life as a pre-occupation with what we are going to do *next*. He might have said a great deal more about the significance of the fact that affinities do exist in life, as well as impulses that seem to be driving us toward a better and more complete life and universe. He refers repeated, and affectionately, to Plato's "Ideas" but he feels no need to update them, or to describe the mechanism by which real and ideal interact. This is his problem as a thinker: dazzling observations and insights that don't build upon one another toward anything definite or dramatic—his problem, and also his strength.

It's been an almost somnambulant day. Hilary is down by the water drawing. And I pass my eyes across selected poems of Ungaretti, Zagajewski, Ensenberger, Lorca, and Elytis. You could almost forget what day it is. We listened to *Rigoletto* and Villa-Lobos string quartets this afternoon.

Reading outloud to each other on the dock after dinner. The wind has come up. *The Greeks and Their Gods*. Three days from a full moon. Later I go down to re-tie the canoe. Bright moonlight, pale stars.

∽

This morning is as pale and muted as the last was clear, bright, and sharp. Something the wind blew in. We're listening to one of Handel's early Italian operas. No plans, though it seems to be a good day to go out somewhere—Radisson, or even Hayward.

∽

Sitting on the ground at Pipestone Falls, grasses poking up at my bare legs, mosquitoes attacking—yet a nice breeze, the sound of the falls, water forever being collected, falling down, running down; and this dappled kind of light, red rocks, not pipestone really. The structure, the stature of an individual plant.

I try to convince Hilary to stop "coloring in" her drawing of the falls, because the drawing is good and she'll ruin it. But she thinks I'm merely being impatient.

The goddess of the place. Moss draped across the rocks, sprays of grass in *dishabille*. White bark of the young maple trees, covered like a map with continents of pale blue lichen. A damselfly on a driftwood log at the edge of the stream, long black wings with an elegant white dot on the tip. And the water moving down from the vast monotonous forests into the narrow bed of the stream, over the shelves of red rock.

We flushed a grouse on our way down here. He seemed to have flown only a few yards, but I couldn't locate him in the trees or the underbrush on the hillside.

What are we looking for? The appearance of something? The return of something? Yes, and it's already here.

∽

Midday. Out for a drive. The Chippewa River is wide. Orioles in the trees. The fields are a yellow-green with diaphanous patches of pale orange here and there. A longing to go down the river; here is a part of Wisconsin where no one but the local farmers pass on a Saturday afternoon. America, not in a political sense, but in the Midwestern sense of there being nothing there. Memories of summer day camp at Grant Town Hall. Kickball. What a drag! But somehow the melancholy fuses with the smell of cut clover and hay to make an indelible impression.

The bright yellow of grasses along the roadside that have not yet grown tired, dried out, or drooped. Billowy white clouds the size of a large barn fill the sky. Moving south and east along gravel roads that follow the river at a distance, we come upon a dead-end with summer cabins at the riverfront. The river itself is fast-moving, full of water, rippling with current; it splits into two channels at one point, with oaks and cottonwoods hanging over the banks and thick grasses along the shore.

Retracing our path we continue our rural zigzag, past the site where, so a rotting sign reads, a hotel was built in 1840; we pass a graveyard–no church in sight, it was demolished in 1949. Down a road which narrows as it approaches the valley, and then comes to a stop at a tiny white frame dwelling sitting on the crest of a hill overlooking a bend in the river. Two broad green fields to one side with a stand of pines coming up the middle. The door to the cottage is open, but there's no vehicle in sight. A big red STOP sign painted on the side of a shed where the lane narrows to a two-rut track and runs off into the woods. It's obvious we're on private property, so we turn around and make our way back up the hill. On the way we pass an old log shed standing at the edge of the woods, surrounded on both sides by a sea of nettles, with a single ten-foot shrub to one side that's dotted with clumps of white flowers. It looks like a Japanese tree lilac, but it's really nothing more than a splendid sumac.

What makes this rural scene so attractive, aside from the spectacular panorama of the river valley, is the fact that there is absolutely no recreational clutter; no boat trailer, no cooler, no volleyball or horseshoe pit–not even a woodpile. Under the brilliant blue sky it looks like a dream image, and the grass that runs off down the hill has been meticulously cut as well.

On our way out I spot two sandhill cranes feeding in the field. Is this not a dream? An Oriental dream?

ళ

Driving the heron away from the dock again and again as we come down to swim, read, or sit. But now a kingbird lands on a post five feet from my head.

Here, in Fowlie's book on Surrealism:

> In his solitude, which is his inheritance, the modern artist has had to learn that the universe which he is going to write or paint is in himself. He has learned that this universe which he carries about with him is singularly personal and unique as well as universal. To find in oneself what is original and at the same time what can be transmitted, became the anxiety and the occupation of the modern artist.

As if artists at other times did not need to be original, or at least distinctive! As if originality did not always spring from the recesses of the self! As if there were no miserable, unappreciated, solitary artists begging for a morsel of patronage or a bit of cash in Racine's day.

On the other hand, the association of modern-ness with solitude, with the further emphasis on the need to bring this "inner universe" forth into the light of day—it all sounds a little like something out of Ortega's book.

"Poetry must be made by all and not by one man," says Lautremond.

"Poetry," Fowlie writes, "is the history of man's dis-interestedness. Among all the occupations of man, which have no value or use in the material sense, this art of poetry is the most impressive."

But, clouds in the distance across the lake. The wind is dying down, as it did *not* die down last night. One more day of this and that, the eagle passing, the color of a wave—all sorts of summer colors, in fact. Green, blue, evening pink. A hot evening, a moonlight swim perhaps, things piling up, an enormous mass of treasure, you drew my face, and a slow-moving fly that I kill with my big toe. We'll be missing the wind in a minute.

Too hazy for stars.

∽

The sounds of the morning. Water dripping through a coffee filter into the thermos; the spring of the toaster as the bread goes down. The motorboat in the distance. The common yellowthroat in the slough, who feels we are not paying him sufficient attention, although he never shows himself. And a great-crested flycatcher is whooping somewhere out in the forest nearby. The first we've heard of him in the five days we've been here.

A gray day, pleasantly cool.

Last night we read outloud on the dock about Zeus, Hera, and their possible connections to earlier fertility goddesses. Hera comes off as a rather lackluster goddess, which is too bad, Hilary says. But the Greeks have Artemis, Aphrodite, and Athena as well. Still, it's not the same. It shouldn't be this way.

Drifting in the canoe as gray waves of clouds move across the sky.

As I begin to read about Apollo, the most "Greek" of the Greek gods, (though he's not of Greek origin,) Hilary falls asleep.

The burglar alarm at the neighbor's cabin goes off at 2 AM. A very loud wailing siren that doesn't stop. I call the sheriff.

The siren stops finally. We hear and see nothing from the direction of the cabin, and go back to bed.

❧

Jump in the lake. It's a morning ritual. A shock to the neck, the chest. The gray weather comes almost as a relief, it had been *so* gloriously clear and bright. This morning we'll sweep the cobwebs off the rafters (not a good morning for the spiders) and also paint the dock. The sense of being "right here" is certainly diminishing as we move into the tag-end of the weekend. Not that I'm thinking about home or work, but I've been calling resorts near Estes Park, Colorado, to line up a few nights at the start of our next vacation, which is coming up in August.

"Life is a constant problem of deciding what we are going to do," says Ortega, but there are times when this is not so much of a problem. Here at Blueberry Lake the options are limited, but choice. Go swimming, play bocce ball, read a book, paint the deck, cook a meal, go for a drive or a walk, take a nap.

Home from our walk, I go out to find the blackburnian warbler that's been singing all morning in the yard. And I do catch sight of him, a tiny orange pellet way up in an aspen tree. I also see a hummingbird harassing a phoebe for no apparent reason, which fits in nicely with a heron eating a chipmunk and a gray fox with a muskrat dangling from his mouth. The Being of beings. And Hilary beat me at bocce ball, so life is pretty rough all the way around. On the other hand, we're going to make fresh pasta tonight with the aid of the cabin pasta-maker. A fine, heavy, machine. Pesto in the fridge that Hilary mixed and froze last summer.

Evening approaches, the sky clears. Maybe we'll see some stars tonight after all. But no. We read out loud about

Apollo—too much data (confusing data, I might add) about who the Hyperboreans were, and hardly a thing about who Apollo was. A canoe ride down to the other end of the lake, around an uninhabited island. The moon is one day from full. Before turning in I go down to the dock in the dark—a cool evening, and the moon is hanging half-hidden in a rift of clouds.

FILM LIFE

Sometimes I have to remind myself how much fun it is to go to the movies. On dark winter evenings it takes a considered act of will to leave the house, drive downtown or out into the suburbs, (after having stopped by the drugstore for a jumbo box of Dots), find a place to park, etc. etc. If you're too early then you wait and wait, but it's worse if you're late, and end up craning your neck from the lower edge of the screen. When I'm torn between seeing a movie I've heard conflicting reports about, and sitting quietly at home in front of the fire with some obscure and innocuous Baroque oboe sonatas on the stereo and a copy of *The Charterhouse of Parma* in my hands, I must remind myself how it inevitably happens, time and again, that, sitting in a theater as the lights go dim and the curtains open, a shiver of anticipatory glee will pass through me. Yes, being out is fun.

166

Movies are fun. Even bad movies present us with the challenge of determining what, exactly, is going wrong.

For years I was haunted by a scene from a movie I'd seen from the back seat of a car in early childhood: Orange light against a mud wall, a man slamming the heavy wooden shutters of a window shut, danger lurking everywhere. I wasn't actually *haunted* by the scene, but it stuck with me, and I wondered what film it was from. Many years later, while watching John Ford's *The Searchers* (1956) at a revival house, I sat transfixed as an isolated frontier family, surrounded by Indians, began to board all their windows shut, and that fascinating and meaningless moment of *frisson* arrived when the childhood memory and the adult experience converge.

No doubt I fell asleep in the back seat at some point during my first exposure to *The Searchers*: I couldn't have been more than four or five at the time. The first film I saw from start to finish was *Perry the Flying Squirrel*, which is not in any film-guide I know of, and not long after that I saw *Tom Sawyer*. From that film I remember one scene in particular, once again a scene of incipient terror, in which the people on the hay-wagons realize that Tom and Becky have been left in the cave, and also the one where Tom hits Indian Joe in the forehead with a brass doorknob and sends him plummeting into the blackness of the cave's abyss.

In those days I wanted to see *Rio Bravo* because Ricky Nelson (of *Ozzie & Harriet* fame) was in it, but my mother wouldn't take me. She bought me a comic book of the film instead, seemingly oblivious to the fact that I didn't know how to read. Well, it had a nice cover.

I'm just old enough to have witnessed the demise of the Saturday serial. Every Saturday the theater in the town where I lived showed a matinee, and before the feature we would be treated to a new episode of a serial adventure involving a submarine. The series was called (rather unimaginatively, it occurs to me now) "Adventure on the High Seas." The idea was to get us to come to the theater every Saturday, to see what would happen next, but the episodes teetered uncontrollably between the incomprehensible, the ludicrous, and the banal, so that to even my ill-formed and childish sensibility they were simply a waste of time.

The feature films shown in those days, on the other hand, offered a splendid range of entertainment, from the scene of blood dripping out of the pneumatic tube at the end of *Sink the Bismark*, (it almost looked red!) to the spectral beings in *Thirteen Ghosts* that you could only see if you looked through the green part of the cheap plastic glasses provided by the theater. *Merrill's Marauders*, *The Longest Day*, *The Blue Max*, *The Guns of Navarone*, these were the great war films I remember from that era, with lighter works like *Call Me Bwana*, *The Odd Couple*, and *Flubber* thrown in from time to time. There were Elvis movies like *Viva Las Vegas* and *Girls, Girls, Girls,* adventure flicks like *Jason & the Argonauts* and *Journey to the Center of the Earth*, and an unforgettable tree house in *Swiss Family Robinson*. I watched Marlon Brando sulk his way through *Mutiny on the Bounty* twice, the sea was very blue, and I felt horrible when Steve McQueen lost his showdown with Edward G. Robinson on the very last hand in *The Cincinnati Kid*. I went to *The Pawnbroker* (I may have been all of 15 at the time) and came out saying to myself "What the hell was *that* all about?" Seeing *Psycho* had me petrified for weeks. But in those days going to the movies was almost invariably fun.

It occurs to many of us at some point that films are not only fun, but also "art." You see films that are so true to life, or at least to teen-aged life, and so full of the anguish or heroism that you feel or admire but lack the ability to act upon or express coherently, that you want to shout out their excellence; others seem so far off the mark that you must condemn them vehemently as if they threatened the well-being of civilization itself. I hated *M*A*S*H* for what seemed to me to be its adolescent irreverence (I still do), and *Bonnie & Clyde* was a genuine disappointment—too frivolous—but I loved *Patton, The Last Picture Show, 2001: a Space Odyssey, Midnight Cowboy, Bananas,* and *Cabaret*. Then there was *Five Easy Pieces, A Thousand Clowns,* and finally *Chinatown*, which, to a young college student, seemed to have greatness written all over it.

At about this time my nascent aesthetic interest in films was piqued by another source. Charles Champlin, the film critic of the *Los Angeles Times,* hosted a weekly television show called "Film Odyssey," in which he introduced a series of great European films from the Janus collection to home   viewers. I saw films on this show that seem to have vanished from sight entirely, like the Czech comedy *Intimate Lighting*, as well as such classics as the ponderous *Ivan the Terrible* and the fascinating and exotic *Rashamon*. I recall mercilessly disrupting my little sister's junior high slumber party one Friday evening because the family TV was in the living room, and I simply *had* to watch a film they were showing called *Jules & Jim*.

In those days film history was a young but serious discipline unsullied by an uncomprehending semiotic fascination with popular culture, and this made it possible to view *Pandora's Box, Chimes at Midnight, Hiroshima Mon Amour,* and *The Age of the Medici* on the big screen, at revival houses that have long since reverted to, or been converted into, racquet-ball courts (the St. Clair), emporiums of folk music (the Cedar), church basements (Xanadu), lecture halls (Minneapolis Institute of Arts), and first-run art-film theaters (Uptown). Of course, the arrival of VCRs has made it possible to view almost any film at any time, if you're willing to drive halfway across town to find a copy, and this is a great blessing. The question now becomes, and especially for the young: "What *should* I watch?"

In an effort to answer that question the American Film Institute recently concocted a three-hour program highlighting what they consider the hundred best American films ever made. Jodie Foster, Dustin Hoffman, Cher, Woody Allen, Leonard Maltin, and Candice Bergen were among the wide range of luminaries who spoke in defense of the choices. The clips were brief and choice, the commentary was almost invariably personal and emotional rather than cinaesthetic in orientation; and, if the films themselves were not always worthy of the rank to which they had been assigned, this is only to be expected. When thousands of film professionals are voting, most, if not all, idiosyncratic masterpieces are likely to fall through the cracks: your odd favorite, *Earth Girls Are Easy*, will give way to *my* odd favorite, *Stop Making Sense*, and vice versa, while *Lawrence of Arabia*, a grand and slightly commonplace film with lots of sand and sky, which both you and I liked only to a degree, moves up in the rankings.

A more serious defect of the AFI list as it stands is that it deliberately ignores films from Europe, Japan, and other parts of the world. Well, it was the *American* Film Institute, after all, that sponsored the show. The fact that few Americans have seen more than a smattering of foreign films also figured in the equation, no doubt. All the same, there's something not only chauvinistic but pathetically provincial about a program that highlights the 100 "greatest" American films, without any mention being made of the fact that many, if not most, truly great and original films come from other parts of the world.

This being the case, I see no recourse except to come up with a list of my own. The result will be personal: Then again, all judgment is personal. At the same time, my list will escape the leveling effect of polls, which, in the process of arriving at a consensus, remove not only the worst films, but some of the best as well. Who's to say, in the end, which films *are* actually the best? In fact, anyone can, and almost everyone does. All we're really saying is that these are the films that have meant the most to us.

One thing to be avoided, I think, in devising a list of personal favorites, is the tyranny of numbers. After all, can any film be considered "great" which is inferior to, say, sixty-five of its rivals? All memorable films are unique, if very few are perfect, and some intimate and precious works approach perfection without being great at all. For this reason, I've devised categories to highlight the diversity of styles and tones to be found in the world of film, which should also make it easier to choose a film to watch on a particular Saturday night.

SIX "CLASSIC" FILMS

The Rules of the Game (1939, France: Jean Renoir) *The Rules of the Game* remains the greatest film ever made, for the simple reason that it has more life, incidental detail, fluidity, energy, historical nuance, and moral import than any other film. Certainly it has a political dimension as well, with its weak-kneed French "hero," the brittle and aggressive Alsatian gamekeeper, the slightly effeminate Jewish millionaire, the perky French chambermaid, and the naive Austrian countess, but these characters function as personalities, not types, and their behavior is driven by the situations that develop in the course of the film, rather than by a didactic message. Love, betrayal, propriety, aristocracy, violence, diffidence, loyalty, charm, ribaldry, conviviality—it's all there, and it displays itself with a vigor and economy that seems almost to spring from the eighteenth century. Add one or two of those quirks of fate that put all questions of justice, honor, and social position to rest with crushing finality, and you have a very lovely film that holds up to repeated viewings.

Seven Samurai (1957, Japan: Akiru Kurasawa) A superb use of the wide screen and a great action picture, no doubt, this long and unhurried work also exhibits a subtle understanding of courage and cowardice, of niggardliness and sacrifice, of warriors and peasants, of honor and opportunism, and this gives it the depth and stature of an inimitable classic.

La Dolce Vita (1960, Italy: Federico Fellini) Fellini's portrayal of a journalist (Marcello Mastroianni) who's struggling to preserve the thread of decency and sanity in a world of dazzling glitter and decadence, combines a remarkable eye for the cinematic with a sincere and troubled conscience—something which is absent, by in large, from Fellini's later work. A break-through film, in short, which chronicles the early stages of the director's own unfortunate "breakthrough" to a more extravagant and less interesting view of film and life.

Citizen Kane (1941, USA: Orson Welles) In the end "Kane" succeeds on the strength of its complex narrative structure and its dazzling shot-making *élan*, more than its somewhat shallow portrayal of All-American hubris. It survives bad acting (Joseph Cotton and, on occasion, Welles himself) and a gathering shrillness of tone, to present us with images, sounds, transitions, humorous asides, dissolves, and overlays of perhaps unparalleled creativity and interest. Which is not to say that its achievement is entirely technical. It showed the world what a film director could do—yet you can watch it again and again without being bored.

Fanny & Alexander (1983, Sweden: Ingmar Bergman) In this film Bergman brought both his talents and his idiosyncrasies into a more powerful and satisfying whole than at any other time in his career. A sprawling epic set at the turn of the century, the narrative focuses on the members of a fun-loving extended family, several of whom are members of a theater troupe, and (as the title suggests) especially on two young children within that family whose lives change radically when their widowed mother marries the local bishop. The radiant tone of the cinematography suits the generally glowing affection that passes between family-members, friends, and servants who, as the film opens, are celebrating a candle-lit Christmas together. Watching the story develop we are reminded repeatedly of themes and even scenes from other Bergman movies, but in each case they've been expanded and enriched.

Hamlet (1996, Great Britain: Kenneth Branagh) The longest Hamlet at four hours, this is also far-and-away the best Shakespeare film ever made. In fact, Shakespeare or not, it is simply a masterfully realized creative work. Branagh, Kate Winslet, Ian Holm, Julie Christie, Richard Briars, and even Robin Williams and Billy Crystal, give Shakespeare's lines intelligence and emotion, as if the characters might actually be trying to say something coherent. The complexity and interest of the story itself– "Student returns home to find father dead, mother remarried," as TV Guide would have it–has never been more forcefully presented.

NINE COMPACT BLACK & WHITE
MASTERWORKS

L'Atlante (France, 1934: Jean Vigo) In this film about newlyweds on a barge the expressive potential of black-and-white cinematography is put to the service of a poetic and surreal rendering of the beauty and strangeness of becoming a couple. The presence of Michael Simon as the crusty old deckhand adds to the film's ballast.

Knife in the Water (1962, Poland: Roman Polanski) Polanski's first feature film relates the adventures and imbroglios of a middle-aged married couple who go sailing with a young stranger they've picked up hitch-hiking. That's all there is to it—which only goes to show how much can be made out of little.

Rashamon (1951, Japan: Akiru Kurasawa) A bandit accosts a couple traveling through the woods. Later, as each of the protagonists relates his or her version of what "actually" happened to a judge, we see the events unfold before our eyes not once, but three times, colored in each case to reflect the personality, and the vanity, of whoever happens to be telling the story. Needless to say, the three versions bear only a vague similarity to one another. A fascinating meditation on truth, self-image, and compassion.

Shoot the Piano Player (1962, France: François Truffaut) Truffaut's up-beat story of a bistro pianist attempting to hide from both his gangster siblings and his concert-musician past is full of insight, humor, and energy. The jaunty tone and loose camera-style leaven the dark subject matter, so that it comes as a genuine shock when someone actually dies.

Day of Wrath (1944, Denmark: Carl Dreyer) In a city riven with witch-hunt hysteria a young woman marries the local preacher. She falls in love with the man's son, however, and as events unfold, the question arises whether she herself is a witch. It's full of darks and lights, with glowing cinematography and subtle psychological tension. Of all Dreyer's famous films (*Passion of Joan of Arc* (1928), *Vampyr* (1931), *Ordet* (1955), *Gertrude* (1963),) this one, I think, has the best blend of entertainment, religiosity, weirdness, and cinema art.

Treasure of the Sierra Madre (1948, USA: John Huston)
This gritty tale of three men prospecting for gold in the
mountains of Mexico has both psychological depth and rich
local color. Humphrey Bogart's portrayal of the paranoiac
Dobbs is justifiably famous, Walter Huston won an Oscar for
his performance as the wizened old-timer, and even Tim
Holt, who seems out of his league here, is really only trying to
be nice. The film, which contains the now classic line, "We
don't need no stinkin' badges," never flags, and the ending is
worthy of all the hardship, conflict, and tension that leads up
to it.

Alice in the City (1974, Germany: Wim Wenders) A
photographer headed back to Germany from the United States
enters into a brief involvement with a compatriot in New
York and ends up with the woman's nine-year-old daughter
on his hands. A hilarious and somehow true-to-life series of
misadventures ensues. Once back in Germany, they have to
find the little girl's grandfather's house: she doesn't know
what city it's in, but she has a photograph...

La Notte (1961, Italy: Michelangelo Antonioni) This classic
study of a married couple at cross-purposes is exquisitely
filmed, delicately nuanced, and painfully melancholy in effect.
What makes it moving and durable is that we feel, throughout
the film, that the two (played by Marcello Mastoianni and
Jean Moreau) might just care about each other. Therefore,
Antonioni's subtle pacing and stunning cinematography serve
a purpose larger than that of affluent post-war pseudo-
intellectual nihilism.

Open City : Paisan (1946-8, Italy: Roberto Rossellini) In
Rossellini's films narrative and documentary elements come
together in an artless and effective way. This anecdotal
rendering of civilian life in Italy during the German occupation

and after the war, shot on bad film-stock and with largely non-professional actors, has been an inspiration to film-makers ever since.

SIX FANTASTIC ENSEMBLE FILMS

We All Loved Each Other So Much (1977, Italy: Ettore Scola) A group of friends who had fought together in the Italian Resistance movement subsequently meet up by chance. Their lives have diverged radically from one another; some have abandoned their ideals and prospered, others have retained their commitment to a vision of social justice that has not, perhaps, always served them well. Affection and irony abounds as, through a series of flashbacks, we follow the chain of events that led each member of the group to his or her current circumstances.

A Sunday in the Country (1984, France: Bertrand Tavernier) A married couple and their two sons visit the man's painter-father at his nearby country estate. Father and son do not really get along, and the daughter-in-law is out of her depth, even before her husband's brash sister arrives unexpectedly. Shot in an unusual sepia tone, this film is like an Impressionist painting of a Chekhov short story, which is saying a good deal. Even the lengthy scene of the housekeeper snapping beans is memorable.

Dark Eyes (1987, Italy/USSR: Nikita Mikhalkov) And speaking of Chekhov, this complicated retelling of the Russian master's story "Lady with a Dog" describes the attempts of a dissolute Italian architect to redeem himself by pursuing a relationship with a Russian woman of a very different background whom he's met at a fancy spa. This is the best of Mikhalkov's many fine and lyrical films.

Rio Bravo (1959, USA: Howard Hawks) This long Zen Western finds sheriff John Wayne looking for recruits who are "good enough" to help him defend the town jail against an expected raid by local outlaws. He comes up with an inexperienced kid (Ricky Nelson) a gimpy old man (Walter Brennan) and a drunk (Dean Martin). Deftly mixing comedy, violence, romance, and even a musical interlude or two, Hawks exploits every cliché in the book, and the result is magnificent. Who says fine art has to be boring?

Amarcord (1974, Italy: Federico Fellini) Fellini's affectionate rendering of his own small-town adolescence in Rimini is a masterpiece of interwoven caricatures: crude, funny, and touching.

American Graffiti (1973, USA: George Lucas) A comic picture of small-town adolescence in Northern California during the early days of rock-and-roll. With a very young Richard Dreyfuss and Harrison Ford.

EIGHT GREAT ROMANCES

Casablanca (1942, USA: Michael Curtiz) Everyone knows about Casablanca, but it's surprising how many people have never actually seen it from start to finish. The core of nostalgic romance is dwarfed by a wide array of character actors and sketchy sub-plots concerning Germans and refugees from Vichy France who pass through North Africa *en route* to safer places. It's difficult to tell who's a crook and who's not, and there are very few genuine heroes around, yet every scene strikes an uncanny balance between sincerity and cliché—perhaps because no one on the set knew quite what was going on.

The English Patient (1996, Great Britain: Anthony Minghella) Although the North African episodes of this widely praised film are more fully realized than the Italian ones, the overall effect, once the characters have been sufficiently burned, mutilated, left to die in caves, and blown up in public places, remains one of considerable beauty and poetry. This is the magic of film.

City Lights (1928, USA: Charlie Chaplin) Chaplin's silent rendering of a blind girl selling flowers to a tramp who loves her but lacks the wherewithal to help her out is very funny, and very sad stuff.

Red (1994, France/Poland: Krzysztof Kieslowski) A young fashion model (Irene Jacob) and a retired judge (Jean-Louis Trinagnant) cross paths more than once in this study of love, fate, and coincidence. The most successful of Kieslowski's Red/White/Blue trilogy, it's a satisfying mix of troubled solitude, murky romance, abject bitterness, and unabashed sentimentality (the puppies), all of which has been brought to the screen with considerable élan.

A Room with a View (1986, England: James Ivory) This film, largely set in turn-of-the-century Florence, and sporting a stunning cast, is so pleasant and so unabashedly romantic that a second viewing may be required to establish how *good* it really is.

Pierrot le Fou (1965, France: Jean-luc Godard) Godard is both the bad boy and the great innovator of post-war French cinema, but above all else, he's a comedian. In this totally unreal parable of modern living, a bored bourgeois Frenchman (Jean-Paul Belmondo) runs off with a baby-sitter (Anna Karina) who seems to be doing a little gun-running on the side. Part romance, part musical, part gangster movie, part gender study, part essay in existentialism, it epitomizes the schizophrenic creative response of nerdy French intellectuals to the culture of the New World giant whom they both idealized and despised.

Sense and Sensibility (1995, England: Ang Lee) The classic and perfect Austen romance. With Kate Winslet, Emma Thompson, Hugh Grant, and a host of equally gifted actors.

Un Coeur en Hiver (1993, France: Claude Sautet) In this unusual film Sautet, a past master of the subtleties of the human heart (*Vincent, François, Paul and the Others*) explores the inter-relations of a pair of violin-makers and the concert performer (Emmanuelle Béart) who's in need of their services. The soundtrack of Ravel chamber music compounds the atmosphere of attenuated romanticism, and the presence of students, mentors, and agents gives the film a multi-generational resonance.

FIVE GREAT FILMS ABOUT CHILDHOOD

Queen of Hearts (1989, England: Jon Amiel) A young Italian couple uproot themselves from their village to escape family pressures and set up a coffee shop in London. The story is told from their young son's point of view, and there are one or two supernatural elements in it, but by in large it's a comedy of Italian family life, full of arrivals and departures, squabbles and reconciliations, personal crises and dramatic reversals of fortune.

My Father's Glory / My Mother's Castle (1991, France: Yves Robert) This duo of films details the summer vacations of a school-teacher, his wife and child, and his wife's sister and brother-in-law in the hills behind Marseilles at the turn of the century. Based on Marcel Pagnol's autobiography, it's a staggering example of simplicity, sincerity, and charm.

Toto the Hero (1991, Belgium: Jaco Van Dormael) An old man relives his youth and young manhood through a series of flashbacks in which a comic-book character plays a significant role.

Small Change (1976, France: François Truffaut) Truffaut returned to form in this brilliant anecdotal rendering of the lives of a bunch of school-kids, their parents, and their teachers.

Stolen Children (1992, Italy: Gianni Amelio) A good-hearted Sicilian police-officer is given the job of escorting two tough young kids to an orphanage. The orphanage doesn't want the kids–they're "from the South"–so he decides to take them home for the weekend. This is not a happy film, and it builds slowly, but it has a rare quality of "lived" time, and it's full of complexity and feeling.

FIVE GREAT WESTERNS

Unforgiven (1992, USA: Clint Eastwood) The first ten minutes are brutal. The web of conflicting interests and loyalties that develops in response to the opening sequence brings to life every theme the genre has to offer with an honesty, depth, and humor seldom seen in the world of film. Eastwood, Morgan Freeman, Gene Hackman, and Richard Harris star.

Missouri Breaks (1976, USA: Arthur Penn) Penn's background in the theater is evident throughout the course of this lyrical, occasionally violent, and well-plotted re-telling of

FILM LIFE

the classic cattle-rustler/hired-gun conflict. Jack Nicholson is the rustler, Marlon Brando is the hired gun, and they both have fun with their roles, but the beauty of the film is drawn from a deeper source of understanding about poverty, greed, propriety and lawlessness that's Penn's own.

My Darling Clementine (1946, USA: John Ford) Ford is the undisputed king of the Hollywood Western, and it's difficult to chose from among solid and entertaining productions that stretch from *Stagecoach* (1939) to *The Man Who Shot Liberty Valence* (1962), but this film, with Henry Fonda as Wyatt Earp, Victor Mature as Doc Holliday, and Walter Brennan as the malevolent head of the Clanton clan, has no really bad scenes, (most of Ford's films do) and a long string of very good ones, from a barn-raising to a bar-room surgical operation to a classic rendering of the shoot-out at the O.K. Corral.

Red River (1948, USA: Howard Hawks) John Wayne's best Western pits him against his own adopted son (Montgomery Clift) on the first great cattle drive. Classic and slightly unconventional.

Jeremiah Johnson (1972, USA: Sydney Pollack) The West of the mountain men, in which Robert Redford battles Indians, winter, American cavalry, and his own ignorance in an effort to survive. No heroism, little story, but only a growing sensitivity to nature, and a growing weariness in the face of the difficulty of carving a life from the wilderness.

FIVE GREAT CRIME FILMS

The Big Sleep (1946, USA: Howard Hawks) Bogart and Bacall star in the most satisfying and fully realized Hollywood detective film, which is famous both for its snappy dialogue and its incomprehensible plot.

L.A. Confidential (1997, USA: Curtis Hanson) An altogether absorbing tale, its considerable cinematic virtues are overshadowed by the growing tension and complexity of its storyline.

Chinatown (1974, USA: Roman Polanski) A gorgeous color classic mix of crime, politics, romance, and decadence set in Los Angeles in the thirties, with Jack Nicholson and Faye Dunaway.

Night Moves (1975, USA: Arthur Penn) A subtle portrtait of an ex-football star (Gene Hackman) turned detective who is hired to find and bring home an eight-year-old girl (Melanie Griffith). In the process he uncovers a smuggling operation and the truth about his friends, his marriage, and his own past. Low-key, confusing, and effective.

The American Friend (1977, Germany: Wim Wenders) A very slow and uneasy story about a frame-maker with a terminal illness (Bruno Ganz) and an American entrepreneur (Dennis Hopper), loosely based on themes from the novels of Patricia Highsmith.

FIVE GREAT ADVENTURE FILMS

Sorcerer (1977, USA: William Friedkin) Friedkin's remake of *The Wages of Fear* focuses on the background of the four men—a Palestinian, a German, a Frenchman, and an American—who will eventually take up the challenge of driving over-ripe nitroglycerin through the jungles of Central America. The beauty, economy, exactitude, and restraint—in a word, the art–of the shooting make this film a genuine, if little known, cinema classic.

The Man Who Would Be King (1975, USA: John Huston) The Kipling tale effectively retold with Michael Caine and Sean Connery in the lead roles.

Only Angels Have Wings (1939, USA: Howard Hawks) Pilots in the Andes during the early days of air-mail, with Cary Grant, Rita Hayworth, Jean Arthur, and Thomas Mitchell.

North By Northwest (1959, USA: Alfred Hitchcock) Cary Grant in the classic Hitchcock tale of mistaken identity.

Les Miserables (1996, France: Claude Lelouch) This epic work has enough prison escapes, Nazi attrocities, love stories, cruel injustices and dramatic turns of fate for three normal films.

A SMATTERING OF SCREWBALL COMEDIES

His Girl Friday (1940, USA: Howard Hawks) The second, and perhaps the best, of Hawks three classic screwball comedies (see also *Bringing Up Baby* (1938) and *Ball of Fire* (1942)) here editor Cary Grant tries to get his star reporter and estranged wife Rosiland Russell back on the job, and back in his life.

Women on the Verge of a Nervous Breakdown (1988, Spain: Pedro Almadóvar) A madcap farce in which a woman attempts to re-establish contact with her drifting lover.

Something Wild (1986, USA: Jonathan Demme) A recently divorced man (Jeff Daniels) encounters a young woman

(Melanie Griffith) and accompanies her to her high school reunion, among other places.

Miracle of Morgan's Creek (1944, USA: Preston Sturges) War-time teen (Betty Hutton) gets pregnant after an all-night party, has no idea who the father might be, and sets a long string of manic and hilarious events in motion.

Red Rock West (1993, USA: John Dahl) Nicholas Cage needs a job, but as it turns out, impersonating a man hired to kill the bartender's wife is not a good way to go about getting one.

SEVEN PEASANT FILMS

Christ Stopped at Eboli (1983, Italy: Francesco Rosi) A beautiful and far from sentimental rendering of the experiences of a doctor exiled to the harsh and poverty-ridden fringe of southern Italy during the Fascist era.

Local Hero (1983, Great Britain: Bill Forsythe) A frustrated minor functionary for a Texas oil company tries to buy a remote Scottish village. The longer he stays, the longer he feels like staying.

Il Postino (1994, Italy: Michael Radford) A simple-minded peasant delivers mail to the famous poet Pablo Neruda. Soon they're discussing metaphors and metaphysics. Throw in a little love and a little left-wing politics, and you've got a masterpiece.

Latcho Drom (1996, France: Tony Gatlif) A semi-documentary rendering of the movement of the Gypsies from Northern India to Spain by way of Egypt, Turkey, Romania, Belgium, and Provence, told entirely by means of musical set-pieces.

Powwow Highway (1988, USA: Jonathan Wacks) The modern West as seen from an Indian Reservation, this funny, spiritual, and entertaining film is a true rarity.

Tree of the Wooden Clogs (1978, Italy: Ermanno Olmi) Peasant life at the turn of the century, by the director who remained true to the neo-realist ideal. It may not be great, but it sure is long.

L'America (1996, Italy: Gianni Amelio) A sharp and cynical Italian businessman sets up a phony business in Albania at just the wrong moment. First he loses the tires off his jeep, then he loses the senile Albanian who's fronting as president of the business. Before long the business is gone, and then...but I don't want to give too much away. An exploration of values, ideals, simplicity, and civilization that moves on the highest level of dramatic sophistication.

A FEW MUSICALS

Don Giovanni (1972, USA: Joseph Losey) A dramatic filming of the classic opera with Palladian villas for sets and a knockout cast.

Cabaret (1971, USA: Bob Fosey) Great tension and excitement in this musical drama set in Germany between the wars.

Cover Girl (1944, USA: Charles Vidor) Gene Kelly as a possessive nightclub owner with Phil Silvers as his sidekick and Rita Hayworth as his undiscovered star. Songs by Jerome Kern, including "Long Ago and Far Away," and a snappy performance by Eve Arden as a fashion agent looking for an unforgettable face, make this, for me, the most entertaining Hollywood musical.

1776 (1972, USA: Peter H. Hunt) This Broadway musical based on the signing of the Declaration of Independence is wonderfully ridiculous.

Seven Brides for Seven Brothers (1954, USA: Stanley Donen) Spectacular dancing and an agreeably absurd plot. The scene where the brothers are all chopping wood in the snow while they sing that mournful song "I'm just as lonesome as an Old Polecat" is one of the high points in film history.

A film analyst (or a psychoanalyst) examining this list might observe that it includes an unusual number of films by acerbic or edgy directors (Kurasawa, Hawks, Fellini, Penn, Godard, Polanski). Yet is seems to me I've highlighted plenty of lyrical and romantic and even silly works as well. And while it may be true that there are no films from the realm of German Expressionism in the bunch, it strikes me that other directors—Dreyer and Vigo and Welles, for example—have put the same effects to better use.

A more serious objection might be raised, that I've entirely ignored the work of Audrey Hepburn. Well, how about *Roman Holiday?* Or better yet, *Robin and Marion?* Now there's a charming film for you.

SPAIN IS DIFFERENT

In the late forties travel agents initiated a campaign to encourage tourism in the Iberian Peninsula. The banner slogan was simply "Spain is Different." This phrase might have led one to ask "Different from what?" but the implication was presumed to be obvious: Spain was different, not only from China or the Yukon—an assertion that no one would contest—but from its next door neighbors Italy and France, with whom it shares a European heritage extending back to Roman times. Perhaps the historical reality underlying this elusive "difference" was illuminated by another common phrase of the time, "Africa begins at the Pyrenees."

In the succeeding decades Spain became the most frequently visited country in the world, although this was probably less because it was different, than because it had a sunny coast that could be developed in such a way as to allow tourists from Northern Europe to relax *without* departing too radically from their familiar habits and routines. Yet even today that bland, enigmatic slogan "Spain is different" captures something of the feeling, exotic yet strangely familiar, that visitors to that country experience time and again.

On the other hand, whatever it may happen to be in relation to its neighbors, Spain is emphatically and unequivocally itself. It would be tempting to suggest, going further, that Spain is lost in the Dream of Itself, but this would convey a degree of unreality and illusion that one does not feel when hiking in the Sierra de Gredos or exploring the back-streets of Vejer de la Frontera, regardless of the prominent role "unreality" assumes in the works of Lope ("Life is a Dream") de Vega, Miguel Cervantes, Salvador Dali and Juan Miro. Spain isn't a dream; it's very real.

Ernest Hemingway once gave a short story set in Madrid the name "Capital of Europe," but Madrid is hardly even the capital of Spain. And Spain is, at best, a country cousin in the European family, one that has spent long periods in isolation, or in the grip of African and Middle-Eastern cultural currents, or struggling to establish a distinctive European identity in the face of those influences. During the Middle Ages the famous cry was *"Santiago, y cierra España!"* that is to say "St. James, and close Spain!" But if the country has chosen to go its own way culturally, it exhibits little of the self-conscious and sometimes haughty self-absorption of the French. Spain dwells in itself not as the best thing going, but as the only thing going. In fact, as a result of its peculiar history and geography, the country to which Spain might most profitably be compared isn't France or Italy, but Greece. Like Greece, it has a Moslem past. It lacks Greece's rich pagan heritage, but it benefits from its Medieval Christian associations, its close proximity to the main currents of European history, and its relative youth as a locus of civilization. It may be true that Spain has been "in decline" for three or four hundred years, but it's also true that its "golden age" of Imperial splendor was a reactionary and somewhat artificial one in any case. On the other hand, in the early twentieth century the Spanish language became a leading tongue of world poetry–a not insignificant kudo for any culture–and, having recovered from the extended paralysis of Francoism, it now exerts itself, and enjoys itself, with both the energy of an adolescent people, and the bearing and "class" of a rooted and dignified one.

For the tourist, a visit to Spain is likely to elicit reflections on this order at every turn, and this is especially true for those who, like me, command nothing of the language beyond "dos cafe con leche," and "cana de vino blanco." In a word, while the specific artifacts of Spanish culture and history demand only an intermittent attentiveness, simply *being* in Spain is an endlessly fascinating and absorbing enterprise.

PAINTINGS: MADRID

The airport: The pale dusty brown of the barren hills on the far side of the river beyond the runway. The deep tomato-red of the runway vehicles bringing in the luggage. The caramel-colored marble of the terminal floor itself. The rich green ornamentation punctuating the glossy tile surface of the walls; the natty yellow-green jackets of trim black-haired men with five-o'clock shadows who stand waiting for their bags, many of them already engaged in rapid and melodious conversation on their cell-phones. You feel the uncanny electricity of being in Europe again, compounded by the absolute newness of the rich blunt colors, of what can only be called the old-fashioned modernity of Spain.

Madrid: With a population upward of five million people, it's a major European metropolis, but the historic center is relatively small, and one might even describe it as shabby. It boasts not a single familiar icon–no Eiffel Tower, no St. Peter's or St. Paul's; no castles, no canals, no Trafalgar

Square. The Royal Palace is huge, but there seems to be no good reason for touring it. A few plazas, a few unassuming monasteries. The Puerta del Sol, which is often described as the center of Madrid, is a narrow and undistinguished semi-circular plaza that everyone seems to be walking past on their way somewhere else. The two things that are most likely to make a visit to Madrid worthwhile are the Prado and the bars, and both of these underscore, rather than challenge, the notion that Madrid is an extravagantly provincial place. For the traveler this may not be such a bad thing, however. Quite the reverse.

The Prado is frequently referred to in guide books as "one of the world's great art museums." While there is no reason to quibble with such an assertion, it would be more accurate to suggest that the Prado is the best place in the world to see Spanish art. Although the range and depth of its collections do not compare favorably with those of the Louvre, the Uffizi, or the Metropolitan Museum in New York, its displays of Velázquez and Goya are unquestionably in a league by themselves. Throw in a few El Grecos, Murillos, and Zurbaráns, some van der Weydens and Bosches, a Titian or two, and you have ample material for a morning's thought.

I was hoping that a face-to-face encounter with the major works of Velázquez, who has always struck me as a sober-minded and uninteresting painter, would illuminate elements of the master's works not to be found in the pages of books. It didn't happen. Certainly the originals are bigger, more subtly colored, and more impressive than reproductions, but for me they remain, in the end, dumb, inert, like a wine that hasn't "opened up." The many royal portraits are neither beautiful nor psychologically penetrating, it seems to me, and the famous renderings of drinkers and dwarfs seem badly arranged on the canvas. Velázquez's most famous work, *Las Meninas*, is one that I've looked at again and again in books without becoming even the slightest bit engaged, and my encounter with the original was no different. I must confess I liked the peach-colored walls of the Velázquez gallery better than I liked the paintings themselves, which, quietly begrudging and even dire, seem to have been painted by a man who liked neither people nor the vanity and ostentation that can make them interesting and lovable in spite of themselves. Clearly I'm missing something.

With Goya, on the other hand, the virtues are obvious. Color, flair, sensitivity to the atmosphere of groups and crowds, as well as to nuances of character that manifest themselves in the corner of a mouth, the crossing of a leg, or the glint in an eye. Goya's work is infused with a slightly twisted sensuality—this is most evident in the series of lithographs called *Los Caprichos*, but it's present in many paintings as well—and there's also a prominent vein of hysterical superstition to be found there. The "Black" paintings, extracted from the walls of Goya's house after his death and later installed in a special gallery in the Prado, are among the few modern paintings that convey the living presence of daemonic paganism without becoming ridiculous. In Goya's work, we feel the recognition that the promises of the Enlightenment, of reason and industry and restraint, will never overcome the irrational forces that drive peoples lives. What Nietzsche predicts and celebrates and demands, without really knowing first-hand, Goya shows us time and again in concrete form. The pull between beauty and perversity, between peasant concreteness and erotic-superstitious atmosphere, charges many of his works with a primal energy that owes nothing to the artificial Gothicisms of the Romantic North. On the other hand, that energy differs from the energy we feel in many of Picasso's works in that it's being directed toward the illumination of an entire world—our world—rather than being squandered in outbursts of personal caprice.

Picasso's most famous painting, *Guernica*, hangs not in the Prado, but in the Centro de Arte Reina Sofia, which is down the hill near the train station. This art center is located in a former three-story hospital, to which two glass-walled elevators have been attached *on the outside*. Well, why not? It makes the building look more modern, and after all, Felipe II kept his books at El Escorial with the bindings facing in.

We've all seen reproductions of *Guernica* so many times that we may have come to wonder what all the fuss is about. In the eyes of many it symbolizes the horror and brutality of modern warfare, even though, (as critic John Berger observes in his study *The Success and Failure of Picasso*) little of the imagery in it can be said to be specifically modern. A bull, a horse, women's faces in unspeakable anguish, all elongated, cut-up, and rearranged: hundreds of Picasso's paintings and lithographs could be described in similar terms.

Yet size and compositional complexity set *Guernica* apart. It's as long as a canoe and as tall as a ballroom door-jam; it hangs by itself high up on the wall of a long gallery on the third floor of the *Reina Sofia* museum. There were two policemen standing next to it when we arrived, and the tension generated between these two armed, uniformed men, the painting itself, and the small group of people standing silently in front of it, seemed to add to the work's immediate aesthetic impact.

Guernica is one of those paintings which the eye can neither take in nor turn away from, and must therefore roam in a vain and restless pursuit of harmony or completeness. The screaming faces, the dangling light, the injured child, the bomb, the open window high up in the corner, full of light but out of reach. Five minutes, ten minutes go by. The policemen are clearly bored—no anarchists in the crowd today—but you stand transfixed by the sheer *life* of the thing in front of you. You could pull away, but you don't, because everything else in the room, however vivid and modern, seems colorless and "art-like" in comparison with this wrenching vision of fractured black, white, and gray shapes.

Only one painting that I saw in Spain had an immediacy of impact comparable to *Guernica's*, and that was El Greco's equally massive, and almost equally famous, *The Burial of the Count Orgaz*, which hangs by itself in the chapel of the Church of St. Tomé in Toledo, where it has hung for four hundred years. There's a ticket booth on the crowded plaza outside the chapel, it will cost you $1. 30 to see the painting, and the entire scene is reminiscent of a side-show at a county fair, where the bearded lady and the South American reptiles are waiting just beyond the curtain, and you scrutinize the faces of the customers leaving the tent to see if they look disgruntled, or satisfied that they've gotten their money's worth.

Once inside the darkened chapel, you can muscle your way to a bench in the front row, where the dazzling beauty of the painting can be fully appreciated. I use the word "dazzling" because the canvas has a sparkle and color that make it impossible to accept the assertion that it has never been cleaned. The size of the canvas—it must be fifteen feet tall— makes it necessary to "roam" the canvas, but unlike the similarly immense *Guernica*, which instills a feeling of chaos and suffering and excitement, *The Burial of the Count Orgaz* elicits a feeling of harmony, sobriety, and order which is nevertheless active and musical, rather than static and musty. The upper half of the canvas has the elongated figures and the conventional "mannerist" colors that render many of El Greco's paintings slightly iconographic and boring. In the center of the lower half St. Stephen and St. Augustine, both dressed in stunningly elaborate yellow and gold vestments, are lowering the limp and pallid body of the Count into a tomb. Across the middle of the scene we see the faces of twelve or fifteen aristocratic-looking Spaniards with trim beards, black clothing, large white ruff collars, and stern, alert faces. Scholars have devoted much time and energy to the task of exposing who each of these well-individuated figures might be, but what strikes you in the end is how similarly unperturbed they seem to be with regard both to the dead man lying in front of them and to the heavens opening up above their heads. Neither arrogant nor indifferent, they seem to be—each one of them—singularly self-assured in the company of death, the saints, the angels...and one another.

As I sat in the dark on the wooden bench in the Chapel of St. Tomé in the holy city of Toledo, my eyes moved back and forth from the scene of death, up across the ribbon of serious faces to the harp-playing angels and the distant figure of Christ the King, and a scheme began to take shape in my mind in which aristocrat and peasant, conventional life and inner life, order and chaos, were spread out in different directions. The self-confident aristocratic individualism of El Greco's well-ordered masterpiece (which, strange as it may seem, is simultaneously social and mystical) was pointing toward the chaos and civil war of Picasso's disordered masterpiece, (which, though it commemorates a historical event, is itself entirely "inner," albeit in a mythic and collective, rather than an individualistic way). Nearer to the center of the scheme

Velázquez's chilly realism ("…he allowed no sentimentality to reach his clear, logical canvases," Hugh Thomas writes) rings false, or else it doesn't ring at all; while Goya's peasant-understanding of people, his natural lyrical style, and his personal familiarity with the pre-rational underpinnings of human life, remind us at different times of Breugel, Tiepolo, and Bosch.

Can these canvases, these elements, be fused into an intelligible vision of Spain? At some other time, perhaps. Today, after staring at length at a succession of painted images, (with a break in Retiro Park to the east of the Prado before lunch, and later in the day at the Botanical Garden to the south of it) we turn our attention, with relish, to the tapas bars.

TAPAS

What is this thing called tapas? A tapa is a morsel of food on a plate. It's small and choice, it can be as simple as a paper-thin slice of cured ham, or as complicated as a little stew. We might call it an appetizer, but that would be to imply that it precedes a meal, which would be misleading. A tapa accompanies a drink. More than that, it accompanies an approach to time that's uniquely Spanish.

Though its origins are obscure, it's generally agreed that tapas were first served in Andalusia at some time in the nineteenth century. The word is derived from the verb *tapar* which means "to cover," and sherry, a fortified Andalusian wine considered too alcoholic to be served with meals, was the drink that a tapa originally covered. The continuing popularity of the tapa in recent times is attributable, no doubt, to the fact that Spaniards eat dinner very late–ten or eleven P.M. at the earliest–and that they love to talk.

For the tourist, indulging in a tapa or two can be a very satisfying experience. It's cheap, the options for sampling a variety both of dishes and of bars are almost limitless (there are more bars in central Madrid than in the Netherlands), and it offers the opportunity for even the non-Spanish speaker to enter the flow of native life—in a word, to participate.

Following our marathon tour of the three great museums of Madrid, Hilary and I made our somewhat weary way up to the Place Santa Ana, which lies on the top of a little hill in the midst of a warren of narrow and undistinguished streets midway between the tree-lined Paseo del Prado and the bustling Puerta del Sol. The square itself is hardly bigger than a short row of tennis courts. Gravel, benches, a few trees, a children's playground on the lower end of the sloping space. At the upper end of the square stands the elegant white Gran Hotel Reina Christina, too classy, too big for the space it looks out on. (Bullfighters stay here, the guidebooks tell us.) On the other three sides of the square, and extending out into the neighborhood on side-streets where vegetables and fish are sold and where students and adventurous tourists stay, are the tapas bars.

I ought to interject here that in Madrid nearly all bars are tapas bars. Any narrow establishment you walk into will be likely to have *calamares, bouquerones, tortillas, pinchos, queso, jamon,* and *chorizo* on the menu at very reasonable prices. I might also point out that whereas in the United States a bar is frequently, if not quintessentially, a place to be loud, to watch sporting events, and perhaps even to get drunk, in Spain a bar is, by in large, a place to gather and converse.

Our first stop in the Santa Ana neighborhood was an unprepossessing little establishment off the square called *La Costa de Vejer*, which is famous for its prawns grilled with garlic. Once we'd made it clear to the bartender than we didn't speak a word of Spanish, the man relaxed and became loquacious. In the end we got our *gambas*, which arrived, not *ala plancha*, but bubbling in butter in small brown earthenware dishes accompanied by two beers and a complimentary loaf of bread. Very fresh, very fine. We spent the rest of the trip trying, without success, to find better.

We then made our way to the south side of the square, where the bars are lined up one after the other; tables had been set out on the sidewalk and even in the street, and most of them were already occupied. We entered one bar and stood for a few minutes contemplating the hand-written tapas menu, but in the end the multi-colored chalk put us off. We peered down into the expansive subterranean *Cerveceria Alemana*, (allegedly one of Hemingway's favorite haunts) but it was too well-lit, too classy. The bar next door was a narrow working-class establishment. We took two vacant stools against the wall, ordered white wine and canapés, (slices of bread covered with thin stripes of ham), picked away at our complimentary plate of green olives, watched the passing scene, and left forty-five minutes later with a miniscule tab.

As the evening progressed and the sidewalks filled the Place Santa Ana took on an almost carnival atmosphere. There were people everywhere—in the park, at the sidewalk tables, in the glass-fronted lobby of the hotel. Although the side streets were relatively dark, they too were illuminated at irregular intervals by shafts of light streaming out from the open doors of tile-fronted *bodegas* and *cervecerias*. We ventured out away from the square in search of a bar famous for its *pimientos de Padrón*, but we ended up at the only vacant table in a warmly lit neighborhood place called *La Casserole*, simply because it looked inviting. We ordered a carafe of white Valdepeñas wine and two tapas: a metal dish of boiled potatoes covered in a tasty pumpkin-colored sauce, and a plate of grilled green peppers. To our left two elderly gentlemen were chatting desultorily as they worked their way through a heap of fried fish—a time-honored Friday night tradition, no doubt. Four attractive young women had planted themselves at the table to our right—their boyfriends were at the bar, they were waiting for a bigger table. A glamorous elderly woman was holding court at the table behind us. Men and women would come up to hug her or ask her for an autograph. I never saw the woman, I was facing the bar, where every stool was occupied and the crowd of middle-aged men was thick. A tired-looking man who was playing the slot machine beside the door went out into the night; small groups came in and passed through the bar on their way to a restaurant in the rear. The room was glowing with yellow light and there was a din of voices, a constant and melodious staccato like a flock of colonial birds that feel comfortable and safe on their reedy islands. It was beautiful; no, it was enchanting, and we felt not the slightest bit uncomfortable or out of place at our little table in the midst of it all. The two men to our left finished their plate of fish and rose to leave. The four young men came over from the bar, politely asked two women down the way to change tables with their girlfriends, slid a now empty table next to the one just vacated by the two men, and sat at last in a group with their female companions. I was gratified to see, when the waiter brought their tapas, that they'd ordered the same plate of potatoes we'd ordered. They also ordered a dish of chopped meat that they ate with their fingers, and which I later deduced from a photograph in a cookbook was a spicy Moorish pork dish called *pinchos moruno*.

What were the young people talking about? Soccer? Literature? Who was the woman sitting behind us that everyone seemed to know? And what about the two middle-aged women who had just moved and were now seated at the shuttered window next to us? They were speaking in serious, anguished tones like characters in an Almodovar film discussing an irrational mother-in-law or an imminent divorce.

And what, after all, were we talking about?

There is something both staggering and bizarre about being transported from the suburbs of the most remote metropolis of the North American interior (Minneapolis) to the noisiest and most animated night-city in Europe (Madrid) in the space of little more than a day. Every street, every sign, every face, shimmers with a challenge and interest that induces an exhilarating and giddy alertness unaccompanied by any genuine advance in understanding beyond the simple and ever-expanding realization that Spain is LIKE THIS! But sitting in the bar at *La Casserole* it became clear to us that we had never felt as comfortable in public anywhere in Europe as we did in Madrid. It wasn't the bemused indifference of the French, the boisterous neglect of the Italians, or the child-like hospitality of the Greeks that we experienced in *La Casserole*, but (and this feeling came to us again and again in the course of the trip) a combination of courtesy, openness, and reserve, that made us feel as if we were adults no less deserving than anyone else of a pitcher of Valdepeñas and a plate of fried fish. Not welcoming, not disdainful, it was simply "you're there and we're here, and we're all out enjoying ourselves, and we'll see what comes of it."

I realize that this impression runs counter to the traditional image of the haughty Spanish aristocrat puffed up with machismo; nevertheless, our experience repeated confirmed the remark George Orwell made in the thirties about the Spanish people: "I defy anyone not to be struck by their essential decency; above all, their straight-forwardness and generosity." Yet it may be that these two qualities are not as remote from one another as they first appear. The poet Juan Ramón Jiménez once wrote an essay extolling the virtues of aristocracy, in which, curiously enough, he disassociated it entirely from wealth, class, and ancestry. "Aristocracy," he wrote, "is a state of man in which are united in supreme union, a profound cultivation of the interior being and a conviction of the natural simplicity of living—idealism and economy."

In the past, chronic poverty and desolation have forced the Spanish people to cultivate "the interior being"—there wasn't much else to cultivate. Writing in the mid-fifties, when the Economic Miracle was building steam in Northern Europe, the Spanish scholar Salvador de Madariaga observed that the peculiar orientation to modern life Spain alone had retained offered a valuable resource and model to her neighbors:

> ...from the spiritual point of view, Spain is and will remain for ever a reservoir of human energy due to [the] human sense that insists on the here and now of the whole manhood of man. When weary of its machines and of its techniques, ironed and flattened out by the drive of its acquired motions and disciplines, sad in its plenty and unsatisfied in its surfeit, the spirit of the West feels at a loose end, let it turn to Spain and her people—who, less dependent on the past, and less hopeful of the future, live fully in the present and can by giving themselves to the present turn the present into eternity.

Of course, since the death of Franco Spain has taken dramatic strides to join its bourgeois neighbors in both production and consumption. And in any case, no one, Spanish or otherwise, ever lives fully "in the present." The women and men, young and not-so-young, who surrounded us in *La Casserole* on our first evening in Madrid weren't meditating on nothingness, after all; they were energetically discussing what Pedro said to Alicia at the water-cooler earlier in the day, and whether Princess Christina should have been in such a hurry to marry that Basque handball player; they were planning a baby shower, or a weekend trip to Chinón to tour the anís factories and sample the wares. The future, the past. Yet the fact remains, Spain is different. You feel it everywhere, without knowing at first what it is—only with time does it become apparent that you're experiencing a unique and elusive combination of, on the one hand, a gravity more authentic and ingrained than anything Unamuno ever described; and, on the other, a spontaneity that's fresher and more wholesome than anything you'll find in Picasso's work.

We ordered another pitcher of Valdepeñas and a plate of *boquerones*—little fried fish like smelt with the head and guts removed. I don't remember what we talked about, we were having a good time just being a part of the passing scene at *La Casserole*; I do, however, recall remarking to Hilary at one point, "You know, if it were necessary for us to pack up and return to Minneapolis tomorrow morning, after a single day and night in Madrid, I would still consider this trip to have been worthwhile."

ANDALUSIA

Madrid lies at the center of Castile and Castile lies at the center of Spain, yet many of the things that conjure Spain to foreigners—bullfights, flamenco, sherry, Moorish palaces, Don Juan, tapas—come from that region south of the Sierra Morenas called Andalusia. Córdoba was the largest and most cultured city in Europe in 1000: it just happened to be controlled and largely inhabited by Moslem infidels. Granada was later the capital of the Nasrid dynasty that covered much of Andalusia: it fell only in 1492, leaving to the Spanish a legacy of irrigation works they could not maintain and an architectural heritage they admired and did their best to make use of. In the following century Seville became the bustling center of trans-Atlantic trade and exploration, but the river silted up, the trade fell victim to authoritarian legal restrictions, the colonies rebelled, and the city sank back into relative obscurity, although, like Venice, it continued to work in the European imagination as a hotbed of cultured dalliance, sensuality, and personal destruction. *The Marriage of Figaro*,

Don Giovanni, *The Barber of Seville*, and *Carmen* are all set there, although neither Moliere nor Beaumarchais, neither Mozart nor Rossini nor Bizet, ever set foot in the city.

In the early nineteenth century the port of Cádiz (with a large population of Italian and English merchants, it's true) became a cauldron of liberal ideas and...but enough about the cities of Andalusia. What about the bullfights and the flamenco? What about the poetry of Lorca, Alberti, and Jiménez, Andalusians one and all?

Juan Ramón Jimenez once remarked "That which is only glimpsed is more real, and lasts longer, than that which is fully seen." This isn't entirely true, but I think it would be safe to say that the mind attaches a particular importance to fleeting impressions, and this is because, in the act of filling out and completing those impressions, the mind adds the stuff of its own reality and conviction, thus internalizing the experience and making it solid, even though it remains vague with regard to detail.

For better or worse, our experiences of both flamenco and bull-fighting in Andalusia were fleeting, and this was largely a matter of choice. We walked by the beautiful eighteenth century bullring in Seville on a Sunday afternoon three hours before the *corrida* was set to begin. There were men outside the gates selling tickets. It was the opportunity of a lifetime! Why not secure a couple of seats, for the "cultural" experience if for no other reason?

I can well imagine that the experience of watching a bull-fight might be a profound one, and, having seen the frescos of bull-dancing at the Minoan palace in Knossos, as well as the Mithric bull's-blood temple in the sub-basement of the Church of St. Clemente in Rome, I ought to have developed   at least a glimmer of insight with regard to the continuing spiritual relevance of that animal in the life of a people closer to the ethos of the ancient Romans than any other modern European nation. What troubles me is that they dispatch not one, but *six* bulls at any given *corrida de toros*. The sight on TV of even a single animal being perforated again and again with sharp metal blades can be disturbing. Call it sport, call it art, call it religion, the fact remains that the bull almost invariably loses. This ought not necessarily to deter the matador himself from entering the ring, he's running a genuine risk of losing too, but the spectators who, safe in their distant seats, risk nothing whatsoever, really ought to be ashamed of themselves.

This is a superficial judgment, I realize, and it reminds me of the one I often hear delivered in this country against professional football—that it's brutal, ugly, senseless, and inhumane. I happen to like watching professional football. To me the game seems beautiful, noble, and stirring, and the violence and brutality is very much a part of all that. Then again, I played a lot of football when I was younger, and I still participate in occasional games of "touch." As a general rule, people who denigrate football have never played the game.

In Spain bullfights have traditionally been held, not in bullrings, but in town squares, with makeshift seats and barriers. Anyone who wanted to could have a chance with the bull. Toreadors got their start in local arenas and squares.

This is not to say that bullfights were ever "nice." There's a description of a provincial bullfight in Arturo Barea's autobiographical novel *The Forge* which, to a foreign reader, may seem disgustingly brutal and cruel, although Barea makes it clear that this activity was very much a part of Spanish village life at that time. Even today 24,000 bulls are killed in Spain every year, which suggests that in one form or another, the tradition continues. We may or may not like it: then again, we've never done it.

As luck would have it, my one look at a bullfight came in Ronda, the cliff-top Andalusian town where modern bullfighting was invented in the eighteenth century. Ronda's bullring stands second only to that of Seville in rank and heritage, and it also has a splendid museum, but my encounter came in the older part of town, at a church we'd crossed a bridge over the gorge to visit. A service was in progress, we couldn't go in, but as we turned to leave I saw a bullfight in progress on a television screen in the darkened office of the church. I watched through the window as the bull made one pass after another. It was a mesmerizing sight, and the effect was heightened by the sound of people singing in the church next door. Finally I pulled myself away and we continued our stroll through the largely deserted town. Later that evening we returned to our room, I turned on the television, and there on the screen was the same matador, riding on the horns of the bull. He looked peculiarly small and limp and passive, stretched out across the head of that unruly beast, and the gaudy magenta splendor of his outfit seemed rather inappropriate to the gravity of the situation he was in. The bull finally tossed the man aside like a rag doll—he hadn't been really angry, just momentarily irritated—and the evening news moved on to other things.

Flamenco performances are less broadly appealing to Spaniards than bullfights, to judge from their relative scarcity even in Andalusia. A concert was being staged at the cinema in the village of Orgiva in the Alpujarras Mountains, the day after we passed through. We considered sticking around, but Orgiva is an ugly town (although the surrounding countryside is stunning), and a day is a long time to wait for anything when you're travelling cross-country by car. Besides, the concert was scheduled to start at 10:30 PM, and that meant (or so all the guidebooks warned us) that it would probably start at midnight. The good stuff often doesn't get going until 3:00 AM, and sometimes it doesn't get going at all.

In this respect flamenco resembles America's great indigenous art form, jazz, which is often performed by social outcasts to small groups of *aficionados* (a Spanish word, by the way, which derives from the bull-ring). I've been to many jazz performances, which often start late and build in intensity as the evening progresses, and the inspired ones are so good that it makes the risk of attending a lackluster effort well worth taking. But the concert at Orgiva would have been a shot-in-the-dark. We'd reserved a room for a few days in the town of Arcos de la Frontera, a hundred miles to the west, to coincide with its feria, which we were planning to attend. That would be the time to attend a flamenco performance.

A few days earlier, in Cordoba, we'd passed through the beautiful courtyard of Tablao Cardenal on our way to the Museo Taurino, where the hide of the bull "Islero" that killed the famous toreador Manolete has been hanging for forty years. There were bright green tables set up cabaret-style in the courtyard, with an elevated stage at one end and sound- and light-boards at the other. Here, perhaps, would be the place to catch a flamenco performance. The cover charge, though not unreasonable by American jazz standards, would have crimped our budget for days, however, and the fear that the room would fill up at 11:00 PM with brash Americans wandering over from the fancy and exclusive El Caballo Rojo Restaurant waving their American Express cards was too real to be discounted.

Wandering later in the day through the back streets to the east of the mosque, we came by chance into the expanse of the Plaza de la Corredera, a crumbling, ramshackle seventeenth century colonnaded plaza similar to the ones you see in Salamanca or Madrid, except for the fact that it has never been restored. The west end of the plaza was lined with beat-up cars; one bar was open near the south entrance, two tables had been set out on the cobblestone sidewalk; a woman and her small son were poking sadly at bowls of an oily beef-and-tomato soup. The east and north faces of the plaza appeared to be entirely boarded up–but perhaps we'd just come at the wrong time of the day! In the shadowed southeast corner an antiques dealer had brought his stock out into the open air under the shady colonnade: leaky aquariums, plastic pails, a few wobbly dressers, tilted picture-frames.

Whitewashed plaster was crumbling here and there around the square, the light was harsh, the afternoon sun was unpleasantly hot, and there was dust on everything. Silence. An occasional voice from the interior of the distant bar. I felt that I was standing in a painting by de Chirico. If Don Quixote had come riding into the empty plaza through the far portal on his skinny horse I would not have been surprised. (In fact, we were, at that moment, only a hundred yards from the Posada del Potro, which Cervantes mentions in *Don Quixote*, and where he himself almost certainly stayed. But that tiny *posada* has been "lovingly" restored; it looks like a bed & breakfast in Chipping Camden.)

As we were leaving the square Hilary, (who knows the guide-books better than I do) said, "I think we're near where that flamenco club is. I think this is the street right here." We entered into a narrow street lined with plain white buildings. A tattered postcard had been fastened to the third door to the left. It read "La Bulería," and there was a crudely Xeroxed photograph of a group of performers–the men in suits, the women in flamboyant dresses–attached to it. "10:30 PM nightly."

The street, narrow enough to be entirely sunken in shade, was deserted. The wooden door to which the postcard was attached looked like every other door on the block.

We did not return to "La Bulería" that night. We'd already purchased tickets for the nine o'clock train to Granada the next morning. But on our way back to our *pension* we passed under a window where a guitar lesson was actually taking place.

It's said that flamenco isn't performed, but lived, (and there's an old jazz saying, "If you haven't lived it, it won't come out your horn"); and it follows that to teach flamenco can't be easy. Little is written down. Phrases are repeated time and again, passing from master to student until the rhythm and feeling are right. (Can non-gypsies play flamenco? Can whites play jazz?) There's a famous guitar school in Córdoba run by Paco Peña, and it's possible we were standing under the window of one of the classrooms. Two men, perhaps a third. A rapid passage, then the same passage again; talking, shouting, none of which we understood. Then the short passage incorporated into a longer one. A little slower, working through a difficult turn. The short, then the longer. A repeat, more shouting. I felt like shouting out myself, "Play the whole damn thing for once in your life!"

A few days earlier, in Seville, we *had* heard a street musician sing and play. He was serenading tourists at a sidewalk cafe in the Barrio Santa Cruz, we were standing half a block down the street. Brief though it was, it was deep, and moving, and painful, even at that distance. Later the same afternoon we were approached by a panhandler as we sat at a sidewalk table in front of the Bar Giralda with little plates of grilled swordfish and red peppers stuffed with tuna in front of us. "You like flamenco?" he said in perfect English. "I tell you where to go. Down by the river, across from Triana. It starts at 11:00. Too late for you? No, you'll like it, I assure you, you should go." We later heard the same man talking to other tourists: "...the tapas here are good, yes, but for a meal let me suggest..."

The next morning we passed him again on the street and waved, as if he were an old friend. He looked up at us and smiled, and then returned to the young couple he was cajoling, "...yes, the beaches there are good, but if you really want..."

"He should work for the tourist bureau," Hilary remarked as we passed out of earshot. Maybe he does.

Later that day we went down to the palm-lined quay by the river, where debris left by the midnight revel he'd been telling us about was everywhere. Climbing the steps to the bridge we saw six people curled up asleep, (or perhaps unconscious, considering it was mid-afternoon) in the bushes. It must have been quite a party.

Returning to our *pension* near the Alcázar than night, we found the owner busy practicing *his* guitar in the back room. A CD was blaring, and he was playing along with it, or trying to. Then he'd stop the music and begin again. We could hear him from our room on the second floor. It was hot, we opened the window and turned on the antique oscillating fan, but I could still hear flamenco strains very dimly from below. The music went on long into the night... or so I thought. Odd as it may seem, when I finally turned off the fan, the music also stopped.

To our relief, the fan in our room in Córdoba was a new one. Hilary said, "Thank goodness, this will be much quieter than last night."

"Yes," I replied as I turned it on, "but what I want to know is, can this fan play flamenco?"

THE FERIA at ARCOS de la FRONTERA

Arcos de la Frontera is a medium-sized town–the eastern most of those *pueblos blancos* that figure prominently in Andalusian tourist itineraries. Ronda is far better known, in part because of its historical associations with bull-fighting, in part because of its spectacular cliff-top location, but mostly because it happens to be the only "white town" that can be reached by train from the Costa del Sol. Though poorer and far less heavily touristed, Arcos, like its famous neighbor thirty miles to the east, stands on the edge of a cliff looking south toward the tip of Spain and Africa. To the west the countryside flattens out as it approaches Jerez and the Atlantic. To the east it rises into a series of hills that go by the name of the Serrania de Ronda. These rugged if diminutive peaks catch the moist air from the Atlantic–the nearby village of Grazalema has the highest average annual rainfall in Spain–but by in large the terrain is harsh, rocky, desolate, and covered with either chestnut trees or scrub. Cattle graze there, you can hear the bells clanging, and in the flatter land further to the south there are sprawling ranches where black bulls are bred for the ring.

We chose Arcos as the base for our explorations because it was relatively untouristed, because we'd read about a fabulous hotel on the edge of the cliff that was within our price range, and also because the town would be having its *feria* during our visit. A feria is an annual fair; the one in Arcos is scheduled to coincide each year with the feast of St. Michael, the patron saint of the town. Whether our room would really have a cliff-top view, and what the *feria* would actually consist of, we weren't sure, although we'd received a charming, if slightly fractured, letter from the hotel which ran, in part, as follows:

> ...We'll do our possible you to have a room with a view. Our hotel is in the old area of Arcos, in part of a convent. It has been restored to built the hotel. All the rooms have baths and some of them are with a view.
>
> At the end of September we will celebrate the Feria de San Miguel. September 28 is the last day and you can go there to see people wearing dresses for the Feria, dancing, horses...At night, at 12:00 to announce the end of the party there are fireworks. We recommend you to visit it, it is very nice.

To reach the Hotel El Convento you drive north from the plain across the river and into the lower reaches of Arcos, then left up the long narrow street that leads past bars and banks and hardware stores, all unadorned and perfectly white, to the "old" part of town. A gnarly man wearing a blue shirt and a black watchman's cap will direct you to a parking space in the plaza next to the cathedral. On the far side of the plaza is the edge of the cliff, although a marble balustrade insures that no one is likely to go driving off it. A ritzy *parador* stands on the cliff-edge to the left of the plaza; an alley heading off behind the *parador* takes you to the door of the far more modest but equally well-situated El Convento.

As it turned out, our room had a private, red-tiled balcony with a spectacular view looking south across green hills, tidy olive groves, and brown harvested fields. Once we'd removed two sentimental pictures from the wall and stacked them carefully out of sight in the closet (Spain is the capital of kitsch), and ascertained that we had enough food in the pack to make an evening meal, we returned to the lobby to inquire about the *feria*. The woman behind the counter was young and shy. She had long red hair and slightly crooked teeth; she seemed eager to be of service, but uncomfortable with her English. We spoke slowly, being painfully aware, but unable to communicate the fact, that when measured against our Spanish (which was non-existent), her English was stunningly precise. More than that, it was poetic.

"You should go now," she said, "Haven't you seen women in fancy dresses down in the streets? There will be horses, dancing. It's better in the afternoon. At night, after dark, it's more like..."and she pursed her lips, searching for the right word, "... more like disco."

We weren't quite sure *where* we were supposed to go, but it appeared that if we went back down into the new town all would become clear, so we thanked Estefanía González Ramírez (presuming this woman was, in fact, the one who had written to us two months earlier) and set out on foot through the narrow cobblestone streets lined with whitewashed buildings that appeared uniformly blue in the humid shadows of the afternoon. I was wondering as we walked if this young redhead had made an appearance at the feria yet (it was the fourth and final day, after all), with a boyfriend or husband perhaps. She clearly didn't want to sound disapproving, but the way she'd pursed her lips as she was searching for the word "disco" made me suspect that she spent her evenings at home drinking tea, listening to Italian madrigals on a wind-up phonograph and struggling through the novels of Tobias Smollett and Barbara Pym...in the original.

As we approached the main street of Arcos—the spine of the town, as it were—we caught sight of a family walking ahead of us. The two adults were dressed in conventional black and white clothing, but their little daughter, who was walking between them holding hands with them both, wore a brilliant red dress stacked with flowing flounces from bottom to top.

As we made our way down main-street we caught sight of adolescent girls and young women coming out of doorways where private gatherings were taking place, similarly dressed in colorful and elaborate "flamenco" dresses. Blue, yellow, red, patterned, polka dot, or plain, they were uniformly bright and heavily flounced, and many of them had a distinct sheen. The men, in stark contrast to the women, seemed entirely indifferent to the goings on, to judge by their casual dress. Jeans or slacks, and button-down broadcloth or pique golf shirts.

The nearer we got to the lower end of town the more colorful dresses we saw, and it was clear that the general drift of the crowd was to a part of Arcos we hadn't seen on our drive in. We turned left toward the river with the other pedestrians and soon found ourselves at the entrance to a fairground that consisted of a single sand-packed avenue lined with trees. This in itself was extraordinary—there aren't many trees of any kind in an Andalusian town—but even more extraordinary were the lights, the booths, and the tents that had been set up all along the length of the avenue. An immense brown pre-fabricated bull-ring with a circular wall twenty feet high stood at one end of the boulevard, and at the other were vendor's stalls selling purses, cigarette lighters, cassette tapes and CDs with faded plastic cases, thick Peruvian sweaters (Good heavens, it was a hot day!) and ice cream cones.

All along the middle length of the course, however, were large tents catering to the entertainment needs of the local population. These tents were all the same, in so far as they all sold beer, wine, sherry, and simple foods, and they all had music and dancing, but they differed widely in ambiance. Some were sponsored by the manufacturers of alcoholic drinks—Tio Pepe was one that I recognized; others were sponsored by wealthy families in the community, and they were by invitation only. You could tell because the name of the sponsor-family was printed on the side of the tent, and there was a policeman standing at the door checking invitations. The city of Arcos had sponsored the largest tent, and there was a flamenco dance contest going on inside. We watched for half an hour or so, and the performances were impressive, but all the contestants seemed to be under the age of twelve, and the single song to which they all performed grew tiresome with repetition. There was also something slightly weird about seeing pre-adolescent boys and girls make overt and exaggerated sexual gestures toward one another on a stage in front of their parents and neighbors.

Spain is different. And at this point I might as well observe (Hilary noticed it too) that Spanish women in general, and Andalusian women in particular, exhibit a degree of glamorous and energetic femininity, accompanied by a studied reserve, which is evident in their looks, their gait, and their choice of clothing, and which, to take a single example, is quite unlike the demeanor of the tall, blond, serious-looking Dutch attendants we met with on the KLM flight from Amsterdam to Madrid.

I've used the word "glamorous," but here, as in other aspects of Spanish life, one feels the need to stress the naturalness and interiority of the phenomenon in question. If Spaniards are decent and courteous, it's because that's how they are; if the women are glamorous, it's not because they've been reading *Vogue*, it's because that's how they are.

You may accuse me of trading in cultural stereotypes here, but in fact I'm merely reporting what I have observed, and similar judgments are to be found throughout the literature. To take a single example, H. V. Morton, the most widely read travel writer of his time, and certainly an equanimitous judge of character if ever there was one, covered a great deal of ground in a single sentence when he wrote in 1956:

> The eight centuries of Moorish occupation... is the event that distinguishes the early history of Spain from that of other European countries; it has placed a dark enduring gleam in the eyes of her women, and has given that plaintive eastern undercurrent to her music; among many other things it has possibly planted that streak of cruelty in Spanish hearts which is regularly sated on Sunday afternoons.

Sunday is traditionally when bullfights take place in Spain. The blood of Christ, then the blood of the bull.

We walked from tent to tent back and forth along the avenue. Men (and less often women) in gray bolero jackets and squat flat-brimmed hats rode by on tall, beautiful horses. It was interesting to note that one tent would be absolutely empty, while the one next door was jam-packed with dancers.

Was the music to blame, or some youthful notion of "in"-ness beyond rational explanation?

There were, among the crowds of couples dancing, quite a few who had taken the pains to learn traditional steps, holding their hands arched above their heads like flamingos, shuffling back and forth, now toward, now away from one another; but without exception, those who I saw dancing this way were women. They danced by themselves, they danced with their men, they danced with one another.

As for the music itself, it was all electronic dance music with a heavy bass line and pop-oriented female vocalists. Not a hint of flamenco anywhere. Nothing even remotely similar to the Gypsy Kings, who, aside from the fact that they're French, are themselves a long ways from the heart of the tradition.

We returned to our room, ate a cold dinner of bread, sardines, dry Manchego cheese, and cheap Sangre de Toro wine, and watched the kestrels soaring out from the cliff face below our balcony and back again to their hidden nests. It began to drizzle. We went out for a walk. The upper town was deserted. We entered the open courtyard of a pensioner's home, and we saw, through the window, a group of old men playing cards with a Spanish deck. Swords, Cups, Coins, Clubs. A soccer game was in progress on the television above their heads. Entering a small shop with strings of beads hanging in the door, we asked for chocolate, but the woman behind the counter, after looking in vain for something smaller, held up the only bar she had—wrapped in silver foil, it was the size of a briefcase.

We all laughed, and it felt good to laugh in Spain, in a tiny, badly lit shop, at night, in the rain, on the edge of a cliff.

THE MUSIC OF THE SPHERES

Winter drags and I make vegetable soup. I follow the recipe for minestrone Marcella Hazan gives in her *Classic Italian Cookbook*, which is hardly a recipe at all, although I don't cook the soup as long as she recommends, and I keep the pasta out of it.

Here's how it goes:

1) Heat 1/2 cup of olive oil and 3 tablespoons of butter in a large enameled cast-iron pot. That may seem like a lot of oil, but you may be eating the soup–depending on the size of your family–for two or three days.

At this point, depending on the hour of the day, you may feel the urge to pour yourself a glass of wine. Perhaps there's some Sauvignon Blanc chilling in the refrigerator. If not, open that bottle of not-half-bad Chianti you picked up at the liquor store the other day. No one will be outraged if, uncorking your last bottle of Orvieto, Frascati, or Vernaccia di San Gimignano, you drop an ice cube in the glass along with it.

2) Having resolved this issue to your own satisfaction, chop onions until the chopping board is full. Two onions, if they're big. Bring them over to the pot and throw them in.

By this time you'll notice that the aroma of hot olive oil is filling the air: it's the smell of the Mediterranean. In one of George Simenon's mysteries, *Maigret's Method*, the intrepid Inspector Maigret, during a visit to an island off the coast of southern France, describes the vague disgust he experiences when he encounters that smell. For myself, I love it, and also the way it jumps up at you as you lean over the pot to drop the onions in.

3). As the onions cook you chop the carrots. Four carrots. Maybe five. The carrot is the sweetest vegetable. Great vitality in its bizarre orange color! Dump them into the pot.

One aspect of the soup-making process is missing: the music. What music, then, would be a fitting accompaniment to the simple process of assembling a melange of sun-plant materials in the dreariest part of the year? Several possibilities present themselves immediately. Bizet? Too old-fashioned, somehow, and if the toreador song comes up you'll be whistling it for a week. It could ruin your marriage. Faure? But why a French composer with minestrone? For the simple reason that the secret of living well lies somewhere between Italy and France—in Avignon perhaps? In the end it seems to me that the suavity and the classical grace Faure brings to whatever he does–the chamber music, the piano music, the songs–isn't earthy enough for the task at hand.

How about Puccini? Now we're on to something. Yet no sooner is the name called to mind than the shadow of Giuseppi Verdi looms before us. Verdi is arguably the greatest composer of operas we have. He's an Italian, and he's also of peasant origins. Sounds promising. On the other hand, it would be difficult for us to overlook the fact that his operas have a degree of gravity, of melodrama, of *import*, that might well overpower the humble vegetables bubbling in the pot.

But if not Verdi, then why Puccini? For the simple reason that in moving from the noble physiognomy of Verdi's work to Puccini's somewhat slippery visage, the idea of vegetable soup has become more germane. After all, the garret of the first act of *La Boheme* is one in which the potage we're assembling would undoubtedly be welcome, whereas it would be difficult for us to image the Doge of Venice, or King Philip of Spain, or Aida, getting excited about the beans and the cabbage we're about to drop into the pot. The argument weakens, I will admit, when we turn to consider the gypsies in *Il Trovatore*. But the characters *in* Verdi's operas are of less significance to us, I think, than the character of the operas, and here a contrast in temperament between the two composers becomes obvious. The complexities—some would say the inanities—of his plot-lines notwithstanding, Verdi takes himself very seriously. Puccini, for all his stage notes and compositional genius, does not.

In his book *In Defense of Opera* Hamish F.G. Swanston devotes more space to Verdi than to any other composer. He has little respect for Puccini's work, on the other hand, because Puccini, in his opinion, has nothing to say about life. In the course of his critique of Puccini he unloads a battery of criticisms of which these are only the most succinct:

[Puccini] evidently thought himself capable of great things.

And certainly he was the maker of some of the finest melodies ever offered for an audience's diversion.

Puccini never seemed to realize that through the composition of an opera he can say something as suggestive and stimulating to human thought as other men might through the writing of a treatise or the passing of a social reform.

There is no salvation possible in a Puccini opera, not because the world is terrible, as Verdi believed, but simply because Puccini is a sadist.

Puccini is a perfect example of Thomas Mann's idea of the artist as 'magician.' The audience is charmed by his tunes into accepting all kinds of strangeness and insignificance.

But it is a characteristic of Puccini's psychology that it is self-destructive, claustrophobic and trivializing. He had evidently concluded that it was difficult enough to make a sound musical structure, properly alternating lively and solemn melodies, solo and ensemble situations, without bothering overmuch about meaning.

Swanston seems to be suggesting that Verdi's operas are great because they explore great social and perhaps even metaphysical issues, or at any rate, that they flesh out the terrible world we live in. Therefore, they *mean* something. Puccini's operas, on the contrary, amount to nothing more than a bundle of pleasing effects. They have no broader frame of reference, no import, no *significance*. This view strikes me as wrong-headed in the extreme. We don't love Verdi because of the part his operas may have played in the unification of Italy, for example. We love the drama, the music, the life and energy and even the darkness that rumbles through them. Although Verdi may have believed that life is terrible, his operas convey quite the opposite point of view. And after all, what is Art supposed to "mean," beyond the meaning contained in images that draw life and death, love and loss, spirit and anguish, into a pleasing whole?

> 4) The green beans must now go into the soup. Green beans are the most resilient vegetable. In the minestrone they're indispensable. However mushy the other vegetables may become, the green beans will be less so. Omit them at your peril.

I must confess, (returning for a moment to the issue of meaning), that my own tastes run toward those works that don't mean anything at all. If I'm enamored of French and Italian vocal music one reason–though surely not the only reason–is that I haven't the slightest idea what anyone is saying. The content of an opera or a song can add considerably to its beauty, of course. When Mimi dies at the end of *La Boheme*, for example, I'm moved. When the star drops below the horizon at the end of the first act of *Otello*, shivers run up and down my spine. And you can be sure that when the Commendatore comes to sup with his murderer Don Giovanni in the last scene of Mozart's famous opera, my heart is twisted tight at the awful beauty of the drama taking place before my eyes. But there are more than enough such moments to be found in Puccini's work.

Swanston contends that "the popularity of 'Boheme' and 'Butterfly' is akin to the popularity of romantic novels." Why is it, then, that the romantic literary works upon which both operas are based have long since vanished into oblivion, while the operas themselves remain extraordinarily popular? In the first place, the appeal of Puccini's music is intimately tied to the *sound* of the music; but there is also something distinctive in Pinkerton's callowness, Turandot's hysteria, or Scarpia's wickedness, to mention just three examples, which brings to the operas in which these figures appear a kind of dreadful truth which is not in the least bit "romantic."

On the other hand, any number of Puccini arias could be used to good effect in a romantic film, and several have. One of his most famous tunes "Se Come Voi" has the peculiar effect of reminding me of a winter evening when I was ten or twelve. My brother and I were doing a jigsaw puzzle. The scene—a painting, not a photograph—was of a dusty town on the seacoast of Spain or Mexico. The sea was turquoise-blue. The adobe houses had wrought-iron balconies, there were exotic trees scattered here and there. My parents were leaving the house on their way to a Christmas party. My mother had a black dress and a black checked jacket on; I could smell her perfume. The radio station was having an "all-Beatles" night, so the year might well have been 1965. My brother and I had probably both placed a couple of puzzle pieces in our pockets; we both wanted to have the satisfaction of bringing the work to completion ourselves. A mysterious happiness suffuses this memory. The music, the darkness outside, the perfume, and the sight of the dusty roads and the distant sea, which we poured over in our efforts to complete the scene. This happened to be a moment during which my heart opened itself to an experience of all-encompassing richness, felt it, gathered it in, and somehow or other, hung on. It did all of this without my knowing it, I might add. The puzzle got built, the evening passed, the Beatles broke up, and I never gave any of it another thought. Decades later, I heard Kiri te Kanawa sing "Se Come Voi" and the details of this specific evening surfaced like the triangular fortune in a fortune-telling bowling-ball. What's the connection? I have no idea.

Isn't the mind weird? Wrong question. We should be asking ourselves, Isn't life weird? That such feelings and images can persist in memory, that an operatic aria can summons them from the depths.

5). At this point chop the zucchini, inconsequential and demure. People joke about zucchini. Everyone who has a vegetable garden has too much of it. They get too big. A zucchini doesn't taste like anything much, but it has a subtle presence that can elevate a soup. I love zucchini. It's not up to the level of a leek, but it's getting there.

To put the matter as simply as possible, Puccini's work, unlike Verdi's, (and very unlike Wagner's) has an immediacy which is distinctly "modern." A dangerous adjective, I will admit. If every art category refers to an exaggeration—classicism is arid, romanticism is bathetic, the baroque is mindlessly ornate—then modernism, too, is a bundle of exaggerations—affectations of primitivism, excessive emphasis on pattern and design at the expense of import, decadent sentimentality. If, on the other hand, every age produces works of interest, then the modern age, once again, is no exception. On the contrary, this period, roughly circumscribed by the rise of impressionism in all its forms on the one hand, and the transfer of art attention from Europe to the United States following World War Two on the other, ranks among the most fertile periods in the history of Western civilization. What sets the art of this period apart from others in my view—the music, the poetry, the painting—is the quality of jangled immediacy.

Art historians have frequently characterized this period as one in which artists liberated themselves from the chains of representationalism. This interpretive rubric has provided us with one of our grandest and most heroic images, yet the truth of the matter is quite the opposite. The styles developed at this time—impressionism, surrealism, cubism, to mention only a few—served to disrupt and remove the aesthetic conventions that were *clouding* our vision, and this house-cleaning effort allowed the beauty and the vigor, visual, emotional, cerebral, of life with a capital L to reassert itself.

Artists of the modern period approached their subjects with a degree of fierceness, heedlessness, playfulness, and wonder, which we ourselves, children of a different, and a thinner, spiritual climate, can only marvel at.

Fernando Pessoa, the modernist Portuguese poet, made a note in his journal that typifies this aesthetic:

> *If only I were, I feel it in this moment, someone who could see all this as if he had no relation to it except seeing it— contemplate all of it as if he were the adult traveler who had only today reached the surface of life! If only I hadn't learned, from birth onward, to give accepted meanings to these things, if only I could see them in the expression they have separate from the expression that has been imposed upon them. If only I could understand the human reality in the woman selling fish independent of her being a fishmonger and know that she exists and sells. If only I could see the policeman the way God sees him. If only I could notice everything for the first time, not apocalyptically, like a revelation of the Mystery, but directly like a blooming of Reality.*

Pessoa and many of his contemporaries sensed a positive and vigorous energy within things, which is all but obliterated by the mental habit of naming and evaluating them. Various technical crutches were employed at the time to shed the accumulated weight of perceptual convention—the pseudo-barbarism that animates Stravinsky's "Rite of Spring" for example, or the African angularities of Picasso's "Demoiselle d'Avignon." Still in all, the freshness, the perversions of sense and emotion, the tide of uninhibited expression that leads to the opening of the mind and heart I've just described with respect to Puccini's work, greets us time and again in the work of this period. Puccini himself would undoubtedly be surprised to hear his operas referred to in the company of, say, the animated ballets of Eric Satie, or the fanciful graphic productions—half sketch, half wallpaper design—of Raoul Dufy, or the disquieting algebraic landscapes of Giorgio de Chirico, yet he shares with them an interest in and sensitivity to a domain of experience often referred to as "the irrational," though it might better be termed the "pre-rational."

> 6). And speaking of the "pre-rational," the cabbage lies shredded on the cutting board: Napa or Savoy, if possible. It goes in last, because it needs to cook least. You stir it into the logjam in the pot, it insinuates itself like a fine net between and across and around the hearty vegetables, glistening, oily, and translucent. Give it five minutes to cook, and then add salt, pepper, the canned crushed toma-toes (which give the soup acidity) and enough heated beef broth to turn it all into a soup.

While our minestrone simmers, let me propose, as a lighter alternative (or even an antidote) to Puccini's arch and swooning lines of musical thought, that we turn our attention for a moment to the music of Francis Poulenc. Maurice Ravel once remarked with respect to Poulenc's work, neither condescendingly nor enviously, if I read his character right: "What I like is his ability to invent popular tunes." And it's true that Poulenc can evoke a range of moods stretching from the dourly somber to the perversely pixilated simply by means of melody. His best works tend to be small in scale—piano music, chamber works for woodwinds, and especially songs. As the critic Norman Lembrecht once remarked, Poulenc appears to have had a very short attention span. His harmonies may be classically beautiful one moment, puckish and astringent the next. In this he resembles that subtle and irreverent genius of the eighteenth century, W.A. Mozart. Poulenc rarely builds, elaborates, or "towers" the way Mozart often does, however; rather, he veers freely across the fields of his own imagination, reckless, fun-loving, acerbic, and more or less sincere.

My own familiarity with Poulenc's work may be traced to an afternoon many years ago when a friend of mine, on his way home from work, heard a performance of the *Clarinet Sonata*, fell in love with it, and in due time bought me a recording of it as a gift. I must admit this piece didn't strike my fancy immediately, although the slow movement was clearly a gem. It was, for me, the kind of record that you pull out when you've grown tired of all the things that until very recently you found terribly exciting and played repeatedly. "Now here's something fresh and different," you remark as you place this strange piece on the turntable, preparing yourself for the brashness and petulance, which, as you dimly recall, is inseparable from the beauty. In this way Poulenc insinuates himself by degrees into your psyche. It may take years, but the day will dawn when you hold your four-CD collection of Poulenc's complete songs more precious than all the symphonies ever written. You thumb through the accompanying pamphlet containing texts by Apollinaire, Valéry, and Cocteau, and ask yourself idly whether the time has finally arrived to learn French.

> 7). Meanwhile, the smell of simmering vegetables fills the air; it may even steam the windows. The soup can simmer for hours–Marcella Hazen advises a minimum of two and a half. To my taste it's done in thirty minutes. (Hazen advises that however long you cook it, you put the cabbage in only just at the end.) At this point the soup no longer tastes raw, but the vegetables are still at least slightly firm. All that remains is to set a few pieces of bread out on the table, and prepare the *pistou*. Chop up four or five cloves of garlic, add a few spoonfuls of dried basil (fresh would, of course, be better), moisten liberally with olive oil, and finally, stir in a cup or so of Parmesan cheese. Place a

spoonful of the lumpy mass into your bowl of soup, set the bowl on the table in front of you, and watch the green flecks move out into the hot red sea of floating white and yellow bits as you luxuriate in the heady aroma of garlic and herbs.

Then you eat.

᠅

As I looked down into my bowl of minestrone, I was suddenly reminded of a scene from a French documentary called *Two or Three Things I Know About Her*. The narrator, whom we would be justified in identifying with the film's director Jean-Luc Godard, I think, is sitting in a sunny bistro. An attractive woman at the bar is giving him the eye. His attention moves from the woman to the cup of *cafe au lait* that he's stirring with a spoon, then over to the silent woman again, who deliberately crosses or uncrosses her legs, then back down into the enormous bowl of coffee, which, shot from above, fills the screen. As the hot black liquid swirls in its bowl, the bubbles of foamed milk gather together and break apart, while the narrator muses on nature, the universe, infinity, women, and nothingness, in a peculiarly French pop-existential way.

Socrates expresses the opinion, in Plato's "Theatetus," that the one emotion indispensable to a philosopher is astonishment. Yet we all feel astonishment at one time or another, without in most cases moving beyond that experience to any systematic understanding of what life is really about. Are we all, then, philosophers? It may be significant that, at a remove of fifteen years, I remember the bar, the woman, and the foam on the bowl of coffee that I saw in a famous film. I also remember the effect the scene had on me—the associations were both funny and apt, the somnambulant voice-over was mesmerizing, great truths seems to be swirling in that very ordinary bistro drink. On the other hand, I don't remember anything of what the narrator actually said.

There is a place in life for this kind of aimlessly meditative activity, I think, which allows you to hover pleasantly near to truth, without arriving at anything meaningful or concrete. In fact, I've spent more time than I would care to admit staring into bowls of vegetable soup, down suburban streets, across ice-covered lakes, up into the starry sky, out at the silent and motionless rabbits that gather in my back yard night after night, or into the faces of people I love as they read the newspapers or busy themselves with simple tasks, all the while tossing my own experience this way and that in the hope of unloosing some kind of framework for it all. These sincere, if not very concentrated, efforts have led me to a single simple realization: *The universe is musical, not mathematical.*

Such a remark may seem fatuous coming from someone like me, who doesn't even own a good telescope. On the other hand, it strikes me that the most interesting and complicated parts of the universe aren't "out there," they're "around here." If, as I'm suggesting, the universe is musical, rather than mathematical, then calculating will have to give way to singing, or at least to listening, before we can become really comfortable in it.

I am well aware that this simple and all-encompassing idea isn't new. Concepts like rhythm, harmony, and sympathetic chant have been associated with holiness, meaning, and life itself from earliest times. The words themselves are usually considered to be metaphors, however, and the ritualistic practices associated with them are usually taken to be a means of making contact with other, greater realities beyond music itself. At the same time, it has often happened (in our

Western intellectual tradition at any rate) that musical concepts have first become confused with, and then been supplanted by, their mathematical representations, and this has had the effect of distorting and even destroying the truth-value they contain.

Everyone knows what music is, I think, at least to the extent of being able to distinguish between a popular song and a barking dog, say, or a cement-mixer at work. "Mary Had a Little Lamb" is music; the sound of pebbles trickling down the slopes of a gravel-pit is not. By the same token, everyone knows that the mathematical arts concern themselves with the relations between numbers, lines, and shapes, as opposed to, say, relations between word-types (grammar) or between mammal species (zoology). $2+2=4$ is mathematics. The numbers on your license plate are not.

Although music and mathematics have almost nothing in common, strictly speaking, musical compositions *can* be denoted using mathematical signs and expressions. The problems begin at the point where it is further asserted that music is appealing precisely *because* of the mathematical nature of the tonal relationships it offers to us. We must remind ourselves here that although both music and mathematics are human creations, music is irregular, mathematics is regular; that works of music are unique creations that play themselves out *through time*, while the world of mathematics is a body of anonymous, static, unchanging, and abstract symbols and relationships. Finally, and most obviously, perhaps, the relationships that a work of music sustains exist not between numbers or symbols, but between sounds. Music is inexorably rooted in the human world of hearing and emotion, in which consonance and dissonance, rhythm and timbre, and the recurrent but seldom repetitive patterns of melody and harmony, produce unique and pleasing aesthetic effects. Mathematics, on the other hand, though often admired for its purity, and even referred to from time to time as "beautiful," in both its formulations and its applications, actually serves the function of helping us to describe and make use of other things—tides, grain ledgers, artillery trajectories—that are not mathematical themselves. When all is said and done, mathematics is a practical and symbolic endeavor; music is a real and aesthetic one.

It would appear we're entering onto a strange path here. After all, who in their right mind would suggest that *Don Giovanni*, say, or *The Art of Fugue*, bear the slightest similarity to the binomial theorem or a trigonometric table. And yet, curious as it may seem, it has been argued repeatedly over the centuries that a study of the mathematical relationships which provide the underpinning for musical expression will help us to expose the very structure (which is to say the harmony) of the universe!

Pythagoras of Samos, often referred to as the father of Western philosophy, was the first to probe the relationship between music and mathematics diligently following these lines. We know little about him as an individual—the cult he founded was committed to secrecy and was sustained largely by oral tradition; nevertheless a large body of adages, tales, and esoteric practices were passed down within the movement and eventually committed to writing. They give us a picture of the Master as a teacher of considerable force of personality, who advocated vegetarianism and espoused the doctrine of reincarnation, perhaps as a result of his travels in Egypt, Babylon, and Syria.

Pythagoras is largely remembered today, however, for two things, one practical (mathematical), and the other aesthetic (musical). He discovered that the square of the two short sides of a right triangle equal the square of the longest side—we call this the Pythagorean Theorem; and he discovered that the musical intervals we tend to consider "pleasant" correspond to simple mathematical ratios.

The Pythagorean Theorem is still in common use today, because it happens to be true. Yet the second of Pythagoras's discoveries has had a far greater impact on our culture. One historian of the period writes:

> Pythagoras's discovery of the arithmetical basis of the musical intervals was not just the beginning of musical theory; it was the beginning of science. For the first time, man discovered that universal truths could be explained through systematic investigation and the use of symbols such as mathematics. Once that window was opened, the light spread across the whole breadth of human curiosity-not least in the field of cosmogony. The genius of Pythagoras lay in the comprehensive way he joined the inner man and the physical world, and the physical world and the cosmos.

If Pythagoras's genius lay in the way he brought the inner man, the physical world, and the cosmos together, then his error lay in casting aside this momentous conjecture concerning our latent musical connection to the cosmos, in pursuit of the simpler but also more questionable notion that "number," and not the musical patterns and relationships from which "number" derived its significance, was divine.

Aristotle describes the effect of this shift in emphasis as well as anyone has, and also noted its unfortunate result:

> The Pythagoreans, as they are called, devoted themselves to mathematics; they were the first to advance this study, and having been brought up in it they thought its principles were the principles of all things. Since of these principles numbers are by nature the first, and in numbers they seemed to see many resemblances to the things that exist and come into being; ... since, again, they say that the attributes and ratios of the musical scales were expressible in numbers; since, then,

*all other things seemed in their whole nature to be modeled
after numbers, and numbers seemed to be the first things in the
whole of nature, they supposed the elements of numbers to be
the elements of all things, and the whole heaven to be a
musical scale and a number.*

Aristotle wisely rejected this line of reasoning. He found
"number" to be an inadequate language for describing the
great variety of things and events we meet up with in life. And
yet, although the illogicality of the Pythagorean chain of
reasoning was noted early on by other thinkers of antiquity,
the appeal of his thought remained considerable, because it
advanced a correspondence between the cosmos, which is
chaotic, bewildering, and largely incomprehensible to us, and
the simplest and clearest images and relations imaginable: one,
two, three. Making use of this evident correspondence
between "things" in their chaotic murkiness and units in their
admirable clarity, it became possible to suggest, and even to
"prove," what we all feel occasionally without knowing why:
that there is a harmony in the universe.

The danger involved in such an association can be most
simply suggested by observing that although the universe may
be harmonious (I think it is), there is no real harmony in
mathematics. To say that the universe is musical makes a
certain amount of sense, therefore; to say that the universe is
mathematical, on the other hand, is to take the harmony out
of the universe; harmony is an aesthetic, and not a
mathematical concept.

Pythagoras's error has resurfaced repeatedly in the history
of thought, and it's still very much with us today. In fact, it's
endemic to scientific research, where it serves a largely useful
function. The scientific endeavor itself is rooted in
experience, yet it strives to remove itself from the
irregularities with which nature abounds, so as to approach
the uniformity of mathematical law—simple, precise, and

universal in application. This is an admirable undertaking in many ways. The danger lies in elevating the laws, which are seldom arrived at without considerable isolation and simplification of the phenomena being examined, to the level of "reality," while relegating the varied experiences from which first the data, and then the "law" itself, have been derived, to some lesser state of reality and interest. This is what Pythagoras did when he asserted that "reality is number," when in fact the number was merely being used to describe a complex and continually evolving aspect of creative life; and this is what physicists and mathematicians do today when they suggest that in developing a formula to describe the behavior of a hydrogen atom in a black hole they are beginning to "know God."

Steven Hawking, the well-known physicist and author of *A Brief History of Time*, is one of many eminent scientists who find it difficult to resist dabbling in metaphysical realms that are well beyond their ken. Yet Hawking is also well aware of the limits to which physicists and mathematicians are constrained by their methodology. In a lecture given in Cambridge in 1980 he wrote:

> We already know the physical laws that govern everything that we experience in everyday life. As Dirac pointed out, [in the 1930s] his equation was the basis of 'most of physics and all of chemistry.' However, we have been able to solve the equation only for the very simplest system, the hydrogen atom consisting of one proton and one electron. For more complicated atoms with more electrons, let alone for molecules with more than one nucleus, we have to resort to approximations and intuitive guesses of doubtful validity.

In other words, knowing the laws that underlie the behavior

of simple particles doesn't help us much when we're reflecting on the complex web of entities that make up the universe we actually inhabit. Unlike the world of mathematical formulas, the real world is a shifty place, riddled with anomalies and surprises. The odds against predicting the behavior of even a single organism for any length of time, on the basis of laws operating on the atomic level, make winning the Publishers Clearing House Sweepstakes look like a sure bet. All of which is to leave aside entirely the issue of whether we *understand* anything merely by predicting what it's going to do next. To envision moving from these dark regions of ignorance, reductive thinking, and conjecture to "the mind of God," with or without the aid of mathematics, would require us to make a leap of faith that beggars comparison.

A good deal of valuable scientific work is being done today using fractals and computer simulations to chart complex natural phenomena mathematically. Descartes would have been pleased. Novelty, chaos, complexity, emergence–the vocabulary of these nascent disciplines would suggest that the phenomena under investigation do not recur regularly, nor do they correspond to a mathematical grid. To understand the processes involved in the formation of weather systems, for example, or in genetic drift, requires a sensitivity to elements of evident spontaneity which, insignificant in themselves, may lead to cataclysmic change with the passage of time. Meanwhile, even the gentlest approaches to history, that most complex and important of all fields of knowledge, remain uncharted.

In short, we are intrigued, reassured, and even moved when we uncover regularity in nature, but there is neither truth nor safety in this kind of discovery. In the end, life is not regular, life does not have a formula, and no formula has the power even to hint at the character, richness, energy, or danger it repeatedly confronts us with.

But if it's true, as I'm suggesting, that the universe is musical, rather than mathematical, then life itself must be, not a formula, but a song. In that case God would not be a mathematician, as the physicists like to suggest, but a composer. Better still, he'd be the song itself.

This is an appealing idea, I think, and I would like to stress that we are not trading merely in metaphor here. When we say the universe is a song, we mean to suggest that it has measure and proportion, that it has elements of consonance and dissonance; that it has rhythm—that it flows. This, in fact, is the basis of aesthetic experience. Music in the conventional sense, and by extension the other arts as well, appeals to us only because it conveys, on a small scale but with heightened emphasis and formal clarity, the beauty and trauma of the music we feel and live every day of our lives, and sense in the shapes and rhythms of the universe all around us.

I know of no better definition of happiness than this: to have a song in your heart.

I suspect that Pythagoras would be perfectly comfortable with the world of subtle effects and reverberations I'm attempting to describe here. He had the wisdom to discern that the study of life ought properly to be focused on how its parts best fit together, not only on how they might best be taken apart. From the Orphic tradition that was already ancient in his time he adopted the idea that music has the power to instill order and health in those who open themselves to it. When he applied the word "harmony" to the realm of personal affairs, he wasn't speaking metaphorically. The entire universe was, in his view, veritably quaking with sympathetic vibrations. His error, as I hope I have by this time made clear, lay in supposing that music draws its power from the regularity of number. In fact music is as irregular, unpredictable, dense, and at times as wildly chaotic as is life itself. But it does possess the beauty and the forward-moving lilt that also happens to characterize the universe itself.

The painter Auguste Renoir kept a notebook in which he recorded his observations on life and art:

> *Everything that I call grammar on primary notions of Art can be summed up in one word: Irregularity.*

> *The earth is not round. An orange is not round. Not one section of it has the same form or weight as another. If you divide it into quarters, you will not find in a single quarter the same number of pips as in any of the other three; nor will any of the pips be exactly alike.*

Strange as it may seem, Renoir's remarks, which may have been recorded at the turn of the twentieth century, are directed against a practice of art founded on the principle of ideal proportion—a principle that may be traced back to the teachings of Pythagoras himself. Against the mathematical regularity that Pythagoras divined in musical intervals, and that artists of the classical period cultivated in their painting and sculpture, Renoir thrusts the observed irregularity of everything we experience in life.

> *I propose to found a society. It is to be called "The Society of Irregulars." The members would have to know that a circle should never be round.*

The eccentricities and irregularities that characterize the musical universe we inhabit are not significant or endearing in and of themselves. An unceasing dialectic is at work between order and disorder, harmony and discord, exuberance and restraint, and this dialectic sustains the vital atmosphere within which we live. And, just as there has never been a workable formula for generating music, or establishing just relations between peoples, or guiding the development of a human personality, so, it seems to me, there will never be a mathematical rendering of the song which is the universe itself. Images can do it. Numbers can't. We listen, we act, we suffer, we hone our instrument, we become more adept at sustaining a fabric of harmonious living and interaction. Describing his own passage through life Confucius once remarked: "At fifteen I set my heart on learning; at thirty I took my stand; at forty I came to be free from doubts; at fifty I understood the Decree of Heaven; at sixty my ear was atuned..."

A Norwegian researcher by the name of Jon-Roar Bjorkvold has devoted his career to the cross-cultural study of the role singing plays in childhood development. He notes at one point in his book *The Muse Within* that many African languages don't have a word for "hearing" or "listening." The Bantu, for example, use the word "sikia" to denote the act of sensing with one's whole being. A Swahili-English dictionary, Bjorkvold reports, lists "Sikia: 1) hear; 2) pay attention to, notice, understand, perceive; 3) heed, obey. Mostly of the senses of hearing, but also of other senses except taste."

Bjorkvold writes: "It is through such integrated sensation that "music" is experienced in the African manner—as something one hears and listens to, but also as something one sees, responds to physically (dance), understands through, and even obeys. It is just so, I maintain, that children experience the world from infancy into early childhood."
To me it sounds a lot like Pythagorianism, (or Confucianism, for that matter) but without the numbers.

I doubt whether sensing with one's whole being will ever

return to prominence among the values we espouse as a culture. Incense at the Basilica? The roar of the crowd at the Metrodome? The throb of a virulent rock band at First Avenue? Can these experiences really be said to evoke harmonies of a cosmic order? I don't see why not. It would be a mistake in any case, I think, for us to associate music as a concept too closely with mere sound, or even with movement. Like the Bantu, we've got to take a much broader view.

I had a remarkable musical experience not long ago that was largely visual. Hilary and I were headed east toward the river early one Saturday morning. The sky was cut in two by a thick band of pink clouds; we drove in silence, the sun rose, the snow glistened, the bare trees stood stark and clear. We arrived at William O'Brien State Park at eight and set off up into the hills, skiing. Two ski-skaters in black tights swooped past us before we'd gone a hundred yards. They were the only people we saw on our trip.

We moved alongside a brushy swamp, under a railroad bridge, and up through the woods following the bed of a frozen creek between two graceful hills. A turn to the right onto a side-trail took us higher still, across the steepest grades of the morning, up to the edge of a farmer's fields, and then down again over a roller-coaster sequence of hills thick with red oak and maple. In time we came out of the woods into a pasture. The approach to this spot is a favorite stretch of mine. First you see the light through the trees, then you near the opening, and suddenly you emerge with symphonic grandeur into the sunlight and space of an entirely new world. You climb as you cross the field, admiring the wooded hills on either side, and when you reach the top you see how high you've actually risen. Rolling hills covered with the gray leafless branches of distant trees, purple in the early morning light, stretch off to the distant valley of the St. Croix River. A lake lies in the distance to your right, and a barn roof rises from the midst of the trees, reminding you that this is a park, not a wilderness. Those rows of lofty Norway pines beside the fence were seedlings not so long ago.

There's a good deal of skiing left to do, but I don't think I need to describe it here. The counterpoint of woods and fields, ascent and descent, continues. The sun climbs higher, the snow begins to melt in the track. Feeling the sun on your face, filling your lungs with cold brisk air, sensing a weariness in the knees that tells you you've actually done something. By the time you get back to the car the freshness is gone from the morning. A bucket-seat never felt so comfortable.

On our way back to town we stopped at the studio and showroom of the potter Warren MacKenzie. MacKenzie, whose utilitarian wares are scattered in homes and museums throughout the world, would be among the "living treasures" of American culture, if, imitating the Japanese, we in America had such a designation. He lives and works on a farm outside Stillwater. He's been making pots for nearly half a century, teaching pottery at the University of Minnesota for almost as long. In 1981 *Ceramics Monthly* included him in a list of the world's twelve best potters.

That was a long time ago. You drive past the house and down the hill, and park your car by the pile of chards outside the kiln. His salesroom is open twenty-four hours a day, make your choice and leave your money in the basket. Tea-bowls cost hardly more than a fast-food hamburger.

When MacKenzie has a sale, cars are lined up for half a mile on either side of the sandy road leading to the house. The yard in front of the sales-room is filled with pottery, his own and that of his students and colleagues, set out on wooden planks. There's a certain giddiness in the air, people have put on their old fringed buckskin jackets again, you expect to hear Joni Mitchell's "Blue" or Buffalo Springfield burst from an intercom at any moment. It's a happy scene, but I find it difficult to pick out the pots I want in such an atmosphere.

On the other hand, if you go a few days after an advertised sale, there simply won't be much of interest left.

As luck would have it friends of ours who live nearby stopped in at MacKenzie's place on a whim the week before our ski. The sign on the door said "New Firing Tomorrow." When we arrived the following Saturday morning, the place was deserted and the showroom was full.

Yes, but how to choose? This problem is made more difficult for us by the fact that we already have a great deal of pottery. Seven unique and exquisite tea bowls sit in a row on the back of our stove. The china cabinet is full of porcelain pitchers, majolica bowls, bizarre post-modern beakers, miniscule wedding cups from Japan, etc. etc. Vases of various sizes are scattered here and there, they hold dried flowers or eucalyptus sprigs, or nothing at all. Teapots, serving dishes. What is it that we came here to buy?

It isn't really such a problem. You take your time, wandering among the tables and shelves, holding one piece after another in your mind's eye, and then in your hand, to feel the heft and fit.

There's an element of chance involved in the production of the kind of wheel-thrown, gas-fired functional pottery MacKenzie makes. Chance may not be the right word to describe the natural rhythm, both in the modeling and in the firing effects, that gives the best pots an inner liveliness, yet this liveliness has less to do with a potter's calculations than with an act of awareness which transmits itself through the hands and body intuitively. The effect is human and natural, and also, I think, musical. In a room of a hundred pots, four or five will have this living musical quality. Fortunately for the potter, no two people are likely to agree on which four or five they are.

After twenty minutes of silent perusal Hilary settled on a straight-sided bowl about three inches high with a single thumb indentation in the side. Too big to be a tea-bowl, too small to be a serving bowl, it has an almost ceremonial stature. I can see it filled with black olives or Tuscan bean dip.

I chose a wide-jutting bowl with an airy foot, a simple black tenmoku glaze, and a nice swirl on the inside. Not much you can say about it, really, except that the forces it harnesses are in balance, so that the form seems both "free" and "right."

I wouldn't hesitate to serve minestrone in this hand-thrown creation, although clear Spanish glass would serve just as well. Not that it makes a great deal of difference. And yet, in the musical universe, everything makes a difference. Given the right vegetables, the right bowls, the right music, the right company, things will come together like the bright clear sound of a ringing bell. At that point, I think, we may begin to approach the mind of God.

JAMES SALTER: AN APPRECIATION

For years James Salter appeared to me like a character in one of his books—legendary and obscure. His novels were graced by a prose more limpid and elegant than that of any of his contemporaries, and his sense of what made a scene or narrative significant could only, I thought, be referred to as "wise." And yet for all of that, you never heard anything about him. Was he still alive, even?

Occasionally a sign would appear in a magazine, like a piece of spoor—a brief article about Eisenhower, say, or a recount of a bicycle trip he'd taken across Japan. And once I caught sight of him in a cartoon illustration in the *New Yorker*, dancing in a chorus line at a benefit somewhere in the Hamptons alongside William Styron and Norman Mailer. Even the appearance in 1988 of *Dusk*, a generally fine book of short stories, was hardly enough to convince me that Salter was alive and well and working on something really "major." His early novels, *A Sport and a Pastime*, *Solo Faces*, and *Light Years*, were all vaguely elegiac in tone and peopled with talented men and women whose lives remain unfulfilled in one way or another. Perhaps Salter's own life had become a lengthy "falling off" as well.

I first came across one of Salter's books by chance. At the time I had only recently dropped out of college. Having written a humorous letter of resignation (or so I thought) to the head of the department, who happened to be a friend of mine, my wife Hilary and I shuttled our hand-me-down furniture into her parent's garage and packed off for an extended visit to France.

In those days things were cheap. We ate in restaurants every night, and our most expensive hotel, a room with a green linoleum floor in the Latin Quarter in Paris, cost $8 a night. Day-long walks across the countryside in the Dordogne valley, with workers in rubber boots in the muddy fields and chickens in the hedges; a ride on rented bikes north from Carcassonne to the desolate Black Mountains and the ruined Cathar castles of Lastour; *prix fixes* dinners with *côte du porc* and peppery green beans, all the red wine you could drink, a cheese cart, salad, and a flan at the end; provincial art collections housed in baronial *hotels*, interesting more for the architecture than for the art they contained. The silver flanks of the Alpilles, glistening like sharkskin in the morning light. Spanish workers bent double harvesting long rows of red and yellow tulips by hand; crumbling Roman arenas; and Mte St. Victoire, which we came upon by chance during a cross-country walk through the sage-covered hills east of Aix-en-Provence in search of the battlefield where Marius had defeated the barbarian hordes in 102 B.C. and saved the Roman Republic from devastation.

Life is like art. And history lives. In France, in 1978, to young minds full of naive enthusiasm for European lore, life was art. Sunlight and food, poppies, ruined villages, fruit-stands and bakeries on every street, and strange wizened folk everywhere who could not tell what you were saying.

I returned from that paradise and went to work unloading trucks at a book warehouse. That was where I ran across Salter's novel about mountain climbing, *Solo Faces*. The discovery could not have been more propitious. Though he was an American, Salter wrote in a vaguely French style, (i.e. adjectives and clauses floating freely) and the story itself was largely set in France. I found it encouraging, after years of reading, (and, not incidentally, loving) Burckhart, Hamsun, Leopardi, Flaubert, and many other dead European writers, that a living, and more surprising still, a living *American* writer could be writing so well.

But style itself is never enough. In *Solo Faces* I found a story with enough danger, excitement, triumph and trauma for any thrill-seeking reader. Salter was clearly even more interested in the dark side of triumph, however. The birth of the legend. The hollowness of the relationships built on uncomprehending adulation. The fear of failing to live up to an early success. And the self-absorption that makes the development of lasting personal ties all but impossible.

In a horrible flash of insight, which Salter offers us in a single sentence, almost as an aside, Rand, the once famous climber, comes to the realization that all he ever wanted in life was "to be envied." And the only bit of advice he can offer his girlfriend at the end of the book, who has come to find him unfeeling, remote, almost like an encounter with "empty air," sounds oddly like a mountain climbing cliché:

> *"Well, what you have to do is hold on," he said. "Don't get scared."*

> *"Really?"*
>
> *"I can't tell you any more than that."*
>
> *"Hold on ...," she said.*
>
> *"That's right."*
>
> *He sees it there in the darkness, not a vision, not a sign, but a genuine shelter if only he can reach it. In the lighted room are figures, he sees them clearly, sometimes seated together, sometimes moving, a man and a woman visible through the window, in the dusk, the Florida rain.*

The simplicity and subtlety of Salter's narrative, which probes to the core of a masculine psyche in a style that one might almost describe as feminine, struck me as a rare thing at the time, and I naturally lost no time locating copies of the other two of his books that were available. A *Sport and a Pastime*, (which has recently been re-issued in a Modern Library edition,) had superb renderings of French provincial life, although to my mind the story itself was somewhat thin. *Light Years*, perhaps Salter's *chef d' oveure*, is a scintillating account of the lives of a golden couple living in the Hudson River Valley and in Manhattan. The book introduces us to a large cast of characters, and it spans many years, yet almost every scene conveys a sense of having been conjured, reflected upon, and then realized in simple, carefully selected phrases.

The Salter enigma, which a familiarity with his other books only heightened in my mind, comes down to this: how does it happen that the writer described by one critic as "the contemporary writer most admired and envied by other writers" has no readers? The answer, I think, lies in the fact that Salter's sense of what living is *about* had reached a point of rarefied sympathy for people and things even before he began to write. As a result, his books do not sustain the dramatic and psychological focus that most readers find appealing. As we watch a family disintegrate in *Light Years*, for example, we feel the pathos strongly, but we are also drawn, almost in spite of ourselves, to the beauty and vividness of the events themselves. What Salter is showing us is, in fact, both truer and deeper than either a conventionally tragic or a comic narrative can be. Life flows. It doesn't resolve itself, even though the elements of tension and drama in our own lives do. This unusual focus, which is both broad and impersonal—although it would be more accurate for us to call it omni-personal—explains why Salter is so often praised for the beauty of individual sentences: every stroke of the pen brings a minor miracle to light. It also explains why his narratives seem less to come to an emotionally satisfying conclusion than to merely peeter out.

In the spring of 1998 Salter's long-delayed memoir *Burning the Days* finally made its way into print. A segment ran in the *New Yorker* detailing his adventures working with Robert Redford on the screenplay for the film *Downhill Racer*. Clearly Salter hadn't lost his gift: the piece was suffused with the glowing and incisive descriptions I'd come to expect from him, along with plenty of self-deprecatory wit.

Not long after the book appeared I noticed that Salter was scheduled to give a reading at a local bookstore, and I asked our hardcover buyer to see if he could arrange to have him stop by the warehouse while he was in town to sign some books. Fifteen minutes later I passed the buyer on the stairs and he said "Salter will be here tomorrow at 1:30."

The moment arrived, a friend and I came upstairs to see the great man. Thoughtful, soft-spoken, not tall, dressed casually in a green and yellow hound's-tooth jacket of the type everyone over 30 used to wear in Italy, he sat signing books as we expressed our admiration as coherently, and perhaps as technically, as we could. We asked him what he was reading. Gogol's *Dead Souls*. And he was looking forward to reading Penelope Fitzgerald's *The Blue Flame*. Had we read it? He asked us a few questions, Were we writers? Had we published? And so on. I attempted to convey what I felt to be the unobtrusive wisdom of his work by referring to a passage in *Solo Faces* in which Rand, no longer a hero in Paris, could see both ends of his life for the first time.

> *Paris—it was like a great terminal he was already leaving, with a multitude of signs, neon and enamel, repeated again and again as if announcing a performance. The people of Paris with their cigarettes and dogs, the stone roofs and restaurants, green buses, gray walls, he had held their attention for a moment. The* affiches *with his face on them were vanished but he had stayed on. He saw it clearly as, at a certain place in life, one sees both the beginning and end: Paris had forgotten him.*

A lesser writer would have carried on at length about such a moment of revelation: one sees both the beginning and the end. Salter sets it adrift amid Rand's impressions of Paris in winter, of glory that has faded and turned sour.

When I mentioned the passage to Salter, however, he winced and said "Oh, now you've really depressed me, John," and he seemed genuinely, though not seriously, anguished. "Did I really say that? I say the same thing in my new book." He began thumbing through the pages. When he found the passage he held the book up to show me. It was longer, less concise, than the passage of thirty years ago. Well, the book itself is longer. Salter has given himself the luxury of dilating.

That evening we all went to hear Salter read. Afterwards he answered questions courteously, although he did show a flash of anger when some innocent reader asked him to comment on his famously exquisite style.

"I don't know what all of this is about my style," he snapped, and then added almost plaintively. "Really, have you listened to what I have just read? Could anything be simpler?"

It seemed to me that Salter was not being disingenuous here. Yet he should know as well as anyone that one or two aspects of his style are truly distinctive. He uses lingering adjectives, sustained, implied subjects, and descending half-sentences far more than any other writer I can think of. Let me give you an example, chosen more or less at random:

> *Morning; the sea sound faint on the wind. His sunburned daughters walk on creaking floors. They pass their life together, in a compact that will never end. They go to the circus, to stores, the market shed at Amagansett with its laden shelves and fruits, to picnics, pageants, concerts in wooden churches among the trees...*
>
> *They pass their life together, they pass boys fishing, walking to the end of the pier with a small eel tied, doubled up, on the hook. The mute eye of the eel calls out, a black dot on his plain, silver face. They sit at the table where their grandfather eats, Nedra's father, a salesman, a man from small towns, his cough yellow, the Camel cigarettes always near his hand...*

We note, on the one hand, the long sentences that trip along, adding descriptive material to an established subject, for example, "the daughters." In the first paragraph not only does that subject drop out, but the preposition "to" does also, so that the grammatically free-floating phrase "the market shed at Amagansett" rides on an implied "They" and also an implied "go to..." which the reader must sustain in his or her head in order to make the passage coherent. This habit of piling phrases onto an implied subject is evocative, but it necessitates that the reader proceed slowly, holding things in the mind, and everything would become a monotonous lyric purr except for the fact that Salter is also adept at shifting the frame of reference abruptly, often in the middle of a sentence. We see this, for example, when, in the second paragraph cited above, our attention is shifted first from the two daughters to the boys who are walking past them to the end of the pier, and then, in a reverse telescoping motion, from that image to the "point of view" of the eels doubled up on the fishing hook. Similarly, the grandfather who is introduced in the first part of the final sentence becomes the focus of the second part of that sentence.

These two unusual and complimentary qualities have the effect of sustaining the atmosphere of a scene without giving it any recognizable point of focus. No one *in particular* is seeing or feeling the things Salter describes, in other words, and nothing seems to be farther from his mind than advancing a plot.

When Salter asks, therefore, with respect to his prose style "Can anything be simpler than this?" the careful reader is likely to reply, "On the contrary, can anything be more *complex* than this?" And we have not even begun to consider the role of the pronoun "His" in the sentence devoted to "*His* sunburnt daughters...", or the question of who, precisely, is registering the impressions described in the first sentence: "Morning; the sea sound faint on the wind."

In *Burning the Days* both the strengths and the limitations of Salter's style are made plain. The chapters devoted to his childhood and coming of age, though they contain a number of interesting and illuminating episodes, seem slightly diffuse and poeticized. The sophistication of the rendering is not always well suited to the simplicity of the events and impressions being described. On the other hand, the early chapters do shed light on Salter's lifelong pre-occupation with failure—his father, having returned from the war, could no longer sustain his glamorous pre-war position in the world of New York real estate sales, and spent his declining years in bed. They also give us some inklings of an orientation toward women that's romantic without being entirely self-centered. It would appear that as a young man Salter was shy and deeply concerned about his manhood, as many young men are, but also unusually comfortable around women and well-liked by them. I am almost tempted to suggest that the luminescent style he developed, which reflects an unusual awareness of the radiant beauty of life as it is lived, moment by moment, is the result of his having grown up in an atmosphere of womanly affection. He is himself bold enough, at any rate, to suggest that his boyhood friend's mother, a stylish, fun-loving woman, may have "loved" him. And he describes his adolescent encounters with the opposite sex with a rhapsodic, almost corny romanticism undimmed by a lifetime of cosmopolitan living.

In succeeding chapters Salter's years in the Air Force come vividly to life: the exhilaration and the fear of the early jet fighters, the colorful and dicey life on base, the bonding among the pilots, the sometimes dreamlike beauty of actually being in the air, and the inevitability of both technical and combat disasters. All of this gives him ample pause for thought about living and dying and Fate, about being "good enough."

It is only when Salter enters the problematic world of screenwriting, however, and takes Europe and Manhattan as his locus of life and reflection, that the style and the material come fully into line with one another. Yet it's at precisely this juncture, also, that what can only be called Salter's romantic idealism, with respect both to women and to doing a job right, seems to dwindle and disappear.

One criticism leveled against *Burning the Days* has been that Salter's wife hardly appears in it. In fact, Salter even goes so far as to admit that she was hand picked for him by another woman–his best friend's wife–with whom he was in love at that time, although the affair was never consummated.

She was perfect for me, Paula said, exactly the kind of girl I needed. I believed her. Who else loved me as much or knew me as well? What she did not say was that she saw someone she knew she could be friendly with and who would not be a threat to her.

It's interesting to note that Salter describes the intense heat of his relationship with Paula in the following terms:

She was ready to give anything, do anything, and we were held apart by all that was drawing us together: honor, conscience, ideals. There was no way out.

Ten years later we find him in a hotel room in Rome with film-director John Huston's sometime mistress:

I liked her generosity and lack of morals—they seemed close to an ideal condition of living—and also the way she looked at her teeth in the mirror as she talked... Her cosmetics bag was filled with prescriptions, just as the shelf in her closet was filled with shoes... The things she said seemed to come straight from what she knew or felt, as easily as one might pick up a fork. There was no hesitation or propriety. She said things I wished I might have, things more direct.

Something has changed. Salter is well aware of the change and he's not entirely happy with it. The situation is thrown into stark relief one evening in a Paris hotel room; he makes love to his Italian mistress while, on the television screen beside the bed, his old flying companion Buzz Aldrin is lifting off on the first trip to the moon.

I have never forgotten that night or its anguish. Pleasure and inconsequence on the one hand, immeasurable deeds on the

other. I lay awake for a long time thinking of what I had
become.

But nothing in Salter's world changes, as a result of these
reflections, and nothing seems to hold him for very long. The
death of a child, the publication of a book, a dinner with
Fellini, air combat in Korea, drinks, parties, women, cities.
People and episodes float by like images seen through the
window of a moving train, made beautiful and unreal by the
tint of the glass and the gentle ululations rising up from the
rails. The Japanese phrase *Ukiyo*, which Salter gives to one
chapter of his book, might well serve as a description of the
entire last half of it. *A floating world.* Is this a good or a bad
thing?

Taken in large doses it's a bad thing, I think, because it
numbs the sense and the impact of the events Salter is trying
to describe, like those endless minor heroes in *The Iliad* who,
one after the other, take a javelin to the chest and fall to the
dust, "their armor clattering in a heap on top of them."
Judiciously nursed by the reader, on the other hand, the
import of Salter's narrative remains clear.

At one point near the end of the book Salter all but spells it
out:

> *Hers was a singular life. It had no achievements other than*
> *itself. It declared, in its own way, that there are things that*
> *matter and these are the things one must do. Life is energy, it*
> *proclaimed, life is desire. You are not meant to understand*
> *everything but to live and do certain things.*

To live and do certain things. Although aspects of Salter's life
may strike us as dissolute and naively captivated by glamour
and the trappings of wealth, there is no writer that I can think
of who takes greater care to evoke the palpable heart of all
kinds of people and things. The deftness with which he shifts

his point of view, subtly flitting lightly across a scene, has the effect of vitalizing a landscape or an event.

> We live in the consciousness of a single self, but in nature there seems to be something else, the consciousness of many, of all, the herds and schools, the colonies and hives with myriads lacking in what we call ego but otherwise perfect, responsive only to instinct. Our own lives lack this harmony. We are each of us an eventual tragedy...

It seems to me that in *Burning the Days* we catch a glimmer of this larger pulsing "self" within the human community. Salter neither aestheticizes the tragedy of living nor attempts to embrace it in an act of existential bravado, yet his glowing and insightful phrases elevate us repeatedly above it's tragic imperfections and inconstancies.

During the introduction to his reading Salter remarked that the second half of the twentieth century has produced no great American writers. I was tempted to shout out "What about you?" but that would have been an embarrassment, I immediately realized. And a humorous, yet utterly sincere, comment Salter made on another occasion came to mind:

> The writer's life exists only for a small number. It can be glorious, especially after death. There are provincial, national, and world writers—one should compete in one's class, despise riches, as Whitman says, and take one's hat off to no one.

Buzz Aldrin flew to the moon on the back of a thousand engineers, physicists, and mathematicians. On the other hand, when Salter writes:

Morning; the sea sound faint on the wind. His sunburned daughters walk on creaking floors. They pass their life together, in a compact that will never end.

he has done all the work himself—not only the work of writing, but the anguished work of living with a mind open to both the transience and the enduring import of things. It strikes me that this solitary effort takes us higher.

DEEP FRANCE

I am one of those people who love France and things French with an avidity that even I find suspect. I don't speak French, which may help. But it strikes me that the villages, the landscape, the food, and the common life of the French people exhibit a sensitivity to both conviviality and proportion that belies the common stereotype of shallow conservatism and narcissistic haughtiness (or of shallow *radicalism* and narcissistic haughtiness) that we sometimes meet up with in the media. The French have been cultivating appearances for centuries with seemingly unerring naturalness and *nonchalance*, not because they want to impress you–they don't care a whit what *you* think–but because it's simply how things are done. That, at any rate, was the impression I had gotten from repeated visits to the country during the 1980s. But things do change. The time comes when we must ask ourselves once again, Does *la belle France* actually still exist outside the frames of cliché-ridden romantic films and the pages of travel brochures? In May Hilary and I went back to find out.

We chose to visit the province of Burgundy because it offered several elements of historic and cultural interest—Romanesque architecture, Gallo-Roman archeological sites, and of course, some of the world's finest wines—but nothing that would distract us too seriously from an extended and leisurely romp across the countryside. It also carried the promise, more heavily than any other province we could think of, of the ringing depth and anonymity we were searching for.

The word *burgundy* itself summons images of a deep rich shade of red even for those who have never eaten *Boeuf á la Bourguignonne* or sampled a bottle of Corton or Puligny-Montrachet, and who perhaps have no idea that it refers not only to a color and to a type of wine, but also to a region of France. With Paris to the west, the Rhine towns to the east, France's "second city" Lyon to the south, and the commercial-industrial centers of Flanders and Picardy to the north, Burgundy floats quietly in a sea of rolling green and yellow fields, with a broad valley of world-class vineyards running down the middle of it. Dijon, the largest city in the province, is widely known only because it's a center of mustard production. The region's historic associations with Vercingetorix and the freedom-loving Gauls, with St. Bernard and his monastic Cistercian brethren, and with the dazzling Gothic court of the Dukes of Burgundy, border on genuine obscurity, although each bears the unassailable nobility of a lost cause. Even Parisians will admit that Burgundy and the Lyonnaise, its neighbor to the south, lie at the center of French gastronomy. Less obvious, perhaps, but certainly worth considering, is the notion that Burgundy lies at the center of Europe itself. But be that as it may, it's doubtful that any region of France presents better opportunities to make contact with that inexpressible *je ne sais quoi* the French themselves refer to as *La France Profonde*.

I like the bluntness of "Deep France," the standard English translation of the phrase *La France Profonde* but I'm aware that to the French themselves it carries negative connotations. *New York Times* correspondent Richard Bernstein wrote not long ago:

> *During my years in France, whenever I was going outside one of the major cities, the reaction of my Parisian friends and contacts was a bemused "Ah, you're going to La France Profonde," as if my destination were on the other side of the earth. They refer to this distant place with mockery, embarrassment, and longing, all mixed together. They regard it as a place of origin that they have escaped, grown out of, like short pants; and indeed, one of the historical purposes of La France Profonde was to send forth from its very poverty the stream of rural emigration that enabled Paris to become one of the great cities of the world.*

Although Parisians refer to *La France Profonde* condescendingly, the way we in the United States might refer to a town or region that's "out in the sticks," to many visitors the vast, old-fashioned provinces of rural France exhibit much of what's best in French civilization more openly, and less equivocally, than does Paris, Nice, or Bordeaux. The narrow free-flowing rivers, the loping hills, the fields of bright yellow mustard and pale green alfalfa; the glistening white Charolais cows drinking in the shallows along the riverbank, which make you think of a painting by a minor artist you saw once in a museum in Rouen; the Saturday markets. And the bakeries! Pastries, baguettes. A woman leaving the shop with three large white boxes tied with string and stacked one on top of the other, like something out of Proust–fruit tarts for the Saturday evening meal, no doubt. "Bonjour monsieur," as you enter, and then, as you're about to leave, "Au revoir monsieur, bonne vacances."

This last remark, "Have a nice trip," is delivered in the same cheerful, bird-like cadence as the rest, it carries no hint of annoyance or sarcasm. Everyone knows you're a foreigner, you don't speak French worth a damn. But you're their customer, maybe the first American they've served in a week. A friendly welcome and a friendly farewell.

The provinces are distinctive and lovable, then, not merely as a population pool for the great city of Paris, but as venerable repositories of history and culture themselves, where what's natural and organic commingles more freely with what's artful and humane than perhaps anywhere else on earth. This is an exaggeration, no doubt. But one thing is certain: to truly appreciate *Le France Profonde*, you have to get out into it.

There are many travelers, I know, who would like to believe this, but find it difficult to convince themselves. Perhaps the challenge lies in accepting that it would be worthwhile to spend ten days in France without visiting a major city. Châtillon-sur-Seine, the largest town we stayed in prior to the last night of our trip, has a population of 8,000. The smallest of them—Servoz, Moux, St. Léger-sur-Bibracte—you could take in any one of the three with a single turn of the head.

Our plan was to fly into Luxembourg, rent a car, and drive south into Burgundy, breezing past Metz and Nancy on the freeway the first morning before turning off onto the narrow country roads where provincial life begins. We'd visit one or two Gallo-Roman and Cistercian sites, a Renaissance chateau perhaps, and the tiny wine town of Chablis. At this point we'd circle back into the heart of the wine country surrounding Beaune, passing through the remote and depopulated hills of the Morvan on the way, and continue south to the classic Romanesque structures of Autun, Tournus, and Cluny. How long would this take? Five days? Eight days? We didn't know. The last few days of the trip remained obscure, therefore. We would have no qualms about lingering at an unusually interesting scene if one should turn up. On the other hand, things are sometimes less interesting that you anticipate. We therefore planned, time permitting, either to continue south along the Sôane to Lyon, or else to drive east up into the Alps, before making a final mad dash back to Luxembourg.

We had made no hotel reservations. The small towns of France are full of cheap hotels that are seldom close to being full. And in our determination to really get out into the country, we'd also brought along our camping gear.

Le Camping

The most difficult part of camping in France is stuffing the camping gear—in our case a tent, two sleeping bags, and one foam mattress—into a suitcase. The French countryside is littered with campgrounds; they're marked on the Michelin road map with small black diamonds. Although the precise location of the site may remain unclear, as soon as you approach the town in question you'll see a white arrow indicating the direction bearing the phrase "le camping" and the silhouette of a tent. The campgrounds themselves vary a good deal in size and tone, from urban trailer parks with swimming pools, gymnasiums, and security guards (Beaune) to large-scale commercial enterprises— "EURO•CAMP!"– with green canvas bungalows for rent facing out across the countryside from terraced hills (Meursault), to small grassy swards under chestnut trees at the edge of town with picnic tables and rudimentary toilet facilities (St. Léger-sur-Bibracte). None of the campgrounds that we stayed at had even a tinge of wildness—then again, few places in France do.

On the other hand, in Deep France urban and rural, "indoors" and "outdoors" are not that far removed from one another. This makes it possible to set up your tent near a village, or even within its confines, and still feel that you're actually "camping out."

The most well-developed of the campsites we visited on our trip was on a narrow reservoir a few miles outside the town of Semur-en-Auxois. It had a beach, a diving raft, a concession stand, and volleyball pits like a resort in the Catskills. The camping area was a vast grid of asphalt lanes spreading through the trees and lawn on the side of the hill. There may have been two hundred sites available, although very few of them were taken. The one we chose was at the edge of the compound, a small sward of green surrounded and enclosed on three sides by a choice selection of ornamental shrubs–buckthorns, honeysuckles, currants, junipers–all of which were modest in size and aggressively pruned. The lawn itself was a fresh bright green with clumps of white clover here and there. We had chosen the site because it was private, but also because it offered, on the side facing the lane, a stunning panorama of the Burgundian countryside. Not long after we'd set up our tent, to our dismay, a young Frenchman at the site a few slots down from ours began singing "Here's to You, Mrs. Robinson..." in English while strumming on a cheap guitar.

The municipal campground in Noyers-sur-Serein, in contrast, lay right in the center of the village, surrounded by a long brick wall. Having followed the appropriate signs through the narrow streets of the village, which is sandwiched into a hairpin loop of the river Serein, we parked in front of the open wooden gate of the enclosure and looked inside. One end of the enclosure contained a sandy play area, a stand of tall cottonwood trees, and a collection of outbuildings that appeared to be in very poor condition. The other end was nothing more than a wooded field covered with dark green grass more than a foot high, with dandelions (long gone to seed) here and there, and car tracks crossing back and forth in no particular pattern or direction. A rusty metal trailer with a screen-and-canvas extension stood at the far end of the enclosure, seemingly permanently positioned on the spot. Laundry was hanging from a line behind the trailer, though there were no inhabitants in sight.

We drove in, breaking twigs as we bounced across the rough ground. Grass rushed against the bottom of the car and white dandelion seeds were sent drifting everywhere. We set up our tent near a bench not far from the rear wall of the enclosure, took a closer look at our neighbor's en-campment—there were dishes drying in the sink—and walked back out through the gate out into town.

Noyers-sur-Serein is a village of little distinction, which is why we'd chosen to visit it. It has a museum of local naive art that we didn't explore, and a fine town square with wood-timbered arcades that the antique dealers make use of in displaying their merchandise, but for the most part it's simply a French riverside village that hasn't changed much since the fifteenth century.

We walked along the river embankment as the sun was going down, with the town battlements above us to the right—a succession of round stone towers and lower fortress walls, both long since converted to private dwellings. Three gleaming white Charolais cows had climbed down the sandy bank of the quiet river and were standing knee-deep in water. Other cows were grazing in the bright green field beyond, and off in the distance an impressive chateau caught the last of the sunlight from its perch on the crest of the hill. It has been rumored that an underground tunnel once linked the town and the chateau, so that the lords of the place could make their escape should the need arise. If this is actually true, it seems to me the tunnel is a more impressive engineering feat than the walls themselves: the chateau is at least a mile away.

What is obvious, in any case, is that at one time this region, now so pastoral, was at the center of considerable strife, as petty barons muscled their way back and forth across the pretty countryside.

Of greater interest to me than this bloody and commonplace history, as we strolled along, or sat on the embankment wall looking back at the towers we'd passed, while cheap European cars rattled noisily by and other strollers paused to chat with friends leaning out from windows in the stone walls above them, was the character of the river itself. Though less than twenty feet across, it seemed to flow strongly and steadily, and I had the sense that it did so all summer long, rather than drying to a trickle as so many small streams do. I had noticed this earlier in the trip. Famous rivers like the Meuse and the Somme and even the Seine were in fact tiny streams, but everything about them suggested that they flowed steadily.

What gave me that impression? I don't know. Maybe it was simply the fact that rivers where I come from tend to be either large indomitable creatures—the Mississippi, the Minnesota—or muddy creeks meandering through cornfields with crumbling banks and deadfalls everywhere. Centuries of rural grooming certainly make a difference.

On this score a remark by the French biologist René Dubos may be worth repeating. Dubos was raised in a tiny village in the Île de France, a few hours north of the country we were visiting, in the midst of similarly bucolic scenery. His scientific and ecological interests have taken him to many parts of the world during his long career, which gives this description of his native region a more detached, and less merely sentimental thrust:

Ever since the primeval forest was cleared by Neolithic settlers and medieval farmers, the province of the Ile de France has retained a humanized charm that transcends its natural endowments. To this day, its land has remained very fertile, even though much of it has been in continuous use for more than two thousand years. Far from being exhausted by intensive agriculture over such long periods of time, the land still supports a large population and a great variety of human settlements. Its hamlets, villages, towns, and cities have uninterruptedly nurtured the glories and follies of civilization, despite the ebb and flow of men's fortunes.

This sense of humanized charm presents itself to you repeatedly in the villages and countryside of Burgundy. The quality is perhaps more autochthonic, more deeply ingrained in the landscape, however, than the word "charm" can suggest. The population of the region has been falling in recent decades, it's true, with the closing of antiquated metal-fabrication plants, the increasing mechanization of agriculture, and Paris only two or three hours away, but the countryside looks neither poor nor desperate. The world we looked out on from the modest stone embankment of Noyers-sur-Serein is the world of Proust, Perrault, Montaigne, and Marie de France! It's our world too, of course. We were formed by its tastes, and we feel very much at home within its confines.

We returned to our campsite to find that an enormous flock of crows had settled into the stand of cottonwoods behind the playground. They were making an awful squawking racket that continued well into the night. We set out a cold supper of bread, cheese, and fruit on the bench beside our tent, and while we were eating it a dilapidated van came roaring through the gate into the enclosure. The driver, who didn't even glance our way as he sped past us, had wild black hair and a scruffy beard, and he reminded me of a photograph by Nadar of Theophile Gautier. After rustling around in his trailer for a few minutes, the man returned to his van, slammed the door, and returned the way he'd come. Off for a drink in town with his buddies? Who could say? We heard him return to his trailer-shack late in the night. The crows had quieted down, I could almost hear the river murmur as I drifted back to sleep, and I dreamed of Resistance fighters tunneling under the bright green fields.

The campground at Ste. Marie-sur-Ouche, a village twenty miles west of Dijon, was a single loop set in a field south of town. A Vietnamese man was cutting grass with a push mover in front of a rusty yellow trailer when we arrived. We chose an "unofficial" site at the opposite end of the field, through an open gate and close to the river, from which point we could see the village rising on the opposite bank. The local official who came to collect a fee as we were eating our dinner didn't seem to mind our choice in the least. A large white horse was drinking in a dried-up pool at the edge of the river a few yards beyond our tent. I examined the thin wire fence carefully to make sure that there was no point at which this creature could climb the bank and startle us in our sleep, but late in the night he began whinnying and stomping rocks violently with his huge feet, and I woke up wondering whether we weren't on the verge of being trampled to death.

One campground we chose was set on the hillside a half-mile above the east side of Lac D'Annecy. Forty or fifty sites stretched in three rows along the side of the mountain under pollarded trees, although we had the place entirely to ourselves. We spent the evening watching colorful hang-gliders drift out from the cliffs behind our heads and soar silently down across the lake.

The campground at Servoz, higher up in the Alps near Chamonix, was similarly deserted. Lying on our backs exhausted after an afternoon of high-altitude walking, we could see Mt. Blanc, towering huge and white, through the open door of the tent.

My favorite site, however, was nestled in a valley below the highway just outside the village of Ste. Léger-sur-Bibracte.

The village itself is like a Wild West town stretched along two sides of a dusty and treeless municipal square. There would be no reason to visit the place except that it stands very near the famous hill of Bibracte itself–hence the name. Only in the last few decades have archeologists largely come to agree that this hill, which has served as the setting for Mayday festivals since time immemorial, was also the site at which the Celtic tribes for the first time congregated to elect a leader in 52 B.C., in an effort to defend themselves against a formidable opponent by the name of Julius Caesar. A large modern museum of pre-history has been built in the trees on the flank of the hill, but the hilltop itself is still covered with grassy meadows, ancient and gnarly chestnut trees, and dusty archeological sites.

A seven-kilometer trail climbs up through the woods and fields from the campground to the top of the hill, and I'm sure there's no better way to get into the spirit of Celtic defiance or medieval fertility rites than to take it. We, however, chose to drive. Although the ruins themselves are relatively uninspiring, the view across the countryside from the top of the hill is superb. Even more impressive to me was the shady uncluttered woods at the summit. The grounds have been considered sacred from the time of the Druids until the present day: they've never been built on.

In the evening we returned to our little encampment on the bright green grass under the trees. We parked in one site, set up our tent in a second, and, feeling expansive after a day spent in contemplating the titanic struggle that lies at the root of modern European culture, we ate dinner at a third, on a picnic table overlooking a little duck-pond. In the distance the gentle rounded hills of the Morvan caught the pink evening light; the trees were in their fresh early-summer glory. Pale white clouds stretched across the soft blue sky. The entire scene had the exquisite bloom of a painting by Poussin.

I have made no mention of cooking because we didn't bring cooking gear with us. Every morning we broke camp, washed up, and drove to the nearest town or village for coffee and croissants, our faces still perhaps a trifle smudged with soot from the evening fire, and with one or two tangles of hair sticking out at wild angles. One morning it would be a large modern *brasserie* in Avallon crowded with kids on their way to school playing pinball or gossiping in small groups, and the next a tiny hotel dining-room in Semur-en-Auxois with a big fireplace, heavy walnut molding, glass and silver serving dishes, grumpy half-asleep couples sitting in silence across the way, beautiful print tablecloths, cloth napkins, and yellow striped wallpaper out of a novel by Balzac. Our evening meal would often consist of apples, bread, cheeses, olives, and a bakery quiche, with the addition of a rabbit pate, a chunk of salami, or a can of cassoulet with a big piece of duck confit at the bottom of it. Eating this way can get old, however, even in a nation with the culinary resources France possesses. After two or three days "in the field" nothing sounded better to us than a warm bed and a hot shower at a country hotel, preceded by a leisurely meal in its dining room.

Le Cuisine

The French are well known for their almost religious approach to eating, and also, not surprisingly, for the quality of their food. At the same time it's been repeatedly muttered ever since Elizabeth David introduced the masses of the English-speaking world to the glories of French cuisine in the fifties that the French are, in fact, *too* fussy about such things; and that in any case, restaurants have been going down hill for a long time now. In recent years a new strain has been added to the critical backlash—that the French no longer care about food at all! One sociologist at the University of Paris has remarked: "The French have definitely turned away from the obsession with good food that was characteristic of previous generations. The young in particular regard serious interest in food as old-fashioned, even archaic." And the cultural historian Alaine Lemoise has observed, "Interest in good food has declined to the point that within a few years France will have only about 30 or 40 luxury restaurants. The remainder will be fast-food places and inexpensive Asian restaurants."

These views carry the shock value of all cheap journalism—Man bites dog: French can't cook—but they don't bear any relation to the culinary values that animate the French restaurants that I've visited from time to time over the years. I'll be the first to admit that I am not, nor will I ever be, a food "expert." When we eat out in Minneapolis, Hilary and I are likely to visit an affordable store-front restaurant like Chet's, Giorgio's, Lucia's, 128 Cafe, or the Zander Cafe, and I'm more likely to be impressed than disappointed by the preparations. In France, however, things are very different.

Let me give you an example. We arrived one afternoon in the hamlet of Moux, after several days of camping out, and we checked into the local hotel, which stood on a hillside overlooking the small cluster of buildings that constituted the town. We showered and rested up, looking out the screenless window of our room across the fields and woods to the smoke rising from the chimneys in the village below. A young man was watering down a gravel terrace under the window. We walked up the hill to another terrace behind the hotel, and then up a long flight of concrete steps to the door of the hotel's restaurant. Auto-racing and cycling posters were hanging neatly framed behind the bar. The dining area off to the left was a large room with windows on three sides looking out across the hills and down into the valley beyond the town, where fog was beginning to collect. Pink napkins, white tablecloths, wine and water glasses that sparkled in the low evening sunlight.

Our waiter, a teenaged boy wearing the traditional white jacket, led us to a table at the far end of the room with the formal, but not quite officious, bearing characteristic of his trade, and he preserved this sober-minded and polite but never "chilly" demeanor throughout the meal. He didn't tell us his name, nor did he ask us how we "were this evening." We examined the menu, and ordered from the *prix fixe* selections. Our waiter brought the wine and placed it in a freestanding ice bucket alongside the table before wrapping a white cloth napkin across the top of it. The food was brought to us course by course, and, as the sun went down, we ate.

I'm not going to give you a blow-by-blow account of the meal, but I will remark, *contra* the sociologists and cultural historians I referred to a moment ago, that when I took my first sip of the soup that was my first course, the thought that leaped unbidden into my head was: "They don't cook like this in Minneapolis!"

The dish in question was called *oeufs en meurette*. At the time I ordered it I had no idea what it was, although I'd seen it on a number of sidewalk menu displays and presumed it was a traditional Burgundian specialty. In any case, I was a little surprised when a bowl of rich red broth was set in front of me, in which two poached eggs, not white but red like the sauce, were glistening. Although tiny shreds of parsley had been sprinkled across the surface of the dish, there was something vaguely menacing about that suave and silky lump of barely cooked matter staring up at me from the dish. The single piece of toast resting on the side of the dish was reassuring. Only later, as I began to analyze the complex of flavors caressing my palate, did I notice tiny shreds of bacon submerged in the soup.

What we're dealing with here, my friends, is "bacon and eggs." But in Burgundy they do things differently. First, you chop an onion and some garlic, and then add them, along with a *bouquet garni*, to a pan containing half a bottle of red Burgundy. Simmer for twenty minutes. Meanwhile, you cut and grill the bread, and rub it with raw garlic, and you also fry and drain the bacon. You add the bacon, broken into bits, to the simmering wine for a further ten minutes, then strain the wine and return it to the pan along with the bits of bacon you've fished out of the strainer. Now you can poach the eggs in the wine. But just when you think you're finished, you must remove the poached eggs from the pan and set them aside while you whisk a *beurre manié* into the wine to thicken it and simmer for five more minutes. Finally, you pour the glistening, buttery, slightly thickened wine over the eggs, sprinkle with parsley, and serve.

I found this recipe in a book not long ago. Otherwise I would still not know what it was I was eating that day. I have no idea how the chef at the Beau-Site in Moux actually makes his *oeufs en meurette,* but I do know that the result was remarkably rich and at the same time full of very familiar flavors.

The rest of the meal was similarly subtle and complex, from the pork navarin to the potato gratin laced with something—was it cardamom?—to the home-made green-apple ice-cream served with a side of Calvados. The bottle of Chablis Premier Cru, which would have been well beyond our budget on this side of the Atlantic, did nothing to diminish our dining pleasure. And as a final touch, which may seem a commonplace but is not, every course was served to us piping hot.

We were the only diners at the Beau-Site Hotel that night. We walked back through the formal garden and down the hill to our hotel in the dark. No cars on the road. The air was cool, a few lights in the village. In the morning we were awakened by two swallows fluttering noisily a few feet above our heads, having flown into the room through the open window. When we came down for breakfast I recognized the boy in jeans planting flowers in front of the hotel—he'd been our waiter the previous evening. The owner's son, perhaps. The tall, friendly, blue-eyed man who had showed us to our room, and who had also appeared proprietarily from the swinging kitchen door during our evening meal, was likely the owner himself. He seemed very pleased when, after we'd settled the bill, Hilary told him how much we'd enjoyed our meal and our stay.

Les Vins

Above all else, Burgundy is famous for its wines. In fact the region is widely considered, along with Bordeaux, to be one of the two premier wine-growing regions in the world. It covers a much smaller area than Bordeaux, however, and the consequent scarcity of supply has resulted in generally formidable prices. The system of nomenclature and classification is Byzantine, the climate is unreliable, and the predominant grape under cultivation, the *pinot noir*, is challenging and often disappointing. All of this makes the region perhaps too daunting to be approached, much less explored thoroughly, by anyone who is concerned about how much wines cost.

At any rate this was the rationale that served for many years to justify my almost total avoidance of the region. Couldn't afford it; couldn't understand it; probably wouldn't like it much in any case. A single counter-argument presented itself from time to time in the form of a bottle of fine Burgundy served at the house of a friend of mine who was crazy about the stuff. A Beaune here, a Musigny there. Although I didn't know quite what I was drinking, these infrequent experiences were enough to reinforce what I already knew to be a fact: the judgment of the wine-drinking world is not, by in large, based on fashion and pretense; it is not for nothing, in other words, that Burgundy is considered one of the two supreme wine-making regions in the world. I also began to recognize that the appeal of the red wines of Burgundy comes from a somewhat different source than does that of the red wines of Bordeaux. The *pinot noir* grape, which dominates in Burgundy, often produces a wine that's light, harsh, pinched, shrill, and simple. The prevalent variety of grape grown in Bordeaux, on the other hand, *cabernet sauvignon*, can sometimes have a weight of tannin and complexity that's satisfying, even at the lowest levels of price and production. What the fine Burgundies I was being exposed to offered was that same pinot noir lightness—as opposed to a cabernet's more familiar tannic and oaky richness—which, however, immediately opened out to a wealth of overtones and embellishments that stood in perfect harmony with one another. The effect was subtle and astonishing.

The white wines of Burgundy, on the other hand, have always been considered the finest white wines in the world. And these wines have the advantage of extending from the most exalted productions of Chablis, Meursault, and Montrachet, through the middle range of Poilly-Fuisse and Montagny, down to the humblest Mâcon-Village, all of which are made from the Chardonnay grape. You can work your way up among the whites, in other words. Beaujolais red, on the other hand, has little more in common with Burgundy than the frequently mediocre gamay grape from which it is made has with the elevated pinot noir.

But wine talk is boring. To the traveler, what makes the wine region of Burgundy interesting to pass through is the fact that its noble vintages are scattered, intermixed, municipal, and therefore diffuse. Unlike the chateaux of Bordeaux, which are discrete properties with boundaries, *chais*, and centralized compounds at once domestic and vinicultural—Chateau Margaux over there and Ducru-Beaucaillou over here, beyond the hedge—the communes and properties of Burgundy are split among multiple owners and growers in the manner of medieval strip-farms. To complicate the issue, the production from these small plots is often sold to shippers who combine and bottle them under their own more or less distinguished labels. When you drive the D113, which is a tiny two-lane asphalt road just up the hill from the main highway connecting Cagny and Beaune, you pass the farm workers in their pale blue trucks and their bizarre modern vine-tending tractors, and the signs read Puligny-Montrachet, Meursault, Volnay, Pommard, like the index of a wine-guide. The grapevines stretch away in both directions like a calm even sea of brown and green, divided by rock walls at irregular intervals, and you feel that you're in the midst of something serious, dedicated, and grand. Agricultural, yes, but also grand. You know it, because you've tasted it. It's not the same effect as that of actually drinking a glass of a very fine wine. It merely compliments that other, more personal and sensual experience.

Needless to say, every village along the *Côte d' Or* is well supplied with shops offering samplings and sales of the local product. To those of us who don't speak French, the sheer magnitude of the array of offerings can be intimidating, not to mention the natural, if perhaps self-imposed, feeling that having sampled the wares, you really ought to buy something. Wouldn't it be easier simply to pick up a bottle of undistinguished local wine from the wire rack at the corner grocery store for a few dollars, probably bottled on a very small scale from vineyards out in the flat land on the wrong side of the highway, or up in the hills on either side of the "Côte"? It's surprising how fresh and good even this kind of wine can be.

Late in the day Hilary and I did work up the nerve to enter a shop in the village of Gevrey-Chambertin, attracted by the chalk-board sign, in English, French, and German (but what about the Italians?) testifying to the friendly welcome and the home-spun concern for sincere wine appreciation we'd meet

up with inside. The interior was darkly lit, it had a high
ceiling, and there was dark wood everywhere, so that I almost
felt I'd stepped into a log cabin in the Rockies, or a rustic
Swiss *gite* at the very least. Several bottles shaped in the
bottom-heavy Burgundian style stood open on a heavy wooden
table near the front of the shop, beyond which rows of barrels,
cardboard wine cases, and the bookkeeping paraphernalia of a
family business stretched back into the shadows. An immense
St. Bernard dozed in the darkness under the heavy table. (At
the time it didn't occur to me that the dog is named after the
saint we call St. Bernard, who spent most of his life in
Burgundy.)

A lean young man with short-cropped black hair wearing
jeans and a white T-shirt stood behind the table discussing the
merits of the wine he'd opened for review with two pudgy
middle-aged men from Nantes wearing roadster's caps. (How
do I know they were from Nantes? One of them told me.)
They spoke quietly, almost murmuring; from time to time
they would swirl the red liquid in the glass to summons the
aroma, and then take a sip reflectively.

I walked up next to the Nantiers to examine the price-list
that was lying in a plastic sheath on the table. (Not cheap.)
We looked at the labels. (Premier Cru.) The young man (was
he a clerk, a grower, an oenologist, the owner's son?) turned
his attention momentarily to us. "Yes, I can understand a little
English, if you speak slowly." I suggested that perhaps we
might try one of the '95s (which, being younger, were
cheaper,) but– "Oh, no, we do not consider that vintage
ready to sample yet. It's very big and rough." And he poured
us one of the '94s. And it was very good.

Meanwhile, the three Frenchmen returned to their
conversation. The clerk had produced a detailed map, and he
was pointing out where, on the august slope of Gevrey-
Chambertin, the tiny strip of land was located that had
produced the grapes that had gone into this particular wine.

The strip had a name, as do all strips of land that have been designated "Premier Cru." It was called *Les Cazetiers*.

I mention this fact, not because it's intrinsically important, but merely to suggest how far you can go in defining the source of a bottle of Burgundy wine. The region, the town, the commune, the producer, the shipper, the individual plot of ground, which may be as small as four acres–someday they may even start naming the individual grapes!

The Nantiers left and our clerk, who I liked merely because he was courteous and wore a white T- shirt, came over to us again. I asked to see the map and he showed us the map. He poured us a sample from another strip of land called *Combes aux Moines*, and all I could think of to say to him–very slowly– was this: "We've just been in Beaune, and we've sampled a good many wines there today, but nothing we tasted had the quality and substance of the wine we're tasting here."

Back in Minneapolis a week later I looked up the proprietor whose shop we'd happened upon in a wine guide:

> *Philippe Leclerc walks to the beat of a different drummer (probably from a British rock group). And while he could be taken for a member of the Hell's Angels, there is no doubt that he is a great winemaker. There is a fearsome intensity to him that is translated to his wines... The Les Cazetiers (one of the great vineyards of this appellation) is extravagantly rich and luxurious, is loaded with layers of sumptuous fruit, and has mind-boggling length. As hard as it is to believe, the Combe aux Moines is close to perfection...*

It seems we'd picked a winner.

But perhaps the merit of Leclerc's wines might not have
been so clearly evident had we not spent the early part of
the afternoon at the *Marché aux Vins* in Beaune. This institution
serves the purpose of allowing you to sample the wines from
a variety of vintages and communes without driving hither and
yon all over the countryside. The admission charge is little
more than what a single glass of wine would cost at an
American wine bar, and it seems to me that this may be the
world's greatest travel value. They give you a little silver-
plated *tastevin* when you enter, like the ones traditionally used
to sample wines at Burgundian festivals. You descend a
twisting flight of stone stairs and find yourself in a dark
cavernous hallway with a gravel floor. Barrels have been set
up at intervals, and you can see by the dim candlelight that
there are half-corked wine-bottles sitting on top of each of
them. You've been given a cardboard "scorecard" to keep track
of what you'll be drinking as you move down the row.
Halfway through the *degustation* the circuit winds back upstairs
into a gothic chapel. When you finally emerge from this
second round of samples you'll be in the salesroom, naturally.
The route is clear. Nothing remains but to pour, sniff, sip,
and ponder, before jotting down a few notes, and then
advance at a leisurely pace to the next sampling station.

A complete recount of our slow progress down this dark
tunnel of delights would be too long in the telling. Not
surprisingly, older and more distinguished Premier Cru wines
scored higher than younger wines from less vaunted districts.
Thus, among the whites on my card, the Hospices de Dijon,
Meursault 1er Cru 1991 has the word "best" penciled in,
while the Chambolle-Musigny 1er Cru 1986 has the only "10"
among the reds. Of greater practical value, however, is the
note alongside Marsannay 1991: "7, excellent value." After
all, this is a wine one might almost afford to buy a bottle of.

In the end, we stepped out into the bright lights of the
salesroom, having sampled and compared eighteen of the

many fine wines of the Côte de Beaune. The differences between the wines were many, subtle, and largely inarticulable, and the family resemblances were no less pronounced. We had developed a slightly better command of the basic nomenclature of the region, if nothing else, and we had certainly had a good time. We also got to keep our tastevins as souvenirs!

L'histoire

Burgundy is, first and foremost, the land of the portage. (I'll explain what I mean in a minute.) It's also the land of the barbarians. It's the land of the rise of Christian European, as opposed to pagan Mediterranean, culture. It's also the land where the dream of a particularist Europe stumbled badly.

It would be tedious to elaborate these diverse facets of the region's history in any degree of detail. In any case, that's not how they present themselves to the tourist. What happens is this: You walk along the banks of the Seine on a bright spring morning in the town of Châtillon-sur-Seine. The river, so solid and majestic by the time it gets to Paris, is no more than fifteen feet wide at this point. You pass the church on the hill where St. Bernard, then a student and not yet a saint, heard the voices that inspired his entry into the monastic life. But you barely pause, or perhaps merely climb the steep steps going up to the church for a brief look inside. You're on your way to the local museum, which is housed in a beautiful Renaissance hôtel at the center of town. The walls of that building are covered with ivy, there's a well-kept garden running along the street. Inside, on the second floor of the museum, where the wooden floors creak badly, an entire room has been devoted to a display of the remains of a single Celtic tomb.

The artifacts were unearthed in a field a few miles outside of town, near a hamlet called Vix, and they've been dated to

500 B.C.. To judge from the enormous gold toque, the silver dishes, and the intricately wrought buttons and brooches found on and around the body in the tomb, the dead woman was undoubtedly some sort of princess. But the most curious of the artifacts uncovered in the tomb is a bronze vase six feet high with elaborate Greek *bas relief* all around the edge. Archeologists are confident the enormous vase was crafted in Sicily or Calabria. What on earth is it doing in a farmer's field in the middle of Burgundy?

The answer is to be found in the artifact itself. Bronze is made of copper and tin. Tin comes from England. The easiest inland route from England to the Mediterranean runs up the Seine from the English channel, continuing past Paris to the last navigable point, which is a few miles upstream from the museum. From there goods must be carried overland to the upper reaches of the Sôane, where they begin their downstream journey to the sunny South. It would be reasonable to suppose that the families or tribes who controlled the overland route between the two watersheds would be wealthy and powerful.

At the time when this young woman was buried, Celtic tribes were spread across the interior of Europe from the English Channel to Budapest, while the Romans were a small tribe living on one or two hills near the Tiber river, surrounded on all sides by far more sophisticated Etruscans. The Greeks who had colonized southern Italy were the most advanced people in the region. Yet it struck me, as I stood examining the mysterious dark vessel, that although it was enormous and elaborate and Greek, and obviously very difficult to make, it was less well shaped than the solid, simple, and elegantly crafted personal ornaments, which were both Celtic and dazzlingly beautiful.

Rome developed considerably in the centuries that followed, of course, finally becoming the dominant power in the Italian peninsula. During the last years of the Republic, Julius

Caesar set out to subdue the Gaulic tribes north of Rome, and succeeded to such a degree that he brought not only the Po valley under Roman jurisdiction, but also most of the region we now refer to as France. If you drive south a few miles from Châtillon you'll come to the village of Alésia. It's set on the side of a hill, although archeologists have uncovered remains of a much larger settlement on the top. This ancient city was the last major stronghold of the Celts against Roman domination. Military historians armed with aerial photographs have reconstructed the siege in considerable detail, but for the simple tourist the result is all that matters: Caesar took the city, captured the Celtic leader Vercingetorix, and in so doing brought the entirety of Gaul under Roman domination once and for all.

Looking over the ruins of the city I could not help but

think of similar conflicts between the Native Americans and the conquering Europeans fifteen hundred years later. It's even true that in opening the country north of the Alps, hitherto largely unknown territory, to Roman exploitation, Caesar's conquest has an effect on the Roman imagination similar to that of Columbus's discovery of the new world. At Alésia the *frisson* is heightened by the fact that it's unclear which side we're supposed to identify with. Are we the Romans, or are we the Celts? For Northern Europeans and European-Americans the answer must be that we're both.

The Romans succeeded in subduing the Celts, it's true, but they themselves were overwhelmed in turn a few centuries later by waves of barbarians from the east. The subsequent appearance of Vikings from the north and Saracens from the south didn't make matters any easier for the nascent Burgundian and Frankish kingdoms that had sprouted in the region. In one famous incident (c. 954) Conrad of Burgundy deftly played warring Huns and Saracens one against the other, promising aid to each side in turn and finally intervening to crush them both. He has come down to us in history as Conrad the Peaceful, which may tell us something about the other leading figures of that dark period.

During those unruly times the Catholic Church, more than any other institution perhaps, provided a thread of civilization and continuity. Cloistered monasticism in particular, which had gotten its start in Italy, ran rampant in Burgundy, first with the houses of the Clunaic order, and later with those of the more austere Cistercians.

Monastic institutions have, in recent times, begun to shed their centuries-old image as crusty anachronisms. The cultivation of peace, manual work, solitude, and learning, unencumbered by an excessive and self-centered materialism, was promoted very successfully by Benedict and other early leaders of the movement, and these values seem somewhat in need of reemphasizing today. All the same, it would be difficult for us to properly assay the important role played by monastic institutions in early European life and culture, not only on a spiritual, but also on a practical level. Their central role in preserving documents is well known, of course, but their learned contributions over the years to material culture are hardly less significant. Medicine, agriculture, medicine, wine making, hydraulics.

From Alésia it's a very short drive northwest along country roads to the Abbey of Fontenay. Of the 1500 or so abbeys founded by the Cistercian order in the twelfth and thirteenth centuries this, only the third to be established, is one of the very few that have survived intact. It stands in the woods beyond the town of Montbard. Hilary and I walked two miles through the woods along paths carpeted in flowering myrtle, past the ruins of the abbey's enormous fish farm—Fontenay was famous for its trout—hoping to arrive at the monastery in a properly reverent spirit.

We emerged from the forest onto a large gravel parking lot half-filled with cars. Once beyond this eyesore, the well-kept and extensive grounds of the abbey presented themselves. We explored the famous church, the chapter-house, the cloister, the bishop's residence, the infirmary, the foundry, and other buildings, spread out across acres of green grass in the standard Cistercian pattern, with gravel paths and fruit-trees in the courtyards. The scene was impressive, and quite unlike the airy and pastoral ruins so widespread in England. In fact, the grounds are so well groomed—the place is now used as a private conference center—that the abbey complex seems more like a modern college campus than a medieval monastery, and I had to keep reminding myself that these austerely beautiful buildings, whose architecture and pattern of arrangement are so familiar to us, were built in the twelfth century, in the midst of a landscape so remote that it might properly have been referred to as a wilderness. Then again, the International Institute of Industrial Archeology has affixed a brass plaque to the wall of the abbey foundry identifying the site as "the birthplace of the Industrial Revolution." It isn't merely that the monks of Fontenay mined and forged their own iron; evidently they were the first to make use of a waterwheel to pound the metal.

To get a sense of the secular style of the same period we drove half an hour west to the tiny village of Vézelay. It's perched dramatically on the top of a hill, and I can well imagine that during the summer months the single narrow street that winds up the backbone of the hill through the village to the cathedral must be unpleasantly crowded with tourists, yet on the sunny May morning when we were there it was deserted. Shops selling local cheese, wines, postcards, CDs, ice cream, and costume jewelry lined the street. Pale blue wisteria hung from walls and doorframes. The facade of the cathedral itself finally came into view: a pleasantly odd, irregular, construction, seemingly neither Romanesque nor gothic, but somehow strangely Byzantine.

Vézelay was at one time a major pilgrimage site, and it was down this narrow street that penitents set off on the famous route to Santiago de Compostela in northern Spain. The second crusade, led by Philip the Fair and Richard Lionheart, started off for Jerusalem from the valley beneath these walls. Now pilgrims come here to view the capital carvings on the columns in the interior of the church.

It's certainly well worth the trip. The interior of the cathedral, which is made of a light stone with dark ribs in the Italian fashion, is surprisingly beautiful, and the capitals themselves—more than a hundred in all, mostly devoted to scenes from the Old Testament—are naive, charming, vigorous, and fraught with meaning like the figures on a pack of tarot cards. Cramped as they are into spaces no more that a few feet wide, and towering thirty or forty feet above your head, it would be difficult to tell what many of them depict without the aid of the *Blue Guide,* which identifies them all. We spent an hour or more craning our necks to examine and admire them, and when we later sat on a stone bench in front of the church looking out across the green fields down the long road that once lead either to Spain or Jerusalem, I felt I had caught a faint glimmer of the fabulous, crude, romantic, and bizarre world which medieval Christendom was. Or perhaps it was simply the pain in my neck, or the crazy sound of bees buzzing in the white blossoms of the chestnut tree above my head.

There are many other historical sites in Burgundy of which I might make mention, from the cliffs at Solutré where, thousands of years ago, prehistoric man drove vast herds of horses to their death for no apparent reason (the Solutrian era is named after the site), to the factories at La Creusot where the enameled cast-iron pots many of us use in our kitchens today are manufactured; but the most distinctly Burgundian of them all, perhaps, is in Dijon, where the tombs of the last two dukes of Burgundy are on exhibit.

There is something strange about seeing a tomb in a museum, even if the museum is located in the palace of the individuals buried there. The tombs of Philip the Good and Charles the Bold are remarkably beautiful nevertheless, and more than that. What the sculptor has done is to carve, out of marble, in miniature, the full-bodied images and visages of the men and women who mourned the death of these two dukes. You can walk around the two royal figures, rendered in full, reclining above the tombs where they lay, and you can scrutinize their polychrome limbs, their impassive faces. But it is the mourners, much smaller, in white, who appear distinctive, animated, individual, and alive. They stand in groups of two and three, 18 inches high, under the coffins, speaking in low tones about the loss, either personal or political, and every face looks different, every visage has personality. These two tombs may be the greatest tombs in the world. Greater than the Pyramids? Well I don't know. But they do convey how profoundly death looms over and dominates the living in its anonymous and irrevocable finality, without obscuring the fact that life, even when it is small and colorless, is infinitely more varied, interesting, and lovable.

Yes, but who were these men? Who were the Dukes of Burgundy? We return again to the issue of the identity of Burgundy itself.

The first Burgundians came, if historians of the era are to be believed, from southern Sweden or Norway, by way of an island off the coast of Sweden called Bornholm, (but until relatively recent times "Burgundarholm"). They settled in Poland, South Germany, and finally, very soon after the sack of Rome by the Goths in 410, in an area surrounding the city of Geneva. Members of the ruling clan of the Burgundian tribes were known as Nibelungs, which is to say sons of Nifils, god of the northern mists. It was these Nibelungs who, in 436, were defeated by the forces of Attila the Hun, in a battle that's been described as "the most important theme of the epic of northern Europe."

This epic defeat, which appears in Beowulf, the Icelandic sagas, and of course in Wagner's *The Ring of the Nibelung*, does not concern us at present, however. The Burgundian state of those early years lay entirely east of the Sôane. The Burgundy that does interest us arose later, as a kind of "middle kingdom" between France and Germany, (neither of which actually existed at the time,) following the death of Charlemagne in 814. This kingdom had associations with both Spain and Provence from an early date, and it stretched from the North

Sea to Italy. The history of this middle zone is riddled with bewildering intricacies, but we must number among its offspring the Low Countries, the kingdom of Savoy, (from which modern Italy developed,) and the Duchy of Burgundy, which rose to an unusual degree of prominence during the Hundred Year's War, at a time when the French monarchy was at low ebb. In those days Burgundy included much of what we now call Belgium and the Netherlands. Those familiar with Shakespeare's historical plays have at least an inkling of the role played by the Burgundians as an ally of the British against the French. The single most telling detail, perhaps, is this: when Constantinople fell to the Turks in 1453, the Pope sent out an appeal to initiate a new crusade against the Infidel, and this appeal was directed, not to the king of England, or to the king of France, nor to the (German) Holy Roman Emperor, but to Philip the Good, Duke of Burgundy.

The Duke did not initiate a new crusade, however; rather, he held a lavish party in honor of the invitation, in which elephants were included, and 28 musicians leaped from the crust of an enormous pie. Profiting from the wealth that merchants and industrialists in the Low Countries derived from the textile industry, yet retaining an older chivalric ceremonial tradition, the Burgundians were acknowledged masters of such extravagant entertainments.

More generally speaking, one historian of the era writes:

All aristocratic life in the later Middle Ages is a wholesale attempt to act the vision of a dream. In cloaking itself in the fanciful heroism and probity of a past age, the life of the nobles elevated itself toward the sublime...The court was pre-eminently the field where this aestheticism flourished. Nowhere did it attain to greater development than at the court of the

Dukes of Burgundy, which was more pompous and better managed than that of the kings of France.

Burgundy interests us less as a political entity in any case, than as a home of music and culture quite different from the contemporary culture of Italy or France. Composers Machaut, Dufay, Binchois, Ockegham, and Josquin des Prés were Burgundians one and all. It's an all-star line-up. And the Flemish painters of the period—the van Eck brothers, the Limbourg brothers, Hans Memling, Roger van der Weyden, to name a few—also flourished under the patronage of the Burgundian Dukes.

One modern observer has noted:

Burgundy, the forgotten kingdom, was no historical backwater. In the fifteenth century it had a flourishing culture able to rival the Italian cities of the Renaissance. A real Quattrocento of the north was taking place there, a cultural explosion of astonishing power and range: a polyglot, polymath, polyphonic and polycentric culture.

But Charles the Bold, the last of the Burgundian Dukes, failed to achieve his goal of consolidating the Duchy and gaining international recognition as an autonomous kingdom. Abandoning his support of the British attempts to defeat the French at a critical juncture, he turned his attention, and his military forces, toward the conquest of Lorraine, which lay between the two parts of his own domain. On January 7, 1477, two days after an ill-timed and disastrous winter attack on the city of Nancy, his body was found in a ditch, naked and gored by wolves. It was not long before his entire domain had been absorbed, either through conquest or marriage, into the kingdom of France.

History, we're told, is a tale told by the winners. At any rate, bad history is. Genuine history concerns itself with the continuing life of the past, and in this respect the history of Burgundy is certainly worth a note. The artistic flowering of the region during its heyday is distinctive for the modern observer, I think, in the subtlety and exactitude of its handling of themes that are attractive precisely because they're distinctively medieval. Greenness, rootedness, chivalry, and religious fervor reach a level of sophistication here from which we may still have things to learn. The bluntly literal and the naively fabulous seem very comfortable with one another, and certainly less self-consciously aesthetic than in contemporary culture south of the Alps. The Burgundians draw nature, beauty, and the symbolic mystery of an unspoken medieval paganism together into a pleasing whole. The kingdom itself has long since vanished, but the *mystique* remains.

And in what, precisely, does the mystique of Burgundy consist? Clearly it's neither the sunny, boule-playing, rosemary-and-garlic mystique of Provence, nor the urban, bourgeois, tasteful but somewhat materialistic mystique of the Low Countries, but something in between. Noble, yet rural. On the highest level of refinement, yet earth-bound, and perhaps at times even austere. Anonymous, or at any rate content to retain its regional flavor, which certainly evokes certain aspects of character you're not going to find in Paris or Geneva. It's like a *mille fleur* tapestry expanded to three dimensions, *The Romance of the Rose* spilling out of its walled garden across the face of the countryside. Peaceful. Delectable. *La France Profonde*.

Selected Bibliography

Alain, *The Gods*, trans. Pevear; New Directions, 1974.

Jacques Barzun, *From Dawn to Decadence*; HarperCollins, 2000.

Richard Bernstein, *Fragile Glory: a Portrait of France and the French*; Knopf, 1990.

Carlo Betocchi, *Selected Poems*, trans. Salomon; Clarke & Way, 1964.

Roberto Calasso, *The Marriage of Cadmus and Harmony*, trans. Parks; Knopf, 1993.

Rene Dubos, *A God Within*; Scribner, 1972.

Lawrence Durrell, *The Greek Islands*; Viking Press, 1978.

Kitty Ferguson, *Steven Hawking: Quest for a Theory of Everything*; Bantam,1992.

Wallace Fowlie, *Age of Surrealism*; Indiana U Press, 1960.

W.K.C. Guthrie, *The Greeks & Their Gods*; Beacon Press, 1955.

Jorge Guillén, *Cántico: a Selection*, ed. Giovanni; Little, Brown, 1965.

Martin Heidegger, *What is Philosophy?*, trans. Wilde & Kluback; College & University Press, 1956.

Iliad, trans. Lattimore; U of Chicago, 1951.

Odyssey, trans. Fagles; Viking Press, 1996.

Odyssey, trans. Fitzgerald; Anchor, 1963.

Satires & Epistles of Horace, trans. Bovie; U of Chicago, 1959.

Kenko, *Essays in Idleness*, trans. Keene; Columbia U Press, 1967.

Henry de Montherland, *Selected Essays*, translated Weightman; Weidenfeld and Nicholson, 1960.

Ronsard, *The Salad*, trans. Berry; North Point Press, 1980.

Salvador de Madariaga, *Essays with a Purpose*; Hollis & Carter, 1954.

H.V. Morton, *A Stranger in Spain*; Dodd, Mead, 1955.

José Ortega y Gasset, *What is Philosophy?*, trans. Adams; Norton, 1960.

Robert M. Parker, jr., *Parker's Wine Buyer's Guide*, 5th ed.; Simon & Schuster, 1999.

Fernando Pessoa, *The Book of Disquiet*, trans. Adam; Pantheon, 1991.

Jean Renior, *Renoir, My Father*, trans. Weaver; Little, Brown, 1962.

James Salter, *Solo Faces*; Little, Brown, 1979.

— *Burning the Days*; Random House, 1997.

George Steiner, *The Death of Tragedy*; Oxford U Press, 1961.

Jules Supervielle, *Selected Writings*; New Directions, 1967.

Hamish F. G. Swanson, *In Defense of Opera*; Penguin, 1978.

John Toren was born and raised in the Twin Cities area. He studied anthropology and European history at the University of Minnesota. He has worked as a teacher and a wilderness guide, and has written articles for many publications and anthologies. He has earned his living for many years as a warehouse manager, during which time he and his wife Hilary have made many trips to Europe and the American West. He also writes and publishes a seasonal magazine called MACARONI, where many of the essays contained in this book originally appeared.